Gothic Remixed

Gothic Remixed

Monster Mashups and Frankenfictions in 21st-Century Culture

Megen de Bruin-Molé

BLOOMSBURY ACADEMIC
LONDON • NEW YORK • OXFORD • NEW DELHI • SYDNEY

BLOOMSBURY ACADEMIC
Bloomsbury Publishing Plc
50 Bedford Square, London, WC1B 3DP, UK
1385 Broadway, New York, NY 10018, USA
29 Earlsfort Terrace, Dublin 2, Ireland

BLOOMSBURY, BLOOMSBURY ACADEMIC and the Diana logo are trademarks of
Bloomsbury Publishing Plc

First published in Great Britain 2020
Paperback edition published 2021

Cover design: Eleanor Rose
Cover images © Getty Images

A catalogue record for this book is available from the British Library.

Library of Congress Cataloging-in-Publication Data
Names: Bruin-Molé, Megen de, author.
Title: Gothic Remixed : Monster Mashups and Frankenfictions in 21st-Century
Culture / Megen de Bruin-Molé
Description: London ; New York : Bloomsbury Academic, 2020. | Includes
bibliographical references.
Identifiers: LCCN 2019010101 | ISBN 9781350103054 (hb) | ISBN 9781350103078
(epub) | ISBN 9781350103061 (epdf)
Subjects: LCSH: Gothic fiction (literary genre)–21st century–History and
criticism. | Literature–Adaptations–History and criticism.. | Film
adaptations–History and criticism. | Appropriation
(Arts)–History–21st century. | Monsters in literature. | Cultural
industries–History–21st century.
Classification: LCC PN3435 B793 2020 | DDC 809.3/8738–dc23
LC record available at https://lccn.loc.gov/2019010101

ISBN: HB: 978-1-3501-0305-4
         PB: 978-1-3502-3446-8
         ePDF: 978-1-3501-0306-1
         eBook: 978-1-3501-0307-8

Typeset by Integra Software Services Pvt. Ltd.

To find out more about our authors and books visit www.bloomsbury.com
and sign up for our newsletters.

Figures

Contents

Acknowledgements

In her 1831 preface to *Frankenstein*, Mary Shelley writes: 'Invention, it must be humbly admitted, does not consist in creating out of the voids, but out of chaos; the materials must, in the first place, be afforded'. I cannot think of a better description of the process of academic writing. Like Victor Frankenstein, I am blessed with a wealth of material, and an unreasonably supportive family. Tom de Bruin (my Igor) put in many hours of unpaid labour listening to my ideas, copy-editing my drafts, and re-programming my citation software. I am also deeply indebted to Catherine Spooner and Anthony Mandal for their comments and advice on my early draft, to the two anonymous reviewers who provided extensive and insightful feedback on the manuscript, and to the fantastic team at Bloomsbury and Integra for guiding the project through to publication. Above all, this book would never have come to be without the constant encouragement, advice, and support of Ann Heilmann.

The College of Arts, Humanities, and Social Sciences (AHSS) at Cardiff University provided me with a three-year grant to conduct this research. I am especially grateful to the postgraduate and early-career community at Cardiff, who welcomed and supported me in my research and teaching. Special thanks are due to Catherine Han, Daný van Dam, and Akira Suwa, my PhD siblings. Thanks also to Marija Grech, Chris Müller, and Jernej Markelj, who patiently listened to more than their share of concerns and frustrations. Thanks to my fantastic network of friends and colleagues for their encouragement, for their suggestions, for their generous sharing of unpublished research and ideas, and for their eagerness to talk about monsters!

Early parts of Chapter 3 appear as '"Now with Ultraviolent Zombie Mayhem!" The Neo-Victorian Novel-as-Mashup and the Limits of Postmodern Irony'. *Neo-Victorian Humour: The Rhetorics and Politics of Comedy, Irony and Parody*, eds. Marie-Luise Kohlke and Christian Gutleben (Amsterdam: Brill/Rodopi, 2017), 249–76. Parts of Chapter 5 first appeared in the article '"Hail, Mary, the Mother of Science Fiction": Popular Fictionalisations of Mary Wollstonecraft Shelley in Film and Television, 1935–2018', *Science Fiction Film and Television* 11, no. 2 (2018): 233–55. Like all academic texts, this book is the material afterlife of many conferences, conversations, and unexpected convergences over the years.

Last but not least, thanks to Tim Kok and Jur Wolven for pre-ordering *Pride and Prejudice and Zombies* for my birthday back in 2009. None of us could have imagined where that gift would eventually lead.

1

Frankenfictions

*How can I describe my emotions at this catastrophe, or how delineate
the wretch whom with such infinite pains and care I had endeavoured
to form? His limbs were in proportion, and I had selected his features
as beautiful. Beautiful! Great God! His yellow skin scarcely covered the
work of muscles and arteries beneath; his hair was of a lustrous black,
and flowing; his teeth of a pearly whiteness; but these luxuriances only
formed a more horrid contrast with his watery eyes, that seemed almost
of the same colour as the dun-white sockets in which they were set, his
shrivelled complexion and straight black lips.*

(Shelley [1831] 2015, 48)

It has been over two hundred years since the publication of Mary Shelley's
Gothic novel *Frankenstein*, and since the birth of her infamous monster
(described by Victor Frankenstein in the epigraph above). Although he may
not be as mutable as the vampire or the zombie, Frankenstein's creature remains
one of the most immediately recognizable figures in horror fiction, and he
finds a spiritual successor in the cyborgs, androids, and other artificial life
forms that populate contemporary science fiction. In the twentieth and twenty-
first centuries the name 'Frankenstein' has gained broader currency, becoming
a euphemism for a wide variety of different practices and products, from
genetically modified plants, proteins, or animals, to unnatural-but-powerful
combinations of objects and ideas, or simply 'a thing that becomes terrifying
or destructive to its maker' (*Oxford Living Dictionary*, s.v. 'Frankenstein').

Frankenstein's monster is an adaptation of the human form – an
appropriation or re-compilation of its basic components into something new –
and uncertain. From the late twentieth century, the 'Franken-' prefix has been
applied to hybrid food, storms, animals, Stratocaster guitars, and now to the
amalgam of classic and contemporary narrative that is described in this book:
'Frankenfiction'. The Frankenfictions I discuss in this book are commercial
narratives, which insert zombies, vampires, werewolves, and multiple other

fantastical monsters into classic literature and popular historical contexts. More broadly, Frankenfiction is also a hybrid genre at the intersection of adaptation and remix, which both disciplines consider to be peripheral and 'monstrous'.

Frankenfiction was first defined rather narrowly, with the 2009 novel *Pride and Prejudice and Zombies*. This novel reproduced roughly 85 per cent of Jane Austen's *Pride and Prejudice* (1813), using the remaining 15 per cent to turn the Regency romance into the story of a zombie uprising (Grahame-Smith and Austen 2009, 3). Because Austen's novel was in the public domain, both the act of appropriation and the millions in revenue the mashup produced were entirely legal, but its popularity provoked concerned responses from many critics. In a market already flooded with increasingly loose adaptations of *Pride and Prejudice*, zombies were a step too far. Could this even be counted as an adaptation? Was it acceptable to disfigure Jane Austen's work in this way, and did the mashup's success among readers of diverging classes and tastes somehow signal the aesthetic decline of Western culture? To these questions, proponents of the mashup responded by gesturing towards adaptations like Helen Fielding's novel *Bridget Jones's Diary* (1996) and the Bollywood musical *Bride and Prejudice* (2004). Were such texts more acceptable as reimaginings of *Pride and Prejudice* than a cut-and-paste horror novel? Where do popular culture and contemporary criticism draw the line between adaptation and appropriation, and why? This book sets out to address such questions in critical and conceptual detail.

Although I often use the term 'Frankenfiction', I also conceptualize this genre as 'historical monster mashup' or 'gothic remix'. As the following sections will make clear, however, the terminology of remix studies is often inadequate in describing the practice of Frankenfiction. In this book I occasionally privilege remix terminology over adaptation terminology because of the deliberately derivative way these professionally produced Franken-narratives insert fantastical monsters into public domain texts. Frankenfictions are rarely secretive about their appropriations, though the type and range of texts they appropriate are incredibly diverse. *Pride and Prejudice and Zombies* was followed by a brief 'literary mashup' craze, and though this particular mode of fiction soon lost its marketing appeal, the range of texts that perform a similar recontextualization of past fictions and figures continues to grow, and to raise similar questions about the ethics and aesthetics of mashup. Frankenfiction includes direct appropriations of classic literature, like the bestselling Quirk Classics novels, but also literary-historical dramas like the Sky/Showtime TV series *Penny Dreadful* (2014–16), or the depiction of monsters through an historical aesthetic in Travis Louie's paintings.

In every instance, Frankenfictions lead us to revisit scholarly definitions of adaptation, historical writing, irony, and 'literary fiction'. Too traditionally literary to be of interest to remix studies, and not literary enough for adaptation studies, Frankenfictions tend to be used as peripheral examples in both fields. No other study has yet attempted to collect these texts into a new (if still liminal) category. Considering the gap in current scholarship, this book seeks to provide a rationale for why Frankenfiction should be considered a hybrid but distinctive genre, at the intersection between mashup, remix, adaptation, and appropriation.

Gothic remixed

As part of the growing popularity of the fantastical monster in contemporary culture and fiction, we find Frankenfictions – adaptations, remixes, mashups, and other 'monstrous hybrids' – that resurrect old texts and narratives specifically to feed a pervasive, commercial desire for the monstrous (Gunkel 2016, 163). This popular, mismatched genre is particularly apposite to current fears and concerns, encouraging familiar questions about authenticity, historicity, appropriation, and the nature of art in the age of popular monstrosity. It also presents a question of specific relevance to Gothic studies: what does it mean that our historical monsters have moved from the margins to the mainstream?

On the face of it, this statement seems like an oxymoron. How can the monster, a figure that traditionally represents marginality, 'difference made flesh' (Cohen 1996a, 7), become an emblem of the dominant ideology? David McNally suggests that in a global capitalist society, artists' and creators' fears shift from the threat of outside difference to that of monstrous sameness:

> What is most striking about capitalist monstrosity, in other words, is its elusive everydayness, its apparently seamless integration into the banal and mundane rhythms of quotidian existence. [...] In such circumstances, images of vampires and zombies frequently dramatise the profound senses of corporeal vulnerability that pervade modern society, most manifestly when commodification invades new spheres of social life. (McNally 2012, 2)

McNally suggests that it is precisely the popular and the mainstream that are the 'monsters' in our twenty-first-century neoliberal culture, as concerns over the rise of conservative meme activism, the decline of traditional literacy, the prospect of a 'post-truth' society, and 'the angry swamp monster of right-wing populism' all converge (Hartcher 2017, para. 1). Our fictions project similar fears about the future of historical and personal integrity, truth, civil liberty, and originality. The growing popularity of Frankenfiction – a monstrous genre that uses the tropes and conventions of literature and historiography to happily parody the distaste that these disciplines conventionally exhibit for the popular and the commercial – seems to confirm this assessment. In many ways, then, Frankenfictions are the face of a new age in popular storytelling.

Of course, the manifestation of the monster as the uneducated masses can also be readily found in nineteenth-century fiction. In Elizabeth Gaskell's *Mary Barton*, we read the following:

> The actions of the uneducated seem to me typified in those of Frankenstein, that monster of many human qualities, ungifted with a soul, a knowledge of the difference between good and evil.
>
> The people rise up to life; they irritate us, they terrify us, and we become their enemies. Then in the sorrowful moment of our triumphant power, their eyes gaze on us with mute reproach. Why have we made them what they are; a powerful monster, yet without the inner means for peace and happiness. (1849, 189)

Here, Gaskell's first-person narrator identifies the monster with the popular, and with the products and consumers of mass culture. They may possess 'many human qualities', but they lack 'a soul' or moral compass, bestowed through a humanist literary education. Without this 'inner means for peace and happiness', the masses are framed as powerful, but directionless and monstrous. This image is strongly echoed in twenty-first-century intellectual discourse surrounding Brexit or the election of Donald Trump as US president – a discourse which *The Guardian*'s David Runciman described as 'just another version of the old fear of the credulity of the untutored masses: they will believe anything' (2016, para. 22). Once again, the 'new' phenomenon of Frankenfiction and monster mashup reveals an older parentage, and the thrills, fears, and cultural crises they embody point back to a much longer tradition of popular appropriations and revivals.

Like *Frankenstein* itself, Frankenfictions owe a debt to the Gothic fictions of the eighteenth century. In many ways, Frankenfiction is simply a new iteration of these older trends. In her 2006 monograph *Contemporary Gothic*, for instance, Catherine Spooner describes Gothic fictions through various metaphors that show how readily this mode of historical revival reflects the context of adaptation, remix, and Frankenfiction. 'Gothic', writes Spooner, 'has throughout its history taken the form of a series of revivals', and 'like Frankenstein's monster, these revivals seldom take exactly the same shape they possessed before' (2006, 10–11). From this perspective, Frankenfiction is simply another iteration in a long line of Gothic hybrids. Although its appropriative tendencies have increased with each generation, Spooner compares contemporary Gothic pastiche to 'Ann Radcliffe's liberal quotation from Shakespeare and Milton, or Horace Walpole's collection of medieval curios' (2006, 12). The Gothic, in other words, is a genre already well suited to discussions of the ethics and aesthetics of historical appropriation. It has been concerned with these subjects since its inception.

In the second edition of Horace Walpole's *The Castle of Otranto* (1764), the first work of fiction to receive the label 'Gothic', Walpole outlines the emergence of a new, hybrid genre that is clearly echoed in Frankenfiction. *Otranto*, writes Walpole in the author's preface, represents:

> [A]n attempt to blend the two kinds of romance, the ancient and the modern. In the former, all was imagination and improbability: in the latter, nature is always intended to be, and sometimes has been, copied with success. Invention has not been wanting; but the great resources of fancy have been dammed up, by a strict adherence to common life. But if, in the latter species, Nature has cramped imagination, she did but take her revenge, having been totally excluded from old romances. The actions, sentiments, and conversations, of the heroes and heroines of ancient days, were as unnatural as the machines employed to put them in motion. ([1765] 2004, 21)

Like Frankenfictions, Gothic fictions are concerned with the uneasy juxtaposition between conflicting audiences, tastes, and generic conventions. Jerrold Hogle describes Walpole's 'choice of the Gothic label for this uneasy marriage' of two romances as 'a marketing device designed to fix a generic position for an interplay of what was widely thought to be high cultural writing (epic, verse romance, tragedy) with what many still regarded as low by comparison (servant-based comedy, superstitious folklore, middle-class prose fiction)' (2002, 8). Frankenfictions like *Penny Dreadful* or Kevin J. Weir's GIFs (short for graphical interchange format) perform a similar manoeuvre. Like Gothic fictions, Frankenfictions are often associated with the demands of the bored or uneducated for 'artificial excitements'. E.J. Clery goes so far as to suggest that the Gothic 'originates in the problem of boredom and satiety [...] in which the rapid growth of the reading habit in the middle class breeds obscure longings for novelty' (2002, 29). This mirrors accusations levelled at Frankenfictions like *Pride and Prejudice and Zombies*.

Moreover, the multimedia nature of many Frankenfictions echoes that of early and Victorian Gothic fiction, which was considered to include 'an array of media – novels, plays, poetry, paintings, opera and optical technologies' (D.J. Jones 2011, 12). As we will see in Chapter 4, the way some mashup artists paint onto, reproduce, or digitally layer existing artefacts resembles techniques pioneered by the magic lantern – a projection technology developed in the seventeenth century, which had an impact on 'the cultural life of Western Europe' that is 'difficult to overemphasise' (D.J. Jones 2014, 13). David J. Jones argues that the magic lantern 'and other optical media were Gothic artefacts [...] from their very inception' (2011, 17), not only because many eighteenth- and nineteenth-century lantern shows adapted Gothic stories and themes, but also because of the way such technological affordances allowed for 'many Phantasms and terrible Appearances', 'projections of painted Figures', and other special (and spectral) effects (Defoe 1840, 352; cited in D.J. Jones 2014, 14). Similarly, nineteenth-century Gothic's status as 'an intricately interrelated network of evolving media' with 'complex synergies which linked and help these in tension' invites comparisons to our contemporary, networked culture (D.J. Jones 2011, 12).

While I recognize Frankenfiction's debt to the Gothic tradition, however, I am also hesitant to unequivocally label *all* Frankenfictions as 'Gothic fictions'. In part, this is because Frankenfiction often problematizes the use of the term 'Gothic' to describe what is, essentially, highbrow contemporary horror. I discuss this problem at length in Chapter 3. What truly separates Frankenfiction from earlier, Gothic texts is its position between the postmodern 'end of history' and the digital recycling revival. As I argue throughout this book, Frankenfiction, like Gothic fiction, addresses Romantic visions and concerns. It simply does so with a (post)postmodern set of tools.

Monstrous adaptations

The critical debate about the semantics, ethics, and aesthetics of what I define as Frankenfiction mirrors discussions currently taking place in two distinct academic disciplines: remix studies and adaptation studies. Ostensibly, these two disciplines have much in common. Both consider how existing objects and ideas are recycled and revised. In practice there are numerous, if subtle, distinctions between them. Where adaptation is an older, well-established critical concept, remix seems newer and more popular. In the past two decades, scholarly interest in remix practices and cultures has intensified noticeably. In

2005, William Gibson – a pioneering author of science fiction, steampunk, and cyberpunk – argued that 'the recombinant (the bootleg, the remix, the mash-up) has become the characteristic pivot at the turn of our two centuries' (2005, para. 11). In 2006, Henry Jenkins likewise described a fundamental 'change in the way media is produced and a change in the way media is consumed' that he termed convergence culture: 'the flow of media across multiple media platforms, the cooperation between multiple media industries, and the migratory behavior of media audiences who will go almost anywhere in search of the kinds of entertainment they want' (2006, 16, 3). Audiences select and reassemble the media they consume in their own individual ways, irrespective of source, and producers expand their texts across multiple platforms in the hope that they will be ever more accessible to new and diverse sets of consumers. These remixed media are the 'monsters' of contemporary culture, both in terms of their massive size and scope, and in terms of the challenge they issue to foundational concepts like authorship and international copyright. Frankenfictions disturb the idea that texts can have a sole author or owner. They appropriate the pieces of other texts and the authority of other authors, pilfering familiar ideas and images while never directly breaking copyright law. Is this what stops some critics from identifying them as adaptations? To create a mashup novel like *Pride and Prejudice and Zombies* may be insolent or even unethical, but it is perfectly legal. While Frankenfictions may sidestep questions of copyright by working with material in the public domain, then, they raise familiar questions about the ethics and aesthetics of artistic appropriation. At the same time, they seem to lack the critical challenge of postmodern remixes from earlier decades, instead suggesting that postmodernism's ethics and aesthetics may be obsolete in the face of twenty-first-century capitalism and convergence. This is a point I will expand on in Chapter 3.

This book takes the questions raised by *Pride and Prejudice and Zombies* as a point of departure, applying them to a broad range of derivative monster narratives. Some of these narratives can be read as adaptations of classic monsters, while others are more appropriately conceptualized as monstrous mashups of classic texts. For both adaptation studies and remix studies, Frankenfiction offers a useful illustration of the politics of appropriation – and, by association, the politics behind the conceptions of originality and authenticity on which both of these academic disciplines are based. In the context of this book, Frankenfiction is perhaps best described as monstrous adaptation: monstrous because it often features fantastical monsters, and also because it transgresses many of the discipline's preconceptions about what it means to be faithful to an 'original' text. In this sense the concepts I discuss throughout the book are applicable well beyond adaptation studies. Frankenfictions are also a kind of monstrous historical fiction: monstrous because they deal even more freely with the 'facts' of the past than most fictional historiographies. This may seem like a strange way to approach any body of work, but especially one that is the subject of an academic study. After all, who cares about bad adaptation, and fantastical history? Even Frankenfictions themselves often dismiss their value and real-world significance as limited. I suggest, however, that fantastical histories are important precisely because the fantastical and the 'real' often bleed into each other in popular and scholarly discourse. That Frankenfiction is an overtly fictional historical account does not absolve it from its impact on perceptions of the past, just as the inhumanity of Frankenstein's creature does not absolve it from judgement by human standards in Shelley's novel.

In *The Politics of Adaptation*, Thomas Leitch suggests that adaptation and historiography are more intimately linked than many scholars have considered. As he argues, even 'history is itself always an adaptation of some earlier history [...] Even journalism, which has so often been called history's first draft, depends on earlier sources and agendas' (2015, 10, 11). All textual accounts are reliant on and related to other accounts, linked together in a 'web of intertextuality' (G. Rose 2005, 72), or 'a multi-dimensional space in which a variety of writings, none of them original, blend and clash' (Barthes 1978, 146). In other words, though Frankenfictions may overtly reference their 'source' hypotexts, downplaying their own authority, even the earliest or most original historical accounts are in some sense 'hypertexts whose hypotexts are unknown' (Genette 1997, 381). This is not a new proposal, but it continues to have enormous implications not only for historiography, or the writing of critical history, but also for the work of historical adaptation, or the writing of fiction set in the past. It implies that scholars should be as attentive to (and critical of) the most popular and fictional of histories as they are to academic histories. This is the approach I take throughout this study, demonstrating not just how Frankenfiction adapts past texts, but also how it impacts our perceptions of the past itself.

In this book, I attempt to stitch together the various objects that I consider to constitute the body of Frankenfiction: derivative, commercial narratives engaged in monstrous appropriations of historical texts and contexts. In many instances, this has proved to be a challenge. After all, many of Frankenfiction's component parts (fakery and authenticity, reality and fantasy, the commercial and the mythic) are constantly straining in different directions. Because of this, as a genre Frankenfiction is in a permanent state of nervous tension, never static or complete. Throughout the body of the book, then, I have framed Frankenfiction largely in terms of what it is not. Like the fantastical monsters they contain, Frankenfictions have traditionally lurked at the margins of academic disciplines like adaptation and remix studies, and on the fringes of well-established genres and modes like the Gothic, historical fiction, or parody. In this Frankenfiction is also monstrous: it highlights the borders of specific categories and conventions by transgressing them. Frankenfiction is a genre at the periphery of other genres, constructed at the spaces where they intersect and break down.

Of course, the monster's traditional function is not to be completely other, but to show us what is normal and abnormal, possible and impossible, within the framework that already exists (Cohen 1996a, 13). Ultimately, Frankenfictions serve to demonstrate that the boundaries between adaptation and appropriation, monstrosity and normalcy, irony and authenticity, fiction and history, and originality and plagiarism are still fundamentally solid – the borders have merely shifted. Frankenfictions force us to confront these boundaries, and reconsider our own presuppositions and beliefs. Most importantly, they do so in familiar language, often appropriating the aesthetics, language, and formal conventions of literature and scholarship.

Like the creature it is modelled upon, the category of Frankenfiction is not neat, comprehensive, or well formed in the traditional sense. It is a messy conglomeration of texts from various media, registers, and narrative traditions. This messiness is intentional. Frankenfiction reminds us that categorization *is* and always should be messy, revealing the uneasy process of divorcing ourselves from the cultural past, and the continually fragmented nature of textuality in the modern age. Using popular forms and aesthetics traditionally thought to indicate the *erasure* of history, marginality, and authorship, Frankenfiction instead uses them in a way that reinforces the mediated presence of the past, the continued proliferation of marginal figures, and the authority of the author. It mixes itself with other texts, linking itself to multiple genres and styles without ever committing to one or the other.

In this context, Frankenfiction's textual promiscuity helps us to make new connections between existing categorizations. For instance, adaptation studies is currently struggling to incorporate the implications of convergence culture and transmedial fictions into its scholarly paradigm. Remix studies offers a range of imagery and terminology that may be useful in this process, as indicated by their productiveness when discussing Frankenfiction. Likewise, remix studies is working to conceptualize its disciplinary boundaries, and trace its history in earlier forms of art. The disciplines of adaptation and historical fiction, which have already grappled with these questions, can offer potential models of approach. Ultimately, this makes each category more complete.

As Leitch argues, discussing the value of studying the widest possible variety of historiographies, '[s]ome kinds of knowledge thus seem to thrive on intimacy, others on critical distance. But no one kind of knowledge is complete in itself, and no one can pursue every kind of knowledge simultaneously' (2015, 13). For scholarship, then, Frankenfiction is also useful because it helps us to track and respond to the rapidly evolving discourses of originality, intertextuality, and history, without first having to redefine the field. In the early twenty-first century, for instance, Frankenfiction speaks to concerns that we are living in an age of post-irony, post-truth, post-history, and post-integrity. On the one hand, it suggests that we may simply be trying to approach these issues from the wrong angle, and with the wrong assumptions. On the other, it points to the possible origins of these situations, using familiar images, themes, and language, and giving us a place to begin revising our views and improving our approach. Through Frankenfiction's academically marginal and monstrous discourse, we can test new theories and boundaries without tearing the old ones down.

Despite its critical and generic indeterminacy, of course, Frankenfictions themselves are not marginal texts. Frankenfiction is a mainstream category in its own right, on the rise in popular fiction since the turn of the millennium. It adopts the most popular themes, forms, and aesthetics of mainstream culture, and finds success with mass-market audiences as readily as it does with intellectual ones. Paradoxically, then, we might say that Frankenfictions are conservative images of marginality in the mainstream. They revive old or outmoded discourses of the monstrous, and profit from popular culture's current nostalgia for historical otherness. This is likely not what scholars of the monstrous envisioned twenty years ago when they defined the monster along socially progressive lines, as a figure that foregrounded differences of a predominantly 'cultural, political, racial, economic, sexual' nature, and promoted re-evaluations of civil rights (Cohen 1996a, 7). Frankenfiction is, and contains, a new kind of monster. By defining its borders we can also begin to more accurately identify and conceptualize these shifts in mainstream culture.

What can we actually say about the Frankenfictions in this book, then, besides defining what they are not? First and foremost, these Frankenfictions are fictional histories, set in a past populated by fantastical monsters. The friendly, fun, and psychosocially complex way Frankenfiction uses monsters belongs to the twenty-first century, where we are surrounded by the popular monsters of the past, and perhaps even bored by their ubiquity. However, when these monsters revisit the past that created them, rather than remaining in the present, they achieve renewed depth. It also makes them 'monstrous' once more, in the classic sense of denaturalizing the natural and drawing attention to boundaries. At a formal and generic level, meanwhile, we continue to see a mainstream, twenty-first-century representation of physical and social monstrosity. That is, certain kinds of monstrosity are now welcomed and exalted, rather than simply accepted. Where traditional monster narratives normally serve a conservative function – after all, in most classic fictions the monster is destroyed and order restored – because the 'monsters' are usually the heroes of Frankenfiction, their punishment is often deferred. Of course, as the examples in this book will show, this punishment is often simply deflected elsewhere. The monsters of Frankenfiction occupy an uneasy position, never fully embracing otherness, but also never becoming fully subsumed under the conservative authority of mainstream popular culture. The texts of Frankenfiction occupy a similar position.

Because of this anachronistic combination of twenty-first-century monstrosity and past setting, Frankenfiction also has the effect of denaturalizing the historical texts it appropriates. Frankenfiction makes the past seem strange and exotic, sometimes revealing the inherent strangeness of history in the process. For instance, Roland Barthes refers to the tendency of socially constructed notions, narratives, and assumptions to become naturalized, or taken unquestioningly as given within a particular culture during the process of their mythologization ([1957] 1972, 142, 148, 128). Monstrous or fantastical histories inherently resist such naturalization, because they refuse to be taken entirely seriously. As we will see, however, it is certainly still possible to politicize both fantasies and parodies.

Finally, Frankenfictions are deliberately inauthentic texts. Frankenfiction delights in fakery for the sake of spectacle and pleasure, and for the sheer enjoyment of the many modes of reflecting pastness. This performance need not always derive from a didactic will to mock or critique the past. Often Frankenfiction chooses past objects and stories not to make a *historical* point about them, but because it likes what they make possible in the present, or simply because they have become familiar enough that they can be effortlessly recycled in a camp parody of our own nostalgia-obsessed culture. Because Frankenfiction self-consciously shows us the trends that have become too tired to reveal any 'deeper' meaning, it can have a monstrous function, pointing to the once-transgressive tropes it now exploits for fun and profit. Frankenfictions are not automatically progressive texts, then, but neither are they automatically conservative. Often they occupy a position in between, serving as relatively progressive texts in a conservative environment.

The many faces of Frankenfiction

Throughout this book, I am to create a space where Frankenfiction and the various texts and theories it interprets can interact with each other, as objects with their own unique historical backgrounds and contexts. In this process we will learn more about Frankenfiction and *Frankenstein*, but also about the particular weaknesses and strengths of the theoretical frameworks that attempt to keep them safely contained within various categories. In the rest of this chapter, then, I will first describe the historical context in which Frankenfiction came to exist. This is necessary in order to examine the ways in which Frankenfiction has been conceptualized by remix and adaptation studies. Differentiating between these two approaches will enable me to move on to a closer discussion of the genre itself. Tracing the genre's often explicit link to the creature from Mary Shelley's *Frankenstein*, I will also question why Frankenfiction is so prevalent in twenty-first-century Western culture, and point to several ways it addresses ongoing problems of categorization across the humanities.[1]

Chapter 2 takes monster studies as its point of departure. It traces the traditional images of the monster in critical theory, and explains how monsters potentially function differently in the historical mashup than they do in other contemporary works. Furthermore, it situates monster mashups within discussions of intersectionality and multiculturalism, using four prominent examples of 'team mashup' – the novel *Anno Dracula* (1992, re-released in 2011), *The League of Extraordinary Gentlemen* graphic novels (1999–2018), the television series *Penny Dreadful* (2014–16), and *The Extraordinary Adventures of the Athena Club* novels (2017–19) – to demonstrate how the mashup attempts to restore a universal significance to the figure of the monster. Ultimately, the chapter asks whether Frankenfiction allows historical monsters to serve once again as progressive political symbols. This potential seems absent from many mainstream adaptations, in which the drive towards artistic authenticity and identity politics has been replaced by self-reflexive irony.

Following from this argument, Chapter 3 explores the ethics and aesthetics of irony in historical monster mashups, comparing polarizing examples from novel-as-mashup texts like *Pride and Prejudice and Zombies, Jane Slayre,* and

Wuthering Bites to examine how they engage with discourses of parody, satire, camp, and authenticity. I argue that Frankenfiction is often divisive not because it is unclear whether it mocks or upholds established cultural traditions, but because it is in fact parodying several different traditions at once. I take the field of neo-Victorian fiction, a genre that is linked with metatextuality and irony (but also with identity politics) in comparable ways, as a counter-example to the novel-as-mashup. This chapter questions whether postmodern irony has outlived its usefulness as a tool of recognitive justice in the case of metafictional or neo-historical adaptations.

Building on the previous chapter's interrogation of irony and authenticity, Chapter 4 steps back to consider the monstrosity of 'historical' mashup itself, as a kind of fictional historiography. It analyses various approaches to authenticity and historical accuracy in the practices of historical fiction and the Gothic: two different but interrelated methods of rewriting the past. In this discussion, visual historiographies generally offer the strongest claims to realism and historical authenticity, and so I look specifically at four collections of visual Frankenfiction that play with historical images and aesthetics. The four artists I discuss in this chapter use the material fragments of history to make the past exotic again, bringing out its strangeness and denaturalizing it. This chapter asks whether such Gothic historical fiction might serve to make us reconsider twenty-first-century attitudes towards historical authenticity and appropriation.

Addressing one final, key perspective on appropriation and artistic authenticity, Chapter 5 analyses Frankenfiction's place in the heavily gendered discourse of authorial originality and ownership. This chapter discusses the gendered figure of the 'creative genius' in its Romantic, postmodern, and twenty-first-century contexts. Ultimately, I suggest that even when its aims are explicitly feminist, Frankenfiction leaves many of the gendered issues inherent in its own appropriations unaddressed. Frankenfiction and other remixed works rarely revolutionize authorship in the ways we might expect.

Each of the five chapters in this book draws on close readings of key texts, placed in different theoretical contexts, to focus on the tensions between contemporary mass culture and academic scholarship. These tensions can be found in the critical terms used to describe Frankenfiction. They can also be found in Frankenfiction's engagement with monstrosity (Chapter 2), with parody and irony (Chapter 3), and with historiography (Chapter 4), and in its conceptualizations of authorship (Chapter 5). Through an analysis of the various texts and contexts these remixes appropriate, and of the ethics, politics, aesthetics, and circulation of Frankenfiction itself, I examine the ways in which these historical monster mashups might serve to address a culture reacting against both the humanist ideals of the eighteenth and nineteenth centuries, and the posthuman leanings of the twentieth century. First, however, it is necessary to consider the history and politics of the terminology that will be employed throughout the book.

Twenty-first-century remix culture

For writers like William Gibson and Henry Jenkins, post-millennial culture is, at its most basic level, a remix culture. This is a culture that subsists on and often encourages derivative works, which combine or edit existing materials into fresh products. Although the *Oxford English Dictionary* tells us that the word 'remix' in its current usage dates back only to the 1960s, the process it describes is arguably far from new (OED, s.v. 'Remix'). For Jenkins, remix culture (here 'convergence culture') essentially represents a turn back to the past. This turn is directed at the long nineteenth century – more specifically, at the effects of the Industrial Revolution:

> At the risks of painting with broad strokes, the story of American arts in the nineteenth century might be told in terms of the mixing, matching, and merging of folk traditions taken from various indigenous and immigrant populations. Cultural production occurred mostly on the grassroots level; creative skills and artistic traditions were passed down mother to daughter, father to son. Stories and songs circulated broadly, well beyond their points of origin, with little or no expectation of economic compensation [...]. There was no pure boundary between the emergent commercial culture and the residual folk culture: the commercial culture raided folk culture and folk culture raided commercial culture. (2006, 135)

Jenkins specifically cites the United States, but his descriptions of grassroots cultural production and fluctuating copyright legislation are equally applicable to nineteenth-century Europe (Rose 2003; Seville 2006; Alexander 2010). It is in part due to this similarity between nineteenth-century 'mixing, matching, and merging' and twenty-first-century remix culture that this book will focus primarily on twenty-first-century remixes of nineteenth-century texts. Another reason is that many of the texts, personas, and objects Frankenfictions appropriate are themselves drawn from the Victorian period, though outlying examples from other historical periods also exist. This Victorian fixation is partly for the copyright reasons I have already mentioned, but it also has to do with the sociopolitical debt twenty-first-century culture owes to the long nineteenth century: an era that tends to be viewed as the birthplace of the modern world.

Frankenfiction is connected to more recent cultural periods and movements as well. Remix scholars have already begun to explore the link between early collage and twenty-first-century remix practices (e.g. Augaitis, Grenville, and Rebick 2016). Marcel Duchamp's *Fountain* (1917) is often cited as an early example of remix-style appropriation in the modern era (Jenkins 2006; Lessig 2008; Navas 2009; van Poecke 2014). Duchamp uses an old object with negative artistic significance (in this case a urinal) to ask new questions about the nature of art and culture. William S. Burroughs's cut-up technique in his *Nova Trilogy* (1961–64) is another example, which in turn was inspired by Brion Gysin in the 1950s and the Dadaists in the 1920s (Knickerbocker and Burroughs 1965, para. 50). These texts assemble other people's words and phrases into new, but explicitly derivative, configurations. Even Frankenfiction existed well before the twenty-first century. Examples might include the 1943 film *Frankenstein Meets the Wolf Man*, 1945's *House of Dracula*, or 1948's *Abbott and Costello Meet Frankenstein*. All take existing properties and characters licensed by Universal Studios, combining them into one story.

Likewise, any vampire text that followed Bram Stoker's *Dracula* (1897) could arguably be considered a remix, simply by virtue of its inevitable comparison to this iconic work – and later to Bela Lugosi's 1931 performance of the titular Count. The same could be said of most adaptations of *Frankenstein*, since many such texts are not 'faithful' enough to the novel they reference to be considered adaptations in the traditional sense. Some have only been recognized as adaptations since the late twentieth century, when adaptation studies definitions began to adopt remix culture approaches. As the 'Adaptations' section of the recent *Cambridge Companion to Frankenstein* illustrates, many of the texts we associate with Shelley's *Frankenstein* are impossible to analyse adequately on a simple one-to-one relationship with the novel (A. Smith 2016). Indeed, *Frankenstein* itself could be considered a remix, reworking the ghost stories from J.B.B. Eyriè *Fantasmagoriana* (1812) that helped inspire its composition (Robinson 2016, 13). On the surface this might seem to lend credence to Botting's statement that '*Frankenstein* is a product of criticism, not a work of literature' (1995, 2), but I would argue that the relationship between literary texts, adaptations, and criticism has never been as straightforward as we may like to think. As yet, however, the history, origins, and manifestations of remix culture remain under-evaluated.

Regardless of how old remix culture can claim to be, as narratives flow more regularly between multiple media, and as audiences become more used to experiencing and participating in a remix culture, Western scholarship clearly needs new ways to classify the various appropriative processes such culture enables. As Bernice M. Murphy and Stephen Matterson argue in their introduction to *Twenty-First-Century Popular Fiction*, media crossovers and adaptations of popular fictions have become especially 'remarkable since the turn of the twenty-first century', traceable to transformations in the 'writing, publication and consumption of popular fiction' that can be linked to 'the technological revolution of the internet age from the early 1990s' (2018, 4). There have always been Frankenfictions, but the proliferation and success of these kinds of texts has reached unprecedented heights.

Frankenfictions represent a reanimation – or, to refrain from imbuing these creations with false life, a re-mediation – of past texts. I have chosen the term 'mashup' as a secondary label because this is the term most consistently used by fans and critics of my selected texts. Establishing a useful critical definition for the broad range of texts I describe in this book is not so simple, however. Any attempt is complicated by the fact that there is no satisfying consensus as to what distinguishes these classifications (adaptation, appropriation, remix, mashup) from each other. The lack of such a definition complicates conceptualizations of the relationship between an alternate history novel like Kim Newman's *Anno Dracula,* a cut-and-paste mashup like *Pride and Prejudice and Zombies,* or Pemberley Digital's gender-swapped retelling of *Frankenstein* for YouTube – a connection that I believe can and should be made. When grouped together, should these monster mashups be classified as adaptations or appropriations, as mashups or remixes, or simply as extended cases of intertextuality? Or, to put it another way, what does it actually mean to define something as one or the other in contemporary academic discourse? Naturally, attempting to classify a thing often tells us as much about our systems of classification as it does about the thing we are trying to classify. A primer on the terminology and discourses associated with the historical monster mashup may not reveal much about the monster, but it will tell us a great deal about the cultures that seek to describe it.

In a remix culture, the terms that make up the label 'historical monster mashup' – the base components of Frankenfiction – seem at first relatively straightforward. Admittedly, as I will expand in Chapter 4, the contemporary English adjective 'historical' has conflicting meanings that blur into each other: both '[b]elonging to, constituting, or of the nature of history; in accordance with history' and 'a treatise, painting, novel, or other work: treating of, based on, or depicting events from history' (OED, s.v. 'Historical').[2] As I will discuss in Chapter 4, the Gothic itself draws upon a complex tradition of remediating history. Still, it is a useful point of departure to say that we are dealing with texts that in some way relate to our concept of history, and are 'concerned with past events' or texts (OED, s.v. 'Historical'). The monster is a figure I will return to in the second chapter of this book, but one we know broadly as 'the bodily incarnation of difference from the basic human norm' (Braidotti 1997, 62). If we take a psychoanalytical approach, monsters represent 'anxiety and instability [...] dark and ominous doubles restlessly announcing an explosion of apocalyptic energy' (Botting 1992, 51). This definition marks a historical monster mashup as a text that contains monstrous figures, but also signals its potential for monstrosity at a sociopolitical level. Again, this is a link that will be questioned throughout the book.

'Mashup', the noun upon which the two preceding adjectives rest, requires a more extensive contextualization – especially given the variability of Frankenfiction as a genre. As I argue throughout this book, rather than being united by a strictly defined set of formal characteristics, what makes Frankenfiction 'mashup' is subjective. This is not to argue that Frankenfictions defy definition entirely, but rather that they cannot be defined through any single, all-encompassing list of features. Not all works of Frankenfiction are mashups in the way this term is traditionally defined, but the moniker serves as a useful indicator of the forms Frankenfiction often takes. A compound word that rather inelegantly refers to a 'mixture or fusion of disparate elements' (OED, s.v. 'Mash-up'), mashup (much like 'Frankenstein') evokes images of ungainly accidents before it does works of art. Mashups are a part of remix culture, though their exact place in the hierarchy of remix is still indefinite (Gunkel 2016, 20). The mashup as we know it today takes its name from the music industry's reinterpretations and recombinations of pre-existing tracks in the late 1960s and early 1970s, but the basic principle has since been extended to other cultural modes of production, including fashion, the written and visual arts, and mass communication (Tough 2010, 205–6). Since the 1990s, mashup, remix, reboot, transmedia, convergence, and a variety of similar terms have been evoked to describe the emerging set of beliefs and practices that is remix culture.

Each classification comes with its own set of problems, strengths, and presuppositions. Remix studies assumes from the outset that nothing is truly original – an assumption that adaptation studies has begun to share. Both theories ask what it means to be artistically original, and to what extent that question is even worth posing. One answer might lie in the histories of objects and the individual ethics of their appropriation. Remix is not traditionally seen as historiography, though it does acknowledge its debt to historical traces. As Eduardo Navas argues, '[w]ithout a history, the remix cannot be Remix' (2009, para. 7). Put simply, remix needs objects to re-mix, and Frankenfiction needs some pre-existing artefact or idea to 'mash up' with monsters in order to exist. Esther Peeren suggests that ours is the age of the 'neo-' and the 'post-' (2008, 1), and we might add the 're-' to this list, but ultimately such terminology reveals our entrenchment in the past, rather than moving us beyond it. The remix itself may not be new, but the need for a new term signals a new way of looking at these processes. The Frankenfiction with which this book is concerned is a particularly useful example in such discussions. As a mish-mash of 'undead' texts as well as a body of texts about the undead, Frankenfiction serves as a self-reflective metaphor for the process of adaptation, and for the recycling of narrative more generally.

Frankenfiction as remix

Relatively few remix scholars have attempted to distinguish the mashup from other kinds of appropriative art – or, for that matter, from any kind of art, given the relational nature of creativity in general. For these scholars, all art (and all information) is indebted to all other art (and information), especially those to which it is categorically or generically closest. Without a certain degree of dialogue and appropriation between and among texts, it would be impossible to identify a novel as a novel, or a Western as a Western. Even Gerald Prince, in his preface to Gérard Genette's *Palimpsests*, argues that any 'text is a hypertext [...] any writing is re-writing; and literature is always in the second degree' (1997, ix). In *Palimpsests* Genette himself problematizes the idea of originality as a feature of 'literarity' or the literary (1997, 9). The indebtedness of art to other art is perhaps even more relevant in popular culture – which John Storey describes in his *Guide to Cultural Theory and Popular Culture* as 'always defined, implicitly or explicitly, in contrast to other conceptual categories' (2001, 1). Part of Frankenfiction's own success has to do with the popularity of its appropriated source texts, through which it is defined and assessed.

Likewise, directly or indirectly academic disciplines are always in dialogue with other academic disciplines. In some respects remix studies is a field closely related to adaptation studies, albeit with a fundamentally different perspective. In the context of this book, it is especially interesting that Frankenfiction has been taken up as an example of both remix and adaptation. Adaptation implies change, but also continuation. Specifically, it concerns a temporal move from the past to the present, repackaging a story so it can better adapt to a new environment. Adaptation studies asks questions about historical accuracy, copyright law, and source–text fidelity, and is interested in texts at a narrative level. It wants to know how the ghost of the old text manifests in the structure of the new text. When this ghost cannot be located, the adaptation is generally pronounced a failure – dead on arrival – or as something other than adaptation.

These kinds of discussions were brought to the fore in 2016 when, after several false starts in pre-production, *Pride + Prejudice + Zombies* (a work of Frankenfiction that was also an adaptation of Quirk Books's *Pride and Prejudice and Zombies*) was released in cinemas. Unlike the mashup novel it claimed to adapt, it was not a success by any stretch of the imagination, earning back just half of its modest 28-million-dollar budget. The film failed at least partly because it never fully evoked the storyworlds it claimed to be a part of, or the intertextual currency associated with them. In a sense, *Pride + Prejudice + Zombies* did *not* have a unified 'soul'; it tried to draw from too many intertextual hotspots, rather than sustaining a more complete or traditional appropriation as the novel did. In this case, a more 'original' approach actually damaged the story the film was trying to tell. Without a clear iconography to ground it, and to consistently identify the texts it was referencing to its viewers, it was left as an empty shell – it 'staggers along like the undead', as one reviewer put it (Brennan 2016, para. 1). While I consider this film to be a useful example of Frankenfiction, then, it was dismissed as a poor adaptation.

Remix studies discards these resurrectionist perspectives from the outset. Indirectly descended from collage and cut-up practices, it claims to be less interested in where a text came from at the narrative level, and more interested in its origins at the formal and socioeconomic levels. It follows the objects that texts appropriate rather than the stories they attempt to tell. In the metaphor of Frankenstein's monster, adaptation studies would be focused on the monster's fundamental nature or soul (is it human or not?) while remix studies would tend to take a more material approach (what manner of being is it, and what humans or non-humans is it made of?). Frankenfiction shows us how we might pair these viewpoints in order to arrive at new, and potentially more accurate, observations and perspectives on contemporary fiction. In the example of *Pride + Prejudice + Zombies*, this pairing allows us to sharpen our definition of adaptation. In the context of this book, claims of lack or deficiency made by adaptation studies often signal useful areas for a remix studies approach to explore.

Unlike adaptation studies, remix studies privileges mediation over the medium: it is intentionally inclusive in its selection of meaning-making texts, but this also results in a decreased focus on the fundamental nature of texts themselves. Consequently, remix scholars are generally less interested in tracing the various threads of appropriation, and instead consider 'mashup as a metaphor for parallel and co-existing ways of thinking and acting rather than exclusionary, causal and reductionist principles of either or instead of as well as' (Sonvilla-Weiss 2010, 8). Where adaptation studies might highlight difference as a means of categorization, remix studies favours a both/and approach to the various practices it describes. As Stefan Sonvilla-Weiss points out, this approach fits well with a networking culture's affinity for defragmentation: 'trying to re-establish alienated modes of common understanding through aggregation, augmentation, reconfiguration and combination of information, quite similarly to what the hard disk does when physically organizing the contents of the disk to store the pieces of each file close together and contiguously' (2010, 9).

As Sonvilla-Weiss's hard disk analogy indicates, this new line of research is also bound up with the language of technology. Moreover, it places its emphasis on the reconfiguration and storage of meaning, rather than on meaning generation. For Eduardo Navas, contemporary remix culture is made possible by the unprecedented availability of information through modern technologies like the computer and the internet, separating it from derivative products of the past. Expanding on Lawrence Lessig's copyright-focused definition of what a remix culture entails (2001, 12–15), Navas proposes that 'remix culture can be defined as the global activity consisting of the creative and efficient exchange of information made possible by digital technologies that is supported by the practice of cut/copy and paste' (2009, para. 1). This intentionally broad definition makes little distinction between various modes of remix production, between their purpose and effect, or between 'high' and 'low' art, though of course these distinctions are still present in the practice itself. This book embraces remix culture's both/and approach in selecting examples of Frankenfiction, but remains wary of the loss of critical focus this approach can enable. Frankenfiction may present sources from different cultures and registers on equal footing, but the decision to do so in the first place signals lingering distinctions between these sources that must be addressed.

In addition to technological analogies, metaphors of genetic manipulation and monstrous bodies abound in remix studies. Sonvilla-Weiss calls the combination of remix and mashup practices 'a coevolving oscillating membrane of user-generated content (conversational media) and mass media' (2010, 9). David Gunkel describes remix still more dramatically as 'the monstrous outcome of illegitimate fusions and promiscuous reconfigurations of recorded media that take place in excess of the comprehension, control, and proper authority of the "original artist"' (2016, xxix–xxx). It takes a very small leap indeed to link these descriptions of membranes, fusions, and reconfigurations to the Frankensteinian monster of Shelley's novel. The Gothic imagery invoked by remix studies terminology is yet another reason that I favour Gothic comparisons when describing the monstrous genre of Frankenfiction. As I will also demonstrate, however, Frankenfiction is not always as 'monstrous' as it claims to be. The original artist may not be in direct control, but Frankenfiction is certainly governed by familiar systems of authorship and authority.

Because of remix studies' catch-all approach to the practices it describes, a shared terminology has become all but impossible to define. In some studies terms like 'mashup', 'remix', 'collage', and 'bootleg' are interchangeable, while in others they indicate different kinds of practices or relationships with their source texts (Gunkel 2016, 20–1). For David Laderman and Laurel Westrup, 'even the most cursory history of sampling, collage, mash-up, and remix points to the long history of interaction between diverse but not wholly divergent practices' (2014, 3). The decision to describe something as one or the other, however, has remained fundamentally arbitrary, defined more by the background of the individual researcher than by any shared set of views (Gunkel 2016, 24–5). As the field develops, this situation will no doubt improve, but for the time being it affords us the opportunity to consider the politics of categorizing Frankenfiction in more explicit detail.

In his introduction to the 2010 essay collection *Mashup Cultures*, Stefan Sonvilla-Weiss lays out an extensive, yet intentionally broad, differentiation between mashup and other remix practices:

    a) Collage, montage, sampling or remix practices all use one or many materials, media either from other sources, art pieces (visual arts, film, music, video, literature etc.) or one's own artworks through alteration, re-combination, manipulation, copying etc. to create a whole new piece. In doing so, the sources of origin may still be identifiable yet not perceived as the original version.

b) Mashups as I understand them put together different information, media, or objects without changing their original source of information, i.e. the original format remains the same and can be retraced as the original form and content, although recombined in different new designs and contexts. For example, in the ship or car industry standardised modules are assembled following a particular specific design platform, or, using the example of Google map [*sic*], different services are over-layered so as to provide for the user parallel accessible services. (Sonvilla-Weiss 2010, 9)

In other words, for Sonvilla-Weiss remix represents the creation of 'a whole new piece' (highly subjective phrasing) from a selection and alteration of many others, which may or may not be attributed or identifiable in the final result. The resulting remix is seen as an 'original' work. Mashup, on the other hand, collects and assembles materials without altering the 'original format' – again, a tenuous concept where narrative is concerned – beyond recognition. For Sonvilla-Weiss, a text like *Pride and Prejudice and Zombies* might well fall into the category of mashup, borrowing as it does such a high percentage of Austen's unaltered text. Most of what I term mashup in this book, however, would for him likely fall into the category of 'remix practice', or at best some combination of mashup and remix techniques. The collection does not mention Quirk Books's literary mashups at all, though Henry Jenkins's contribution, on how fan reading practices can apply to teaching canonical literature, does refer to Sheenagh Pugh's discussion of derivative works like Jean Rhys's *Wide Sargasso Sea* (1966), Gregory Maguire's *Wicked* (1995), and Linda Berdoll's *Mr. Darcy Takes a Wife* (2004) (Jenkins 2010, 112).[3] Frankenfiction fits no category comfortably. It seems to lack the historical reverence and narrative fidelity needed for adaptation, it sometimes lacks the level of transformation and originality Sonvilla-Weiss requires of remix, and in most cases it fails to resort to the direct copying that would fully qualify it as a mashup.

In addition to the difficulty of putting Frankenfictions firmly into the category of 'adaptation', 'remix', or 'mashup', we must take the background of remix scholars themselves into account. Remix studies is a body of work composed largely by scholars working in communications technologies, computer science, media studies, popular music, and cultural studies. When they do cite a narrative or 'literary' mashup, the reference is almost always to *Pride and Prejudice and Zombies*, indicating that while these theories may view the appropriation of text as mashup, the appropriation of characters, plot, or events is not their first concern. In this light adaptation studies, more traditionally home to literature, film, and television scholars, seems as though it should be a more productive approach to identifying and categorizing the act of historical monster mashup.

Frankenfiction as adaptation

Adaptation studies often considers examples of Frankenfiction on a case-by-case basis where it intersects with whatever the real object of study may be: biofiction, heritage cinema, the neo-Victorian, etc. The key reason for the inclusion of Frankenfiction under the label of 'adaptation' here is disciplinary. As narrative-based texts that most often appropriate a literary (or at least textual) past, all historical monster mashups are of potential interest to literary studies, where adaptation is a popular subject. In defining the historical monster mashup specifically as a collection of *narrative* texts, I have also taken a literary studies approach to the genre. As a relatively young academic discipline (though older than remix studies), adaptation studies suffers from many of the same difficulties of definition as remix, or as the historical monster mashup itself. Because adaptive practices are so diverse, and can be found in an extremely wide range of texts, definitions quickly become either too broad or too narrow to be of any use. This is only made more difficult by the fact that many of the cultural pillars such a definition would need to rely on – originality, authenticity, literariness – are themselves contested and unstable. Many critics in the field neglect to define adaptation at all, instead proceeding from the assumption that a specific text *is* an adaptation, generally based on plot or marketing, and extrapolating form and function retroactively.

In a chapter appropriately entitled 'Adaptation and Intertextuality, Or, What Isn't an Adaptation and What Does It Matter?' (2012), Thomas Leitch illustrates the difficulties in conceptualizing adaptation to great effect. Highlighting work by Julie Sanders, Linda Hutcheon, Robert Stam, and Christine Geraghty (among others), Leitch sketches out nine prevalent definitions of adaptation. He deconstructs each definition in its turn, weighing its advantages and disadvantages as a comprehensive overview of the field. Some of these definitions overlap, but many are in direct contradiction with others. Not only does this exemplify the problems and assumptions inherent in defining adaptation as a discipline, it provides a convenient opportunity to consider why many historical monster mashups can and have been usefully classified as adaptations – and why many also challenge this classification. In almost every case, the mashup serves as an excellent example of why such definitions break down. This allows us to comment on the fact that adaptation and historical appropriation are each driven by similar concerns, such as the economic and cultural capital of source texts, legal constraints, or personal and political motives (see Hutcheon 2013, 85–95).

The first definition of adaptation Leitch examines is that '[a]daptations are exclusively cinematic, involving only films that are based on novels or plays or stories' (2012, 89). Leitch constructs this definition based on the tendency of early adaptation studies to focus exclusively on this particular, dualistic transition, often approaching the adaptive impulse as a question of fidelity and influence (Leitch 2012, 89). This definition becomes most obviously problematic in a case like that of *Pride + Prejudice + Zombies*, which deviates substantially from Quirk Books's own 2009 adaptation of *Pride and Prejudice*. Should we consider the film as an adaptation of *Pride and Prejudice and Zombies*, or as another zombie-filled adaptation of *Pride and Prejudice*? This same issue can be seen in the television series *Penny Dreadful*, which initially drew allegations of plagiarism for its mashup adaptation of literary texts, despite being a markedly different type of narrative than Alan Moore and Kevin O'Neill's *The League of Extraordinary Gentlemen* (Faraci 2013). Clearly, the trail of influence was strong enough to cause some viewers to attribute a different source of inspiration for *Penny Dreadful* than its creators anticipated.

The literature-to-film definition may no longer be the prevalent one, but for Leitch many scholarly accounts of adaptation, such as Deborah Cartmell and Imelda Whelehan's edited collection *Adaptations: From Text to Screen, Screen to Text*, are 'still fundamentally dualistic' (Cartmell and Whelehan 1999; Leitch 2012, 89), creating dichotomies between media like film and text that are not necessarily well founded or helpful in the age of convergence or remix culture. As Kamilla Elliot argues in *Rethinking the Novel/Film Debate*, adaptation 'lies between the rock of a post-Saussurean insistence that form does not and cannot separate from content and the hard place of poststructuralism's debunking of content, of original and local signifieds alike' (2003, 3–4). In other words, adaptation is impossible to systematically define, since the presence and recognizability of intertextual crossovers depends entirely on an infinite and highly context-specific set of possibilities. In the face of this challenge, adaptation scholars (largely from film or literature backgrounds) have the tendency to fall back on disciplinary familiarities and case studies, repeatedly using the same limited range of examples to make generalizations about the system as a whole. For Elliot, this practice is 'largely responsible for many of the problems plaguing adaptation studies in particular and novel and film studies in general and for the pervasive sense that adaptation scholars lag behind the critical times' (2003, 4). In twenty-first-century convergence culture, the postmodern 'debunking of content' Elliot describes is reinforced by the increased 'flow of media across multiple media platforms' (Jenkins 2006, 3). It is not necessarily useful to focus on *which* media a text is adapted between, or even *how* this is achieved in a binary, comparative context. Instead, it becomes more interesting to consider *why* this adaptation occurs at all, across any medium. No two texts, or even two performances of the same text, are exactly the same, but the politics of this inevitable difference remain relevant.

As a result of its previous focus, however, adaptation studies now has a distinct reputation as a specialized field within literature and film studies that is difficult to work around. Even though Frankenfictions tend to appropriate material from more than one source, scholarly analysis of these texts still tends to focus on the details by which a dualistic comparison is possible. For example, Bruno Starrs describes the film *Van Helsing* (2004) as 'a loose, analogous adaptation of the stories of Dracula, The Wolfman, Frankenstein, Dr. Jekyll and Mr. Hyde' (2004, 5). He then immediately points out that the film 'merely alludes to some key characters from the Stoker novel, however, simplifying them more radically to permit as many action sequences as possible' (Starrs 2004, 5). This seems to suggest that, were it a *good* adaptation of these literary texts rather than a 'loose' one, it would be more faithful to the character descriptions the novels contain. Such an approach disregards the influence other films, characters, and stories have had on the creation and execution of *Van Helsing*, including the Indiana Jones films, Japanese anime, and the steampunk movement.[4] The text-to-screen approach to adaptation, then, proves inadequate to cover the existing range of mashup texts. In theory, remix studies lacks the fundamentally binary, value-judgement-laden baggage of adaptation studies. In practice such problems still persist, if on a muted scale. Although it is true that many mashups appear to challenge the binary oppositions between high culture and low culture, old and new, past and present, often this challenge is only visible because it foregrounds these established cultural binaries to begin with (Vallee 2013).

The second definition of adaptation that Leitch explores asserts that adaptations 'are exclusively intermedial, involving the transfer of narrative elements from one medium to another' (2012, 91). Leitch advocates this intermedial definition of adaptation for the neutrality of its language, pointing out that the cultural studies approach of many of its theorists 'does not automatically imply such [value] judgements' (2012, 91). The intermedial approach has two key problems, however. First is the difficulty 'in differentiating between adaptation and other intermedial practices' (2012, 92), the latter referring to more subtle types of appropriation and reference. The second problem with the intermedial approach is 'the widespread existence of adaptations that are intramedial' (within the same medium like Stoker's *Dracula* and Newman's *Anno Dracula*) 'rather than intermedial' (in different media like Shelley's *Frankenstein* and Showtime's *Penny Dreadful*) (Leitch 2012, 92). Although it may be tempting to see the historical monster mashup as intermedial given the large number of film, television, video game, and comic book realizations of literary characters and stories, this view ignores the vast variety of literary mashups that themselves take the form of a novel – *Mr. Darcy, Vampyre* (2009), *Jane Bites Back* (2009), etc. Novels like *Pride and Prejudice and Zombies* (2009) or *Wuthering Bites* (2010), which come close to replicating classic novels in their entirety, and which Camilla Nelson refers to as 'differently adapted texts' (2013, 338), further contest this particular definition of adaptation. When we also consider the category of the transmedial – a single story constructed across multiple texts and media, as in the case of *Van Helsing*[5] – this cross-medial approach requires us to 'parcel out adaptation among [the three] instead of considering it as a unified set of texts or textual operations or a unified disciplinary field' (Leitch 2012, 92). In Leitch's mind (and in my own), this creates unnecessary disciplinary division.

'Adaptations are counter-ekphrases' in Leitch's third definition, acting in opposition to the idea that we can represent 'artworks in one medium by artworks in another' (2012, 92). Here adaptations are explicitly unfaithful, and highlight the impossibility of literal translation from one medium to another. Frankenfiction does not fit into this definition very well, for the simple reason that it neither pretends to replicate a particular source (not even in the case of *Pride and Prejudice and Zombies*) nor directly picks apart that claim. For Leitch, every adaptation 'both contests and confirms the status of its source by identifying it as a source' (2012, 93), something ekphrasis, which purports to reflect or recreate the object it addresses, is not concerned with. Because the understanding of adaptation as a *changed* version of the object it adapts is already so widespread in the field, Leitch sees this definition of adaptation as counter-ekphrasis as no longer beneficial, and for the most part the playful-yet-serious tone of the historical monster mashup supports this assertion. This may also be why it is so difficult to find examples of mashup that could be considered straightforwardly as either ekphrasis or counter-ekphrasis. In a postmodern cultural climate, the first option is discarded offhand as artistically impossible, while the second is blatantly self-evident, or unfashionable. Of course, mashups like *Pride and Prejudice and Zombies*, or the photo modifications of Colin Batty and Kevin J. Weir (discussed in Chapter 4), do challenge the idea that all adaptations are fundamentally transformative by reproducing so much of their source material exactly. Their existence suggests that Leitch's assumption about the outdatedness of counter-ekphrasis may be premature.

Leitch's fourth approach at sketching the boundaries of adaptation comes from Linda Hutcheon, who argues (as paraphrased by Leitch) that the status of adaptations 'depends on the audience's acceptance of a deliberate invitation to read them as adaptations' (Leitch 2012, 94; Hutcheon 2013, 6). This is precisely the definition I am now using to engage in an exploration of the mashup's various forms and functions in adaptation studies. It is also a somewhat tautological and self-fulfilling definition, though this is arguably what makes it useful. The self-identification approach assumes that whatever is called an adaptation by its audience, and marketed as such by its creators, must therefore be an adaptation. Most mashups are not advertised as adaptations in the same way a BBC costume drama might be, since such advertising tends to rely on the same binary, text-to-screen model Leitch critiques. Likewise, where costume dramas often emphasize the way they continue the legacy of their source texts, implicitly claiming the power, status, or authority of these sources for themselves, with mashups the focus is more often on the disjunction between texts. Mashups do sometimes satirize the language of costume drama in their marketing, however (i.e. 'Jane Austen like you've never seen her before' or calls to rediscover the classics).

Leitch sees the problem with this particular definition of adaptation as stemming from its 'double focus on production and reception' (2012, 95): it has to be created as an adaptation, and it also has to be perceived or understood as such by its audience. This introduces issues of universality, for the simple reason that even if a text is considered an adaptation by its creators, it is likely that not every member of its audience will agree with this, or pick up on it while viewing. Leitch cites the 1998 remake of *Psycho*, based on Robert Bloch's 1959 novel but exclusively compared to Alfred Hitchcock's 1960 film, as an example of this potential disconnect. The remake copies many shots from Hitchcock's adaptation exactly, and recycles the earlier film's script and music as well. A series like *The League of Extraordinary Gentlemen*, which borrows from a range of obscure Victorian texts in addition to the more readily identified ones, could be offered as another challenge to this definition. In this case full knowledge of the comic's status as adaptation, and all of the Victorian texts it references, is offered as a secondary layer of the text – a collection of 'Easter Eggs' available to the more dedicated reader.[6] The film adaptation of *Pride and Prejudice and*

Zombies also makes a pertinent example of the way an 'adaptation' can be linked to a mashup it only loosely mimics.

My own issues with Hutcheon's self-fulfilling definition of adaptation are slightly different in focus. Like the intermedial approach to adaptation, Hutcheon's conceptualization suggests that 'there appears to be little need' to address questions of fidelity, or of 'degrees of proximity to the "original"' – a promising start (2013, 7). Rather than seeking the relative terminological neutrality of intermediality or remix, however, Hutcheon's approach then directly addresses some of the baggage that comes with the term 'adaptation', emphasizing, in Leitch's words, 'the motives and interests that provide legal, moral, and aesthetic sanction for some kinds of copies, the derivations that are not derivative, but not others' (2012, 96). Hutcheon's definition specifically excludes exact replicas, like 'music sampling' or the 'museum exhibit', and misleading duplicates, like 'plagiarisms' or forgeries, from the category of adaptation (2013, 9, 172). This qualification does not exclude most historical monster mashups, which tend to be fairly overt in their transformation of historical texts, but it does raise several unanswered questions. What, for example, do we do with repackaged or remarketed versions of the same text?

Take the 2009 reprint of *Wuthering Heights*, which capitalized on the popularity of Stephenie Meyer's *Twilight* series. The re-packaged novel featured a red, white, and black cover (in both the UK and US versions) that imitated those of Meyer's books, as well as an embossed sticker announcing it as 'Bella and Edward's favourite book' (Wallop 2010, para. 4). Sales of *Wuthering Heights* quadrupled in that year (2010, para. 5). The edition indirectly invited fans of the vampire novels to read Heathcliff as an Edward figure. This new parallel between Emily Brontë's Gothic novel and the 2005 vampire romance also invites comparisons to Brontë and Sarah Gray's *Wuthering Bites* (2010), in which Heathcliff is reimagined as a vampire. Does this count as adaptation? The question of repackaged versions of otherwise identical texts is addressed in more detail in Leitch's seventh definition of adaptation, which classifies adaptations as performances.

Continuing in the order of Leitch's article, a fifth definition describes adaptations as 'examples of a distinctive mode of transtextuality' (2012, 96). The definition of transtextuality used here by Leitch comes from Gérard Genette's own much-cited and appropriated text *Palimpsests* (1997). In his work on the topic of transtextuality (essentially a structuralist approach to intertextuality), Genette describes the 'perpetual state of transfusion, a transtextual perfusion' of texts (1997, 400), as textual bodies engage with each other in a myriad of ways. On the surface, this also seems to represent an excellent definition of Frankenfiction. Although Genette is primarily concerned with literature, his categorization of textual reference – or transcendence – into five categories (intertextuality, paratextuality, metatextuality, hypertextuality, and architextuality) is easily applied to narrative art across all contemporary media, including the historical monster mashup. The structuralist nature of his approach to these terms by no means invalidates a post-structuralist appropriation of his framework and terminology. In Genette's definition, intertextuality involves the 'relationship of co-presence between two texts or among several texts', or more explicitly, 'the actual presence of one text within another' (1997, 1–2). It is not explicitly clear what Genette means by the phrase 'actual presence'. For him it includes such practices as quotation, plagiarism, and direct allusion. Presumably, intertextuality then includes the extensive quotation of *Pride and Prejudice* performed in *Pride and Prejudice and Zombies*, just as it includes the mention of the author Bram Stoker in *Anno Dracula*, the actual Victorian cabinet cards painted on by Colin Batty, the replicated newspaper clippings and letters that appear in video games like *Assassin's Creed Syndicate* and *The Order: 1886* (Côté 2015; Jan and Weerasuriya 2015), or the moment in the first few minutes of *Van Helsing*, where Dr Frankenstein cries 'It's alive ... it's alive!' in reference to the 1931 film *Frankenstein* (Whale 1931).

Paratextuality, in contrast, refers (for Genette) to the elements surrounding the text but not directly part of the narrative, which a reader must nevertheless encounter in order to access the text (1997, 4). These elements include a peritext (chapter titles, footnotes, illustrations, prefaces, etc.) and an epitext (reviews, interviews, publicity, authorial or editorial discussion, and so forth). As texts that have inherited some of the postmodern tendency for self-reference, monster mashups often employ paratextual elements in their storytelling process. *The League of Extraordinary Gentlemen*, for example, features paratextual references to the next issue that, in keeping with the genre *League* mimics, are in the style of *The Boy's Own Paper* – a British story periodical that ran from 1879 to 1967, and was aimed at an audience of young boys. Consider the following example of *League*'s paratext, from the end of the second issue: 'The next edition of our new Boys' Picture Monthly will continue this arresting yarn, in which the Empire's Finest are brought into conflict with the sly Chinese, accompanied by a variety of coloured illustrations from our artist that are sure to prove exciting to the manly, outward going youngster of today' (Moore and O'Neill 2000, n.p.; see Figure 1.1). *League* also includes its own commentaries, interviews, and publicity, both fictional and real, and its own fictionalized descriptions of the comic's creators. Alasdair Gray's novel *Poor Things* (1992) includes a number

Figure 1.1 Conclusion of *The League of Extraordinary Gentlemen Vol. I*, Issue #2 (2000 paperback edition), © Alan Moore and Kevin O'Neill. Permission given by Tony Bennett at Knockabout Comics. Scan by the author.

of Victorian-style anatomical drawings, which appear alongside the text but do not always comment on it directly. As I discuss in Chapter 4, the visual artist Travis Louie also uses paratextual caption narratives to help frame his paintings in a specific way.

Genette's third type of transtextuality is metatextuality, consisting of explicit or implicit references in one text to another.[7] As one might imagine, there is substantial overlap between metatextuality and intertextuality, which is one reason 'intertextuality' has come to be taken as a blanket term for all of these various textual relationships. In Genette's words – and in another ghostly metaphor – metatextuality 'unites a given text to another, of which it speaks without necessarily citing it (without summoning it), in fact sometimes even without naming it' (1997, 4). Here the reference is implied rather than stated, but is still meant to be noticed and understood as a reference. An appropriate example from Frankenfiction might be a text which attempts to remain faithful to another text's particular style, or to its paratextual purpose. For example, *Penny Dreadful* not only attempts to revive popular literary classics for television, but also seeks to re-establish the 'gothic-horror genre' as a whole, evoking familiar characters, stories and feelings through both direct and indirect citation (Slayton 2014).

The fourth kind of transtextuality described in Genette's work is hypertextuality, which involves 'any relationship uniting a text B (which I shall call *hypertext*) to an earlier text A (I shall, of course, call it the *hypotext*), upon which it is grafted in a manner that is not that of commentary' (1997, 5). This, again, is a very vague definition. Any relationship between one text and another also necessarily serves as a form of commentary, however incidental. For Genette, hypertextuality represents a transformative, modificational, or elaboratory relationship between one text and another text or genre on which it is based. All texts are hypertextual to some degree (1997, 9), but explicit examples of this type of transtextuality might include parody, spoof, sequel, or translation.

It is interesting that chronology should be mentioned explicitly in relation to these non-commentarial hypertexts. One problem with the historical monster mashup arises precisely in the negotiation of such hierarchies between texts. Which is the hypertext and which is the hypotext? Or to put it another way, which text is the 'self' of the narrative and which is the 'other'? The film version of *Pride and Prejudice and Zombies* was allegedly an adaptation of Grahame-Smith's book, not Austen's, and *Sense and Sensibility and Sea Monsters* is arguably based as much on *Pride and Prejudice and Zombies* (which was conceived at the same time) as it was on *Sense and Sensibility*, or on the stories of H.P. Lovecraft or Jules Verne. Genette argues that all literary texts are hypertextual, but for him the definition does not work the other way around, and his subsequent discussion of literary hypertext fails to interrogate the binary categories onto which they fall back. These kinds of discussions are, as always, inevitably bound up in questions of fidelity and literary value judgements. Additionally, as stories are retold again and again, many people come into contact with the mashup long before they are aware of the alleged hypotext, and 'their version' will always hold the most prominent position in their minds. It is conceivable that younger generations of readers, for example, might be more familiar with Newman's *Anno Dracula* or the film *Bram Stoker's Dracula* (Coppola 1992) than they are with the actual text of Stoker's novel, and only come to relate to the latter text through the lens of the former. The same is true of *Frankenstein* adaptations, as the examples throughout this book testify.

Finally, Genette speaks of architextuality, in which a text is designated as belonging to a particular genre or set of genres. For Genette 'the reader's expectations, and thus their reception of the work' are a very important factor in this final category (1997, 5). This characterization is echoed in Hutcheon's description of adaptation as a self-defined category, and comes with the same set of problems. By definition, mashups *all* play with the means by which a text is generically categorized. One could argue that they form their own genre, which consists solely of a mixing between others.[8] Even this distinction, however, is called into question by early instances of photomanipulation,[9] or by the existence of the novel or the penny dreadful, which were creating and challenging genre boundaries long before the twenty-first-century mashup.

Genette's five types of transtextuality can all be found in the historical monster mashup in varying degrees, though as we can see none really comes close to serving as a blanket definition for Frankenfiction, or to distinguishing between adaptation and other categories. As Leitch also points out, Genette himself admits the unreliability of his distinction between these five transtextual modes and the dubiousness of building a definition of adaptation from his taxonomy. Right from the beginning of *Palimpsests* Genette states that 'one must not view the five types of transtextuality as separate and absolute categories without any reciprocal contact or overlapping' (1997, 7). Not even hypertext and hypotext are distinguishable. As Genette writes, 'every successive state of a written text functions like a hypertext in relation to the state that precedes it, and like a hypotext in relation to the one that follows' (1997, 395). Even, allegedly, original texts like the *Iliad* or *The Song of Roland* are simply 'hypertexts whose hypotexts are unknown' (1997, 381). Not even Genette's assertion that there are 'two fundamental types of hypertextual derivation: transformation and imitation' is entirely reliable (1997, 394), as what constitutes a transformation instead of an imitation is highly subjective for any number of reasons. Does a copy-and-paste mashup like *Jane Slayre* (2010) qualify as a subtle transformation, or as a lazy imitation? Often, as I will explore throughout this book, the answer depends largely on the status of the mashup's author(s), and of the text's place in the hierarchy of the entertainment industry.

Leitch's sixth definition of adaptation, which argues that 'adaptations are translations' (2012, 97), is one I personally find very appealing – just as I do Hutcheon's notion of adaptation as interpretation. In my mind, part of the problem with adaptation comes from the word itself, which, as Linda Costanzo Cahir states, implies a shift of what is essentially the *'same entity'* from one environment to another, dissimilar one (2006, 14; cited in Leitch 2012, 98–9, original italics). If adaptations are translations – that is, *'a materially different entity'* that can stand on its own (Cahir 2006, 14, original italics), rather than a simple transposition – then this represents one definition into which Frankenfiction almost fits comfortably, with only a few lingering value judgements and questions of fidelity. Unlike a translation, of course, Frankenfiction is positioned explicitly *in relation* to a particular body of texts, not *in the place* of them, but like a translation Frankenfiction can come to stand in for these texts in specific popular contexts, illustrated by the fact that *Pride and Prejudice and Zombies* has been used in classrooms as a way to introduce students to Austen's novel (Wyett et al. 2013). Viewing adaptation as translation thus provides an interesting perspective from which to view historical monster mashup. Most importantly, it sidesteps the binary comparison between text and source by acknowledging the nuance inherent in issues of fidelity, asking instead 'to what [...] should the translator be *most* faithful? The question is not that of the translation's faithfulness, but of its *faithfulness to what?'* (Cahir 2006, 15, original italics).

In this context, rather than asking whether a mashup like *The League of Extraordinary Gentlemen* is faithful to *Dracula, 20,000 Leagues Under the Sea*, or the *Boys' Own Magazine*, we would instead focus on which aspects of these texts it does or does not emphasize, and in what ways, before moving on to analyse how it stands as a text in its own right. One might also take the literal translations of a text like *Pride and Prejudice and Zombies* into account. In the Dutch version of the mashup, for example, rather than re-translating Austen's text an old Dutch translation was used, with minor updates to the language. This helped to maintain a certain level of linguistic familiarity for the target audience (Van der Werf and De Bruin-Molé 2015). A contrasting example might be *Assassin's Creed Syndicate* and *The Order: 1886* – two video game versions of Victorian London that were released in the same year (2015). Despite many comparable features and a broadly similar narrative, *The Order* was not as critically well received as *Syndicate*, not because its rendering of Victorian London was inaccurate, but because it did not allow the gamer enough flexibility to explore that environment. In other words, it failed as a big-budget video game, but not necessarily as a translation or an adaptation. Much as it appeals to me for its broadness, however, this approach still does not sufficiently distinguish translation (or adaptation) as a unique kind of communication. As George Steiner points out, translation studies has 'widely accepted' the idea that 'translation is formally and pragmatically implicit in *every* act of communication' (1992, xii), not just professionally translated works. There is no fixed meaning even in professional literary translation, as the text itself is translated again by readers, and differently at every reading. Again, there is no pre-adaptation, making an exclusive definition of adaptation difficult. This is an idea I will return to in Chapter 3, where I look at the ways mashup irony is interpreted and misinterpreted, potentially failing to 'translate' well to certain audiences.

If – as with acts of communication – all adaptations are interpretations, perhaps they are also all performances. This is the reasoning Leitch adopts in his exploration of a seventh definition of adaptation (2012, 99). As he suggests, however, this definition is not common in adaptation studies more generally. Hutcheon, who considers diverse things like 'musical arrangements and song covers, visual art revisitations of prior works and comic book versions of history' in her survey of various adaptations, considers 'live performance works' like plays or musical scores to be a 'parallel' case to adaptation, in which variations between performances are a result of 'the production process' (2013, 170). Here, then, we encounter a problem similar to that in Hutcheon's self-fulfilling definition of adaptation – though for the most part her work is exhaustive. What counts as a performance stops where we say it does, which, ultimately, is the problem with any definition or set of terms residing purely in textual, material, and thus literally 'readable' artefacts. Leitch notes, for example, that all films are technically performances of their screenplays. There are, undeniably, many ways that performance can influence a reading in this context.

Though Leitch sees this performance viewpoint on adaptation as problematic for a whole new set of issues it brings to light, he finds it useful from a very specific point of view. Namely, he proposes that adaptations (like prequels, sequels, or other derivative works) in fact treat their initiators as performance texts:

The most servile adaptation still implicitly proclaims its progenitor incomplete and in need of realization; otherwise why produce the adaptation at all? Even adaptations in the same medium as their alleged originals, like translations into a new language, pose as bringing these original works to new life by supplying something they notably lack. (Leitch 2012, 99)

This definition also provides an interesting context for the historical monster mashup, shifting its focus from one of pure nostalgia to one of cultural or political resonance. As I argue in Chapter 3, this definition is one that neo-Victorian studies has often taken, arguing that such texts use their historical context to fill in the blanks or right the wrongs of history. While this sounds productive in principle, what the mashup is doing is not quite in the same vein. It 'realizes' its initiator text, but in a way that is often self-referenced as a bad or inferior realization. As Leitch rightly notes, then, adaptation 'is the mode of intertextuality that has been defined from its beginnings as a problem child, a mode whose definition has focused on its challenge to the binaries on which both it and its critical discourse have depended' (2012, 101), though of course such contradictions also exist outside of adaptation studies.

Leitch's final two definitions of adaptation are intertwined, and build heavily upon the definitions that come before, splitting them into two broad groups. In the first, adaptations are seen as 'quintessential examples of intertextual practice' (Leitch 2012, 100). In this model, adaptation (and its associated disciplines of film and literary studies) comes to be seen as the central way of looking at how texts relate to each other, and to themselves. Intertextuality is always viewed through the lens of adaptation in this example: the 'principles and practices' of adaptation scholars become 'presumptive models for the whole range of intertextual studies' (Leitch 2012, 100). This rather wishful definition sees adaptation as a mode of narrative at the forefront of textual unification, through a series of binary relationships that are always somehow more than binary. Rochelle Hurst, for example, speaks of adaptation as 'a hybrid, an amalgam of media – at once a cinematized novel *and* a literary film, confusing, bridging, and rejecting the alleged discordance between page and screen, both insisting upon and occupying the overlap' (2008, 188). In other words, an adaptation somehow combines multiple sources and media into a single text, denying that there is any real discordance between the two. Again, this approach is not particularly useful when considering Frankenfiction, though it does represent an extreme example of both the presentation and the breakdown of formal binaries in a single text. Historical monster mashup is not avant-garde in terms of form. It is too mainstream in this regard, like the monsters it contains. Without fail, it presents a coherent story and picture. As I will demonstrate in this book, however, meaning in Frankenfiction is created precisely by drawing attention to the seams in its combinations of register, genre, and medium.

In direct contrast to the eighth definition, the ninth and final definition of adaptation in Leitch's list sees the practice as 'a distinctive instance, but not a central or quintessential instance, of intertextuality' (2012, 102). In other words, adaptation is one of many terms that categorize the interaction between texts, and can itself mean many different things. It may even be an artificial, purely disciplinary construction, which will soon be 'dethroned by another contender' as a key approach to intertextuality among film and literature scholars (Leitch 2012, 102). Leitch refers to this definition as the equivalent of surrender, precisely because it refuses to offer a comprehensive model of adaptation. He thus concludes in an appropriately inconclusive manner:

> After reviewing the problems involved in organizing the discipline more rigorously, adaptation scholars may well decide to defer the question of what isn't adaptation indefinitely. (2012, 103)

Leitch argues that it might also be useful to examine adaptation from the outside in, approaching it from the categories that border it on all sides. This is the approach I have taken in my study of Frankenfiction, examining adaptation from the perspective of monstrous remix, parody, Gothic and historical fiction, and authorship. This approach does leave adaptation studies in the position of having to rationalize 'the field we have fenced in and demonstrating its integrity', however (Leitch 2012, 103).

Frankenfiction as appropriation

While both remix studies and adaptation studies offer useful ways of approaching the historical monster mashup, neither has offered a particularly satisfying way to categorize it. Both are concerned with the integrity of an imagined 'original' or 'source', without being entirely clear what those terms mean. Adaptation implies a 'legitimate' borrowing, as opposed to illegitimate appropriation, but this distinction is increasingly difficult to defend. Remix faces a similar struggle. When Gunkel and other remix studies scholars talk of recombination, they almost always refer to texts that appropriate from a readily identifiable author or author group. This ignores the authored nature of signs and language in general, and the extent to which authorship is 'always anterior, never original' (Barthes 1978, 146).

Part of the problem undoubtedly lies in the way we define how a language, myth, or narrative becomes common knowledge, open to creative appropriation. When Alice Ostriker called women poets 'thieves of language', she was talking about something at once similar to and fundamentally different from the appropriation typically cited in remix or adaptation studies, or even in Frankenfiction (1982, 69). Writing about women's appropriation of classical myth, Ostriker suggests that we must 'look at, or into, but not up at, sacred things; we unlearn submission' to the language and literature that, until quite recently, has been about women rather than by women (1982, 87). This act of revision looks back without validation, but is certainly as interested in where it comes from as where it is now. Like the practice of cultural analysis, it is palimpsestuous, 'a treatment of time that effectively flattens it so that the past is not then but now' (1982, 87). I will return to this feminist perspective on appropriation in Chapters 2 and 5, but for now it serves to highlight the way appropriation, like remix, mashup, and adaptation before it, remains highly politicized.

Julie Sanders's work is perhaps the best-known and most successful recent attempt at distinguishing between adaptation and appropriation, though her definition is still far from conclusive. The closest Sanders comes to a distinction between adaptation and appropriation is in her introduction, where she also contrasts both terms with the concept of citation:

> [C]itation is different again to adaptation, which constitutes a more sustained engagement with a single text or source than the more glancing act of allusion or quotation, even citation, allows. Beyond that, appropriation carries out the same sustained engagement as adaptation but frequently adopts a posture of critique, even assault. (2006, 4)

While citation can claim a kind of academic distance, then, adaptation involves a more intimate and equal relationship between texts. It is also implied that this relationship is positive, whereas appropriation sets itself up as an antagonist to, or as exploitative of, the text it appropriates. Examples of both kinds of relationships can be found in Frankenfiction. Often, as I will show in Chapter 3, they even can be found within the same text.

It is noteworthy that Sanders herself does not claim that either mode of writing always performs one way or another. Nor does she make a distinction between the cultural status of the appropriator and the appropriated. As Richard Rogers notes in his article on the more specific instance of *cultural appropriation* – defined here as 'the use of a culture's symbols, artifacts, genres, rituals, or technologies by members of another culture' – sociopolitical context is key (2006, 474). This context can change the connotations of the term 'appropriation' to mean anything from exchange, to dominance, exploitation, and transculturation (2006, 477).

Frankenfiction represents a palimpsestuous act of appropriation across time, from a past culture. More often than not, however, this appropriation is from one dominant culture to another dominant culture, rather than a dominant culture to a marginalized one, as in Ostriker's examples. In Frankenfiction, twenty-first-century mass culture reads the mass cultural products of the long nineteenth century. In doing so, it reveals that while there are many parallels, some encouraging and some disturbing, between the two cultures, there are also yawning gaps and incongruities in our experiences of them. This is why, although appropriation is perhaps the best fit of the four (remix, mashup, adaptation, appropriation) in terms of scholarly definitions, I still favour the term 'mashup' to describe these works of monstrous historical fiction. Like the term 'Frankenstein', it indicates an uncomfortable, but ultimately successful recombination of things that do not traditionally fit together: adaptation and remix, literature and popular fiction, but also, as the following chapters will show, monstrosity and the mainstream, history and fantasy, irony and nostalgia, genius and womanhood.

Hauntings and illegitimate offspring

In her now-famous manifesto, Donna Haraway introduces yet another metaphor for mashup: the figure of the cyborg. A hybrid of organic and mechanical, nature and monster, Haraway's cyborg rejects historical nostalgia and humanist logic. 'In a sense,' writes Haraway, 'the cyborg has no origin story' (1990, 192). She pits the cyborg against Frankenstein's monster as an example of what she means with this statement, writing: 'Unlike the hopes of Frankenstein's monster, the cyborg does not expect its father to save it' (1990, 192). Frankenstein's monster wishes to pattern himself on his creator, but for Haraway this model of monstrosity is no longer adequate in twentieth-century identity politics. The cyborg, like Frankenstein's monster, is an 'illegitimate offspring', but its parentage – and by association its relationship to patriarchal histories – is 'inessential' (1990, 193). In other words, for Haraway if we are to move forward as a culture we must, to some degree, forget the past. Of course, as subsequent studies in postmodernism, posthumanism, and other 'post-' disciplines have shown, this is neither as simple nor as revolutionary as it may seem. Margie Borschke suggests that despite its 'claim to newness' remix also 'signifies a return, or a repetition of sorts' (2017, 51, 33). Frankenfiction itself demonstrates how the past returns in unexpected ways, even as it is transformed.

Parental metaphors like the one Haraway uses are often evoked in cases of plagiarism or copyright infringement, and are also common in the case of remix (see especially Tushnet 2011; Roth and Flegel 2014). David Gunkel writes that, although the music mashup is 'a derivative and parasitic practice situated in the recorded material of others', its freedom from the single-origin model effectively cuts it off from its origins (2012, 81). Mashups are thus 'orphans cut off from and distributed beyond the authority of their progenitor' (2012, 81). Gunkel also returns to the favoured metaphor of the soul or spirit, arguing that we must '"give up the ghost" [...] let the author finally pass away and rot in the ground, and begin to conceive of writing and related endeavors otherwise' (2012, 82). He suggests that we must move away from traditional models of authority and authorship, and that mashups are an ideal vehicle for this departure. While this may certainly hold true for some kinds of mashup, it is not the case in Frankenfiction. These are Frankenstein's children, not ahistorical cyborgs: they recognize their parents and the promise of their birthright, and are unwilling to let either pass away. Instead, parent and offspring remain locked in an uneasy struggle. As Frankenstein's monster writes to his father, goading him to continue pursuit of his creation into the frozen north, 'My reign is not yet over [...] you live, and my power is complete' (Shelley [1831] 2015, 207). To succeed a text sometimes needs to cling to its origins – however problematic they themselves may be. Audiences and critics still recognize the concepts of originality and cultural heritage, making it necessary that texts continue to address them as well. As I will demonstrate throughout this book, we may boldly declare the 'ghost' of history, the author, or the source text dead, but they all continue to haunt us.

Notes

1   Because English is the primary language of popular global culture in the twenty-first century, and texts in this linguistic milieu tend to have the widest reach and impact, this book focuses on Anglophone examples of Frankenfiction, though the phenomenon itself is not entirely unique to the Anglo-American region. See the conclusion for examples of non-English monster mashup.

2   Sir Walter Scott, one of the progenitors of the historical novel, already comments on this paradox in his Dedicatory Epistle to *Ivanhoe* (1820), writing: 'Still the severer antiquary may think, that, by thus intermingling fiction with truth, I am polluting the well of history with modern inventions [...] It is necessary, for exciting interest of any kind, that the subject assumed should be, as it were, translated into the manners, as well as the language, of the age we live in' (W. Scott [1820] 1877, 17). For Scott, historical fiction is itself a mashup that rejects the antecedent forms it remixes.

3 I use 'derivative' here in the legal sense, which counterintuitively implies originality
   as well as intertextuality. US copyright law, for instance, defines a 'derivative
   work' as 'a work based upon one or more preexisting works [...] in which a work
   may be recast, transformed, or adapted. A work consisting of editorial revisions,
   annotations, elaborations, or other modifications which, as a whole, represent an
   original work of authorship, is a "derivative work"' ('Chapter 1: Subject Matter and
   Scope of Copyright' 2013, §101).

4 Steampunk, which encompasses a wide range of aesthetic and political standpoints
   on nineteenth-century industrialism, is arguably a kind of mashup. Although
   steampunk's diversity makes it difficult to say definitively that Frankenfiction
   should *not* be categorized as steampunk, Frankenfiction is neither as politically
   motivated as much steampunk fiction, nor as involved with contemporary
   technology (see Margaret Rose 2009; Ferguson 2011). Instead, the steampunk
   aesthetic (as appropriated by mainstream culture) simply becomes another easily
   recognizable cornerstone on which Frankenfiction can ground itself.

5 In addition to the animated prequel *The London Assignment*, there is a standalone
   comic book component to the *Van Helsing* adventure (Cf. Dysart and Alexander
   2004). The film itself is also part of a larger 'shared universe' currently being
   developed by Universal Pictures (Kit 2014).

6 *League* scholar Jess Nevins has dedicated painstaking effort to documenting all of
   these sources, and has published several volumes on the series (Nevins 2003, 2004,
   2008, 2018).

7 Genette's definition of metafiction is in contrast to later uses of the term. See Mark
   Currie's influential *Metafiction*, where it comes to mean 'the assimilation of critical
   perspective within fictional narrative, a self-consciousness of the artificiality of its
   constructions and a fixation with the relationship between language and the world'
   (Currie [1995] 2013, 2). While this could indeed still be seen as a reference from
   one text to another critical body of texts, metatextuality is now more commonly
   understood as a text's reference to its own textuality, at a narrative level rather than a
   paratextual one.

8 See, for example, artist Mark Vidler's description of 'genre crossing' in mashup,
   which in Gunkel's words involves 'the intermingling of different source material that
   involves seemingly incompatible styles, production values, and traditions in popular
   culture' (Vidler 2006; Gunkel 2016, 12).

9 Consider the case of the Cottingley Fairies photograph hoax, in which two girls
   from Cottingley, England, convinced a number of people, including Sir Arthur
   Conan Doyle, that they had captured fairies on film (Doyle 1922). Travis Louie cites
   this story as an inspiration for his photorealistic monster portraits (Leavitt 2013,
   para. 6).

2

Adapting the Monster

And what was I? [...] When I looked around I saw and heard of none like me.
Was I, then, a monster, a blot upon the earth, from which all man fled and
whom all men disowned?

(Shelley [1831] 2015, 116)

If Frankenfiction is the monstrous, hybrid offspring of remix culture and adaptation studies, as I argued in the previous chapter, my next step must be to establish what it means to call something a 'monster' in this context. In Western popular culture, the monster has become a mainstream symbol, which ironically makes it more difficult to locate and classify in fiction. As Marxist critic David McNally writes, 'it is a paradox of our age that monsters are both everywhere and nowhere' (2012, 2). This chapter examines four works of Frankenfiction that identify themselves as adaptations of literary monsters, actively attempting to breathe new life into classic symbols of monstrosity, while also straining our established definitions of adaptation and the monstrous. Like many contemporary texts, Frankenfictions adapt familiar monsters, but they often do so differently than other mainstream adaptations. This difference is not really in the types of monsters that are depicted, but rather in the way multiple depictions of monstrosity come together in a politicized gesture.

If we classify Frankenfiction as a monstrous historical mashup, with a metafictional interest in its own parentage that also aligns it with adaptation, we could take any number of contemporary texts as case studies. Many films, novels, and television series have pilfered the past for their monstrous adaptations, especially in recent years. In 2014, Universal Studios announced plans to reboot its own monster movies of the 1920s, '30s, and '40s. *Dracula Untold* (2014) failed to garner critical support, and was subsequently excluded from the official Universal Monsters Cinematic Universe, but the franchise re-launched with *The Mummy* in 2017 – another critical flop (Bradley 2017; D'Alessandro 2017). Undaunted, Universal announced (in a statement later retracted) that *The Invisible Man* would follow in 2018, and as of May 2018 additional films were still in production (Holmes 2018).

Other texts draw inspiration directly from the penny bloods, penny dreadfuls, and Gothic novels of the nineteenth century. *Strange Case of Dr Jekyll and Mr Hyde* (1886) has had at least three serial television adaptations in the last decade – the BBC's *Jekyll* (2007), NBC's *Do No Harm* (2013), and ITV's *Jekyll & Hyde* (2015) – as well as numerous adaptations and character cameos in other media. *Frankenstein* (1818), *The Picture of Dorian Gray* (1890), *Dracula* (1897), and *Carmilla* (1872) have all attracted renewed interest from storytellers, though naturally most of these texts have never truly fallen into obscurity.

While I could apply many of my conclusions about monsters and Frankenfiction to these direct re-imaginings of classic texts, most fall a little too neatly under the model of binary, novel-to-screen adaptation to make them interesting case studies. In large part, they also fail to do anything textually 'monstrous' or politically subversive with the old monsters they appropriate (the queer-friendly webseries *Carmilla*, 2014–16, is one notable exception). For this reason, my attention is focused on another kind of monster adaptation that has also become popular in the twenty-first century, and which locates itself more clearly in the ambivalent aesthetics and politics of Frankenfiction: the monster mash. Films and shows like *Van Helsing* (2004), *Mary Shelley's Frankenhole* (2010–12), *Once Upon a Time* (2011–18), *Hotel Transylvania* (2012), *I, Frankenstein* (2014), *Penny Dreadful* (2014–16), *Castlevania* (2017–19), and even *Monster High* (2010–15), or book series like Kim Newman's *Anno Dracula* (1992–2019), Terry Pratchett's *Discworld* (1983–2015), *The League of Extraordinary Gentlemen* (1999–2019), or Theodora Goss's *Extraordinary Adventures of the Athena Club* (2017–19) – as well as numerous video games, songs, and other media – have helped popularize this genre, which builds new stories through the amalgamation of well-known literary texts and monsters.

Although the specific combination of monsters introduced in these texts may be relatively new, the monster mash has its roots in older 'crossover' narrative (Nevins 2003, 175–84). The Victorians produced many texts that featured an eclectic assortment of literary and historical figures, just as they gave birth to many of the monsters, both real and fantastical, that have since dominated the popular imagination. Jess Nevins points to Mary Cowden Clarke's *Kit Bam's Adventures; or, The Yarns of an Old Mariner* (1849) as 'the first modern crossover, in which characters from different creators are brought together in a story by another creator' (2003, 175). Similar nineteenth-century crossovers include Henry Lee Boyle's *Kennaquhair, A Narrative of Utopian Travel* (1872), and John

Kendrick Bangs's *The Houseboat on the River Styx* (1895) and *The Pursuit of the Houseboat* (1897) (Nevins 2003, 178–9). The use of existing characters and intellectual properties has been the strategy of many an author and film studio ever since.

Alan Moore and Kevin O'Neill's *League* comics are themselves indebted to Philip José Farmer's novel *The Other Log of Phileas Fogg* (1973), which through embellishment and fantasy claims to reconstruct the true story behind Jules Verne's *Around the World in Eighty Days* (1872) (Nevins 2003, 184). Farmer's extended Wold Newton universe has also been cited as an important influence on Kim Newman and his *Anno Dracula* novels, both by the author and by others (Gaiman 2007, 5, author's introduction; Rodgers and Newman 2013, para. 23). Nicholas Meyer's *The Seven-Per-Cent Solution* (1976), which unites the fictional Sherlock Holmes with his historical contemporary Sigmund Freud, was a favourite childhood text of John Logan, *Penny Dreadful*'s writer and showrunner (Thielman 2014, para. 7). Likewise, the Universal monster crossovers have the same general premise as the *Anno Dracula* and *Athena Club* books, *Penny Dreadful*, and the *League* comics, though unlike the Universal crossovers these latter mashups claim a different, more explicitly revisionist agenda.

One could theoretically categorize these monster mashups as adaptations, but their pluralistic approach to source texts immediately foregrounds the non-binary structure of adaptation and remix in general. Instead, I would argue that they are better described as complex additions to the 'storyworld' of each of the literary monsters they adapt. A storyworld is a more recent conceptualization of story building that prioritizes the creation of unique, fantastical worlds as well as plot and characters, and 'shifts the focus from the more traditional literary notion of narrative closure to the open-endedness of serialization' (Hassler-Forest 2016, 8). Dan Hassler-Forest describes this approach as one 'in which a potentially unlimited number of narratives can take place, but this storyworld will always by its very definition exceed in scale any single representation of it' (2016, 8). In other words, in a culture where Frankenstein's monster (for instance) has transcended any single text and become a popular myth, a work that utilizes the character in a new context can be seen to build onto that tradition, rather than overwriting or even re-writing it. The monster mash takes this process one step further by tying multiple traditions or storyworlds together.

The four texts I examine in this chapter each use famous Victorian monsters as a touchstone, weaving in characters and themes from other nineteenth-century texts, and from twentieth- and twenty-first-century criticism. In *Anno*

Dracula – the first in a series of alternate history novels by Kim Newman, originally published in 1992 and re-issued as the start of a new series in 2011 – vampirism becomes a metaphor for the state of human society under capitalism: specifically, Margaret Thatcher's Britain. The monsters in the ongoing comic book series *The League of Extraordinary Gentlemen* (written by Alan Moore and drawn by Kevin O'Neill since 1999) are transformed from the British Empire's social outcasts into twenty-first-century superheroes. The premium cable television series *Penny Dreadful* (2014–16) uses a potentially subversive premise – the idea that all of us are monsters, and that we can find strength and solidarity in our monstrosity – to interrogate the assumption that monstrosity is something we can choose. Finally, Theodora Goss's *Athena Club* novels take an intersectional feminist approach to monstrosity, revising the monster's literary heritage and responding to the fact that 'so many of the mad scientists in 19th century narratives create, or start creating but then destroy, female monsters' (2017, 401, author's acknowledgements).

All four texts indicate that the twenty-first century's definition of a monster is subtly different from that of the nineteenth century, or even the twentieth. Likewise, each of these texts allows us to explore the validity of scholarly claims that the monster has been divested of transgressive potential in contemporary Gothic culture. As I will demonstrate, the way these texts draw in multiple historical monsters to construct their own monstrous communities allows the monster to reclaim its status as an explicitly political symbol of physical, social, or cultural alterity.

From 'miserable wretch' to 'modernity personified': Defining the twenty-first-century monster

'The British Empire has always encountered difficulty in distinguishing between its heroes and its monsters', reads the opening preface to *The League of Extraordinary Gentlemen: Volume I* (Moore and O'Neill 2000). This statement is ambiguous. It might positively signify that Britain finds its national icons among the traditionally monstrous or other (e.g. the foreigner, the woman, the working class subject), rather than the traditionally heroic (the white, Western man). This reading is supported by the fact that the fantastical monsters that make up the titular League are all drawn from popular Victorian fiction; though they are monstrous in various ways, they have all become icons of mainstream British culture.

The more convincing interpretation of this citation is that from the Edict of Expulsion banning Jews (1290–1657), to the policies and repercussions of colonialism, to post-Brexit racial tensions, Great Britain (like many empires) has historically demonized and excluded the people it might better have embraced and valorized. This reading is also borne out by the graphic novel's plot, in which the League is only tolerated by the English government because of the service its members provide as supernatural defenders. In a later instalment set in 1958 but based on George Orwell's *1984* (1949), the members of the League actually become government fugitives and are categorized as 'unpersons' (Moore and O'Neill 2007). *League* thus provides an excellent illustration of how Frankenfiction politicizes monstrosity, linking fantastical monsters to historical otherness. The social symbolism of otherness these monsters evoke, however, is a relatively recent addition to the monster's long legacy in popular culture.

The monster is an instantly recognizable figure in contemporary culture and criticism – a fact that is quite remarkable given the wide variety of the 'monsters' being represented. There are medical 'monsters' like the giant or the conjoined twin; social 'monsters' like the foreigner or the transgressive woman, and fantastical monsters like the vampire or werewolf. Sometimes the metaphors that describe these monsters overlap, until the fantastical and physical monsters become one and the same. In the case of a text like *Frankenstein*, which has accrued many adaptations, even a seemingly singular monster can become endlessly plural in its meanings. This is how the 'miserable wretch' of Shelley's novel can become 'modernity personified' in the television series *Penny Dreadful* (Shelley [1831] 2015, 98; Walsh 2014).

That we can speak generally of 'monsters' at all indicates their prominence as contemporary symbols. Any cultural figure that persists for as long as the monster – with its etymological roots in classical antiquity, deriving from the Latin *monstrare* ('to demonstrate'), and *monere* ('to warn') – can be expected to undergo many changes in symbolism and representation over the years. Before we can engage with the monstrous historical mashup that is Frankenfiction, we must engage with its representations of the historical monster, and before we can do that, we must locate the monster's evolution and emergence into twenty-first-century Western culture. My first task, then, is to define the kinds of monstrosity this book is concerned with.

In the introduction to *Monster Culture in the 21st Century*, Marina Levina and Diem-My T. Bui suggest that 'monstrous narratives of the past decade have become so omnipresent specifically because they represent collective social

anxieties over resisting and embracing change in the twenty-first century'
(2013, 1–2). As the essays in the collection explore, the monstrous change
that is alternately resisted and embraced sometimes relates to identity (us
versus them), sometimes to technology (hubris and hybridity), and always
to territory (spatial, temporal, national, or experiential). For Levina and Bui,
monstrosity has 'transcended its status as a metaphor' to become our culture's
dominant mode of expression (2013, 2). The monster no longer needs to be 'demonstrated' or explained to contemporary audiences – its presence speaks for
itself (see Foucault 1967, 68–70).

    Fred Botting, in contrast, has argued that monsters represent the limits of
social transgression, and that, in the twenty-first century, this limit is increasingly
meaningless (2008, 214–17). Rather than lonely, abnormal, or evil, monsters
in popular culture are now typically friendly, optimistic, or sympathetic. As
Jeffrey Weinstock argues, 'the overall trend in monstrous representation across
the twentieth century and into the twenty-first has been towards not just
sympathizing but empathizing with – and ultimately aspiring to be – the monster'
(2013, 277). This indicates that monstrosity, at least in terms of behaviour
outside of established social boundaries, has been normalized and appropriated
by mainstream culture. One might argue that this increased empathy for the
monster can be a subversive tool, advocating the broad-scale social acceptance of
otherness. Conversely, we might suggest that the twenty-first-century fantastical
monster's lack of a culturally transgressive impulse means that its ability to serve
as a progressive tool has been dramatically reduced. If the monster is always 'us',
it cannot clearly point the way to difference and transformation, as it has within
queer, feminist, disability, and race studies. Jack Halberstam's foundational *Skin
Shows* (1995), for instance, explores the continued link between monstrosity and
race, and Rosi Braidotti examines the intersection between the monster and the
feminine (1997). Margrit Shildrick has spent much of her career working on
questions of phenomenology and embodiment, specifically as they relate to the
monstrous, abnormal, or disabled body (2002, 6).

    As Fred Botting and Dale Townshend suggest, popular horror 'relies on an
increasingly fragile and insubstantial opposition between human and Gothic
monster' (2004, IV:4). Although the 'vegetarian' vampire Edward Cullen,
from *Twilight* (2005), is perhaps the most recognizable example of this, he is
by no means the *only* example – not even if we focus solely on the vampire.
The origins of the all-too-human monster can be traced back to Louis from
Anne Rice's *Interview With the Vampire* (1976), and the character of Angel
in the television series *Buffy the Vampire Slayer* (1997–2003) and self-titled

spinoff *Angel* (1999–2004). Books like Liza Conrad's *High School Bites* (2006), Douglas Rees's *Vampire High* (2010), and Richelle Mead's *Vampire Academy* series (2007–11), as well as shows like BBC Three's *Being Human* (2008–13) and *The Vampire Diaries* (2009–17) on the CW network, also featured friendly, 'everyday' vampires as objects of desire and normality. These monsters are overwhelmingly white, wealthy, and highly educated.

In our twenty-first-century culture of friendly monsters, the monster is often framed as an 'average', liberal humanist individual – a figure which has, of course, 'historically been constructed as a white European male' (Hayles 1999, 4). This mainstreaming of the monster arguably weakens the symbolic power of society's 'real' monsters, specifically those whose difference is 'cultural, political, racial, economic, sexual' (Cohen 1996a, 7). From another perspective, as texts with a close relationship to the Gothic, Frankenfictions can arguably never be unequivocally transgressive or transformative. After all, as Catherine Spooner argues:

> The history of the Gothic has always been bound up with that of consumption, from the eighteenth-century association of the Gothic novel with luxury, a product with no intrinsic use value, to the court battle in 1963 between Bela Lugosi's family and Universal studios over the rights to use the recently deceased *Dracula* star's image in lucrative marketing. (2006, 125)

As popular fictions in a postcapitalist age, Frankenfictions are always influenced by their appeal (or relation) to consumers and mass audiences. Jerrold Hogle likewise points out that 'Gothic fictions since Walpole have most often been about aspiring but middling, or sometimes upper middle-class, white people' (2002, 3). This is a point I will return to throughout the book, as class is also central to the politics and popularity of Frankenfiction.

In the fiction of the late eighteenth and early nineteenth centuries, the Gothic primarily served as a politicized (or consciously *de*-politicized) historical romance, featuring foreign lands and peoples, adventure, and deep, dark secrets. Its contents were rarely considered 'serious' literature, although it did often serve to make readers reflect on contemporary developments (Kilgore 1995). From the middle of the nineteenth century Gothic's monsters took a more familiar turn towards horror themes, specifically the perversion and infection of the 'normal'. This is particularly true of Britain, where, as David Punter so succinctly puts it, the main question asked by nineteenth-century Gothic texts is: 'to what extent can one be "infected" and still remain British?' (Punter 1996, 2:1). The Gothic is, indeed, originally a British phenomenon, although parallel iterations and traditions of the Gothic sprang up almost immediately elsewhere on the European continent, and in North America (Aldana Reyes 2017; Cornwell 2012, 64; Horner 2002).

In the twentieth century, as psychoanalysis became more and more influential in cultural and literary theory, and Freudian readings of Gothic texts and monsters became more prevalent, new texts began to draw on Freudian reflections for inspiration. This embedded self-analysis potentially transformed the Gothic into a tool for interpretation and social commentary in its own right: 'a means of reading culture, not just a cultural phenomenon to read' (Armitt 2011, 10). Although psychoanalysis may have rendered this interpretive function more explicit in twentieth-century Gothic than in previous iterations, Punter argues that 'Gothic was, from its very inception, a form that related very closely to issues of national assertion and social organization, and which even, on occasion, could "take the stage" in foregrounding social issues and in forming social consciousness' (2012, 4).

'By the turn of the twentieth century' into the twenty-first, writes Spooner, 'Gothic had consolidated its position as the material of mainstream entertainment' (2006, 24). By this point, Gothic had become such a central aesthetic in Western culture that to some extent identifying an object as Gothic felt meaningless. Writer and critic Angela Carter famously attested that 'we live in Gothic times', where yesterday's figures and topics of subversion form today's mainstream (1995, 460). Spooner, echoing Carter, writes that the Gothic 'has become so pervasive precisely because it is so apposite to the representation of contemporary concerns' (2006, 8). In other words, the Gothic (like the monster) is currently so popular because we recognize ourselves in its many manifestations. Rather than serving as a ritualistic demarcation between the self or nation and the monstrous other, fantastical monsters often (as McNally persuasively argues) 'dramatize the profound senses of corporeal vulnerability that pervade modern society, most manifestly when commodification invades new spheres of social life' (2012, 2). In these contexts monstrosity tends to become resoundingly bourgeois. As I suggest throughout this book, it is precisely because popular, mainstream culture is so saturated with genres like the Gothic that sub-genres like Frankenfiction are able to emerge.

In contrast with Botting's statements, however, I would suggest that the commercial anti-heroism of the twenty-first-century monster does not necessarily stop it from serving as a sociopolitical symbol. The monster simply 'has a claim on our feelings' *because* of its anti-heroic nature, rather than in spite of it (Hume 1984, 189). Because of its depiction of historical monsters and monstrous communities, Frankenfiction represents a partial exception to the rule of white, mainstream monstrosity. In the storyworlds of Frankenfiction everyone is monstrous, necessitating a re-evaluation of the metaphor. In this process, Frankenfictions often reintroduce discussions of multiculturalism, discrimination, and identity politics into popular culture. I will demonstrate how this is done through close readings of *Anno Dracula, League, Penny Dreadful,* and the *Athena Club* books. First, however, I want to briefly situate the monster's political function more explicitly within the history of the field, to illustrate how and why the monster has been politicized in the past.

According to Chris Baldick, writing about the inception and evolution of the Frankenstein myth, in the metaphor and mythology of classical antiquity monstrosity is displayed to 'reveal visibly the results of vice, folly, and unreason, as a warning' (1987, 10). This stands in opposition to the classical hero's story, which showcases a variety of virtues and a 'pageant of marvels with the great central adventure at its culmination' (Campbell [1949] 2008, 274). Our fascination with mythology's heroes informed the superhero narrative of the early twentieth century (Wolf-Meyer 2003), and our fascination with Gothic monsters is indelibly linked to the overwhelming popularity of the anti-hero at the later end of the twentieth century – a shift in the fictional 'centre of gravity' described by Northrop Frye in his *Anatomy of Criticism* ([1957] 2002, 34).

In the following account of self-discovery in Mary Shelley's 1818 novel, Frankenstein's creature (arguably the first modern monster: see Baldick 1987, 1) highlights a number of the features that might define a sentient being as monstrous:

> And what was I? Of my creation and creator I was absolutely ignorant, but I knew I possessed no money, no friends, no kind of property. I was, besides, endued with a figure hideously deformed and loathsome; I was not even of the same nature as man. I was more agile than they and could subsist upon coarser diet; I bore the extremes of heat and cold with less injury to my frame; my stature far exceeded theirs. When I looked around I saw and heard of none like me. Was I, then, a monster, a blot upon the earth, from which all men fled and whom all men disowned? (Shelley [1831] 2015, 116)

For the creature, monstrosity is indicated by physical and social abnormality. Monsters are 'hideously deformed', deviating from physical norms in ways that range from grotesquely wasted to frighteningly large to uncannily doubled. They are unnaturally 'agile' or dexterous by human standards, and physically resilient. Monsters are not like 'us', the average embodied and socialized citizen. Whether superhuman or subhuman, a prefix always applies in the monster's classification.

Because they are not classed as human, they are also denied the status and benefits of citizenship, generally lacking income or property. They are solitary creatures, without friend, peer, or community – and in the case of Frankenstein's creature, without even a name.

As many scholars in the long critical history of *Frankenstein* have noted, although Frankenstein's creature is a fantastical monster, all of his descriptions could be applied to members – both metaphorically and legally – of the human race. Frankenstein's creature, certainly, is more human than his creator in many ways. It is this shifting and ambiguous border with the monstrous that allows mainstream society to classify itself as 'normal', and that drives its fascination with monsters, real and imagined. This politically charged image of the monster became the cornerstone of twentieth- and twenty-first-century monster theory, which often uses monsters as symbols of various race, class, and gender politics.

In discussing what defines the typical or traditional monster in Western culture, Jeffrey Jerome Cohen's oft-cited essay 'Monster Culture' (1996) outlined seven theses. The first and most important is that the monster's body is a cultural body, which 'quite literally incorporates fear, desire, anxiety, and fantasy' (1996, 4). Monsters may have a real-world presence, which may be legitimately terrifying, but they are always first defined in the realm of narrative and the imagination. These narrative bodies shape (and are shaped by) what we consider to be abnormal and deviant. In this approach to monstrosity, one must 'consider beasts, demons, freaks, and fiends as symbolic expressions of cultural unease that pervade a society and shape its collective behavior', and a culture's fascination with monsters would suggest a desire to explore categories of 'difference and prohibition' (1996, back cover). Although this is clearly not always the case for twenty-first-century monsters, Frankenfiction's tendency to explore themes of identity, alterity, and exclusion seems to be in line with this definition of monstrosity.

Just as the monster's body is constructed by the fears and obsessions of culture, it is also physically marked by what that culture considers as different. This alterity can take any form, but Cohen argues that 'for the most part monstrous difference tends to be cultural, political, racial, economic, sexual' (1996, 7). Because of this inherently (bio)political aspect of the monstrous, through the monster 'the boundaries between personal and national bodies blur' (1996, 10). Again, this tendency seems to be less pronounced in much of twenty-first-century popular culture. Although this allegorical capacity remains in Frankenfiction, the specific way the monster's body is used to represent the body politic in *Anno Dracula* is distinct from *League, Penny Dreadful, Athena Club,* and every other text. With the term 'body politic' I here refer to the metaphor by which a nation is personified, reducing all the people in the nation into a single homogeneous group or person, the head of which is inevitably the government or ruling body. Monsters thus come to stand in for deviant or undesirable elements of the body, or of the collapse of the political system because of said elements.

It is important to note here that the exploration of difference through monsters need not always translate into a politically progressive, or a politically conservative approach. Re-evaluation can lead to rejection or re-affirmation of the assumptions presented by the monster. Although the language Cohen uses throughout his chapter paints the monster as an inviting figure, at no point does he argue that the monster always invites us to embrace progressive political change. In fact, in his very first thesis he stresses that the monster can embody either 'ataractic or incendiary' fantasies: it can spur us to action or lull us into a sense of security (1996, 4). It is true that monsters have often been used to vilify a society's others, and that the dominance of sympathetic monsters is a relatively recent phenomenon, but as the twenty-first-century 'friendly' monster illustrates, examples of both categories can and do exist. A monster is never wholly transgressive or entirely conservative – its position is always relative to other monsters, and other constructions of (ab)normality.

Writing on the relationship between fantasy and mimesis in 1984, Kathryn Hume touched on the problem of cementing a particular monster's symbolism in postmodern culture from another angle. She argued that myth 'gains meaning from being part of a system' (1984, 67), suggesting that the monster's impact and power as a symbol had been reduced because, without grand religious or social motivations to create fear, or to link them to other monsters, they had lost their significance as 'transpersonal' or allegorical symbols. We know that dragons breathe fire and have hard scales because dragon stories tell us so, and monsters like the gorgons 'have an ancestry that links them to a total network of divine and demonic powers'. They are, Hume argues, more than 'ad hoc obstacles' or characters: their appearance signals a specific meaning when they appear along the hero's journey (1984, 67). While this argument has its weaknesses (is there such a thing as a truly ad hoc character?), Hume's observation that classical monsters fit into a larger narrative tradition is a valid one, as is the notion that this tradition loses some of its power as monsters become more nuanced as characters. As Cohen points out, however, every monster is already historically specific, and 'the vampires of Anne Rice are clearly different from those of Bram Stoker, even if they are separated from each other by less than a century and filiate from the same genealogical tree' (1999, xv). By self-consciously depicting a series of specific historical monsters in their specific historical contexts, then, Frankenfictions are able to harness the allegorical power of older monsters without directly reproducing their regressive portrayal of alterity. In this they also indirectly react against the whiteness and privilege represented by the majority of monsters in twenty-first-century popular culture. This is not to argue that Frankenfictions are politically progressive or didactic in terms of identity politics, simply that they are relatively progressive within a particular, popular context.

In addition to drawing on historical monsters, Frankenfictions also create monstrous communities. For Halberstam, the diffusion of the monstrous into the mainstream simply means that it is composed of a 'conspiracy of bodies' rather than one body (1995, 27). We are now faced with a community of monsters, while past narratives often focused on the singularity of the monster: its difference and exceptionality. This is aptly illustrated by Frankenfiction, which brings together a variety of monstrous bodies to construct its own collective concept of monstrosity. Although each monster may only be an individual, in a mashup narrative individual monsters need not shoulder the responsibility of representing the ultimate other or the body politic on their own. Instead, they create symbolism through their interaction with each other, by taking turns playing the different roles of various 'monstrous' or excluded groups in society. Often this process is reductive: the female monster comes to stand in for women in general, the male monster for men, the Indian monster symbolizes all people of colour, and so forth. Certain monsters also draw on existing critical or psychoanalytical readings to create meaning. For instance, the werewolf is often a symbol of toxic masculinity, but may represent other individuals with repressed identities or sexualities. Other depictions are more subtle. For instance, *The Extraordinary Adventures of the Athena Club* features multiple manifestations of the female monster, using them to comment on the way class and race, as well as gender, shape one's identity. Taken together each of these monstrous communities, built from the pieces of older ones, signals a renewal of the monster's power as an oppositional, social metaphor for alterity.

Of course, by arguing that the monsters in Frankenfiction are unique I do not mean to imply that they are entirely new. Well before it became the subject of twentieth-century scholarship, fantastical monstrosity can already be seen to have a complex sociopolitical function. For instance, Baldick argues that '[l]ong before the monster of Frankenstein, monstrosity already implied rebellion, or an unexpected turning against one's parent or benefactor' (1987, 12). He links the monster's implied rebelliousness to its frequent personification of the 'body politic' – most directly relatable, in the context of *Frankenstein*, to the French Revolution (1987, 20). Baldick describes how the monster frequently served as a metaphor for both the overthrown government and the revolting masses, and also how the conglomeration of individuals into governments can be perceived as inherently monstrous. For Baldick, the ready applicability of the monstrous body of Frankenstein's creature to political revolution *and* oppression enables its enduring proliferation as a myth (1987, 20). The continuing myth and metaphor of Frankenstein's creature is reflected in twenty-first-century Frankenfiction, as well as the late twentieth century's disinterest in the morally and politically upright hero.

I am also not suggesting that the model of monstrosity presented in Frankenfiction should be applied across other texts. As scholarship in the field reveals, monstrosity is always multiple, as are its definitions. An overwhelming amount of scholarly work has been conducted on monstrosity and the monstrous in the two decades since the publication of Cohen's essay. The wealth of scholarly work on monstrosity is also reflected in the wide variety of monster films, novels, and other art that has been produced in recent decades. Because of the monster's position as an indicator of category crisis, however, no one definition of monsters has come to dominate the field. Instead, multiple and contradictory approaches have served to describe the monster's function in popular culture. Using the 1991 film *Silence of the Lambs* as an illustration, for instance, Halberstam demonstrates 'the distance traveled between current [late twentieth-century] representations of monstrosity and their genesis in nineteenth-century Gothic fiction' (1995, 1). For Halberstam, while the monster always foregrounds physical difference and visibility, 'the monsters of the nineteenth century metaphorized modern subjectivity as a balancing act between inside/outside, female/male, body/mind, native/foreign, proletarian/aristocrat' (1995, 1). Twentieth-century horror, on the other hand, favours 'the obscenity of "immediate visibility"', and its monsters are 'all body and no soul' (1995, 1). For Halberstam, this shift signals the increasing impossibility of attaching any overarching symbolism to postmodern monsters; like the concept of the human, our definition of the body, normal or monstrous, is at once too basic and too abstract to mythologize.

Weinstock, in contrast, highlights the monster's increasing invisibility in the twentieth and twenty-first centuries. In contemporary monster narratives, physically monstrous characters often take on the role of the hero, who is unjustly ostracized from society for their deformity. Likewise, human characters who seem perfectly normal, intelligent, or affluent are often revealed to have a violent and amoral monster buried within their psyche. Weinstock frames the situation as follows:

What follows from this decoupling of monstrosity from appearance is an important cultural shift that aligns monstrosity not with physical difference, but with antithetical moral values. Monstrosity thus is reconfigured as a kind of invisible disease that eats away at the body and the body politic, and manifests visibly through symptomatic behaviour. (Weinstock 2013, 276)

This fear of the invisible monster is manifested in contemporary narratives of the serial killer, the corrupt politician, the conspiracy theory, the virus, and the environmental apocalypse, and represents a world in which 'evil is associated not with physical difference, but with cultural forces that constrain personal growth and expression' (2013, 276–7). Monstrosity is whatever threatens the liberal humanist subject.

Both Halberstam and Weinstock offer valuable approaches to understanding contemporary monstrosity. If the monster allegedly 'dwells at the gates of difference' as Cohen proposes (1996, 7), what does it mean when popular culture returns to the historical monsters we have already confronted, those we no longer repress, and whose multiple meanings and categories of identification are not only accepted, but exploited? Asa Simon Mittman suggests that the domestication of the monster does not always result in its 'de-monstration', for 'while it is a common trope that we live with the ghosts of the past, so too, we live with the monsters of the past' (2013, 6). We not only live with the metaphorical (and perhaps literal) monsters from our own pasts. Our mediascape is populated with monsters appropriated from other cultures, times, and parts of the world. 'As we cannibalize the Others of others,' Mittman argues, 'as we tear them apart and stitch them back together, we continually redefine the parameters of the monstrous' (2013, 7). Adaptation does not necessarily erase a character's social or moral monstrosity, but it does redefine it. The redefinition of identity is always a political gesture.

Proceeding chronologically, in the rest of this chapter I will illustrate how monstrosity is appropriated and adapted across four very different works of Frankenfiction. *Anno Dracula, The League of Extraordinary Gentlemen, Penny Dreadful,* and *The Extraordinary Adventures of the Athena Club* each possess radically different aesthetics and aims. Despite their many differences, the way all three texts appropriate historical monsters and historical monster criticism is worth a more thorough analysis. Each takes a similar premise (literary monster mashup) and presents it through different media (written text, graphic narrative, and television). This serves to provide a good overview of the monstrous in different kinds of Frankenfiction – which also spans multiple media – while also illustrating Henry Jenkins's point about the free and steady 'flow of media across multiple media platforms' in twenty-first-century convergence culture (2006, 3).

'Ourselves expanded': *Anno Dracula* and the neoliberal vampire

Kim Newman's 1992 novel *Anno Dracula* is set in London, 1888. It melds fact and fiction, combining characters from *Dracula* and other literature with fictionalized historical personalities like Oscar Wilde, Marie Corelli, and Bram Stoker himself. Appropriating all but the last few chapters of Stoker's novel, and beginning on 'an alternate timetrack half-way through Stoker's Chapter 21' (Newman 2011, 456, author's afterword), *Anno Dracula* imagines what would have happened if Dracula had succeeded in his plans to conquer England, marrying Queen Victoria, and becoming Prince Consort and ruler of the British Empire.

The consequences of Dracula's victory are dire. He imprisons the queen, calls for the execution of Jonathan Harker, Abraham Van Helsing, and other opponents to his rule, and turns Mina Harker into his first vampire underling. Dracula quickly sires many new vampires, and soon England's undead population numbers in the thousands. In this supernatural England, humans of all social classes clamour for immortality (or rail violently against it), and vampires of other bloodlines also emerge from hiding to claim power and status. Most of the novel's central characters are vampires, and those who are not are defined either by their wish to become vampires, or their staunch opposition to vampirism. *Anno Dracula* is narrated primarily by Jack the Ripper (who is revealed to be the *Dracula* character Dr Jack Seward), by Newman's original character Charles Beauregard, who is an agent of the Diogenes Club from Arthur Conan Doyle's Sherlock Holmes series, and by Geneviève Dieudonné, a 400-year-old vampire from Brittany who volunteers her time and expertise as a nurse at the Toynbee Hall charity. Geneviève is another of Newman's original characters, appearing in different forms across Newman's other work. Occasionally other characters' stories are given a brief space in the third-person narration.

The novel is carefully researched, and in addition to including many historical and geographical details, it is populated with characters from a broad variety of historical and literary texts. Some characters are created seemingly from scratch, some from a single name or sentence. Count Dracula, Mina Harker, Daniel Dravot, Lord Ruthven, and Count Vardalek are all creative interpretations of the characters that first graced the pages of nineteenth-century fiction, but they are based on careful reading both in and around their various texts.[1]

Despite the fact that *Anno Dracula* features many historically monstrous characters (vampires, serial killers, political tyrants), in Newman's novel monstrosity is never synonymous with a monstrous appearance, or even monstrous actions. In fact, the novel goes to great lengths to demonstrate the different ways in which 'humanity' or basic goodness is a feature vampires also possess. This is one of the more emphatic ways in which Newman's interpretation of these monsters stretches the bounds of a 'faithful' adaptation – it adapts twentieth-century readings of nineteenth-century texts, as well as the texts themselves.

In her chapter on Newman's vampire novels in *Blood Is the Life: Vampires in Literature*, Elizabeth Hardaway points to one way that 'Newman's alternate-reality novels, rather than reflecting the external characterization and tone of *Dracula*, instead reflect on that work's subtext' (1999, 177). Many reviews speak of *Anno Dracula* as picking up where Stoker's *Dracula* leaves off, but in actuality it picks up neatly where 1970s scholarship leaves off, linking both Freudian and Foucauldian theories of sex, power, otherness, and foreignness that have been built into Stoker's *Dracula* over the years, and plugging these back into what has now become a Victorian classic. Although *Anno Dracula* plays with traditional concepts of the monstrous, the monsters in *Anno Dracula* do not represent the fear of foreignness, queerness, or general otherness that have often been read into Stoker's *Dracula*. Instead, often they present an exploration, and occasionally a caricature, of such fears.

As Hardaway argues, Newman takes scholarly discussions of homoeroticism in *Dracula* and 'demystifies homoeroticism by bringing it to the surface of the text and making it one more characteristic that vampires and men have in common in *Anno Dracula*' (1999, 179). Newman goes a step further, transforming Dracula from 'a grotesquely romantic outsider' into a power-hungry politician, and giving 'an additional ironic twist to *Dracula*'s homoerotic subtext by making the Dracula of *Anno Dracula* aggressively homophobic' (1999, 179). Indeed, at one point in the novel Dracula decides that he will punish sodomy by execution, and a hysterical public supports him:

> Elsewhere in the papers there were editorials in support of the Prince Consort's newly-published edict against the 'unnatural vice'. While the rest of the world advanced towards the twentieth century, Britain reverted to a medieval legal system. (Newman 2011, 119)

Building on a homoerotic reading of *Dracula*, this passage uses a twentieth-century view to mark homophobia as monstrous, inviting the reader to side with the novel's 'good' Victorians and condemn Dracula's 'medieval' behaviour – echoed in certain Thatcherist and present-day policies. While it is not necessary for readers to recognize such nods to academic theory in order to appreciate

Anno Dracula, in this instance the homoerotic subtext of *Dracula* becomes yet another tool for Newman to use in his adaptation of the novel.

Race is also used as a metaphor for monstrosity, again to distance the vampire from the foreign endangerment of British 'racial stock' that many critics have read into Stoker's novel (Brantlinger 1988, 230; See also Halberstam 1993). At one point, Beauregard asks Geneviève why she dislikes Dracula and his Carpathian guard so much. Geneviève replies: 'No one dislikes a Jewish or Italian degenerate more than a Jew or an Italian' (Newman 2011, 208). Here she identifies Dracula and herself as morally distinct members of the same 'race'. Geneviève is not opposed to Dracula because he is a vampire, or even because he is a foreigner living in Britain. After all, she is both herself. Instead, she disapproves because he is a *bad* vampire and a 'degenerate' foreigner, who conforms to the racist stereotype and discredits the good behaviour of the rest of the group. The way *Anno Dracula* nuances historical varieties of monstrosity through critical theory thus invites the reader to identify with some of the vampire characters, traditionally Othered, and to accept that as with humans, monsters come in moral and immoral varieties. It is immorality and a lack of social responsibility that makes a monster, not any specific racial or sexual characteristic.

Another key example of the relationship between the monstrous and the 'normal' in the novel is in the grudging friendship between the human Inspector Mackenzie and the Carpathian vampire Kostaki, who are each initially disdainful of the other's physical state. These two characters are forced to work together to keep order as panic over the Ripper murders escalates, and they form a strange rapport. The relationship causes both characters to admit that the other is not so different after all. When Mackenzie reacts negatively to Kostaki's suggestion that he become a vampire, Kostaki asks him: 'What is more unnatural? To live, or to die?'. Mackenzie replies: 'To live off others', referencing the vampire diet of human blood. Kostaki retorts by arguing: 'Who can say they do not live off others?' (Newman 2011, 278). In other words, though vampires literally live on the blood of humans, humans are equally capable of metaphorically sucking the life and livelihood of those around them.[2] Kostaki also points out that he and Mackenzie have more in common than Mackenzie and Jack the Ripper do, even though Mackenzie and Jack are both 'warm' (i.e. living and not a vampire). To this, Mackenzie can only respond: 'You have me there Kostaki. I confess it. I'm a copper first and a living man second' (Newman 2011, 278). Against the larger social backdrop of greed, brutality, and mass hysteria, Mackenzie and Kostaki are equally human, and comparably humane. The prime difference between the Victorian vampire and the neo-Victorian one is, in this instance, a question of morality and civic responsibility. Newman goes a long way to demonstrate that whether we are talking about the Victorian era or our own, the difference between man and monster is culturally determined, and is not at all as great as the reader might initially assume. In this he avoids the formula in which (according to Halberstam) 'in the Gothic, crime is embodied within a specifically deviant form – the monster – that announces itself (de-monstrates) as the place of corruption' (1995, 2). Rather than depicting monsters as 'specifically deviant' beings, Newman underlines the monster in everyone.

In a later instalment of the series, *The Bloody Red Baron* (1995), in which we see Dracula's influence extend into the twentieth century, Charles Beauregard speculates that vampires 'are not a race apart. Not all demons and monsters. They're simply ourselves expanded. From birth, we change in a million ways. Vampires are more changed than the warm' (Newman 2012, 79). For Newman, everyone is in fact caught up in 'a painful fusion in which all, warm and vampire, carry the seeds of their own destruction' (2012, 186). Throughout the *Anno Dracula* series, the true monstrosity of the vampire lies in the self-destructive nature of humanity, and not in biological or ideological alterity.

Anno Dracula shows us that there is more than one kind of monster and that, paradoxically, not all monsters are monstrous. Broadly speaking, monstrosity is politically and ethically defined in the novel, rather than in terms of physical or mental difference. The novel also has an overtly political agenda beyond discussions of race and sexuality. In Newman's own words, with the novel he 'was trying, without being too solemn, to mix things [he] felt about the 1980s, when the British Government made "Victorian Values" a slogan, with the real and imagined 1880s, when blood was flowing in the fog and there was widespread social unrest' (2011, 455). In other words, *Anno Dracula* is a direct response to Thatcherism. Retrospectively, Newman thus stakes a clear claim to being a Victorian revisionist, though here he takes a stand against conservative neo-Victorian sentiments of the 1980s.[3] *Anno Dracula* depicts an inclusive Victorian Britain, through the eyes of heroes who believe no one should be allowed to exclude anyone else from citizenship – symbolized through vampirism – or the benefits that accompany it (housing, food, and heath care). It also illustrates the conflict between Margaret Thatcher's celebration of late-twentieth-century austerity as a return to 'Victorian Values', and the rise of both humanitarian aid projects and the welfare state towards the end of the nineteenth century.

Drawing on Alan Sinfield, neo-Victorian critic Kathryn Bird highlights the Thatcher government's 'repeated attempts to "outlaw sections of the population (disadvantaged sections, of course)", including "blacks and 'scroungers'" and the homosexual community, among many other "out-groups", who would "bear much of the brunt of such scapegoating in modern Britain'" (Sinfield 1997, 348–9; quoted in Bird 2014, 3–4). For Bird, writing for the journal *Neo-Victorian Studies*, *Anno Dracula* represents an analysis of the systems of exclusion on which Thatcher's conception of a 'civilized' society is based, and which 'in contemporary culture is intimately bound up with the notion of "Victorian Values"' (2014, 3). Bird's essay also draws on Kate Mitchell's work in neo-Victorianism in support of this assertion. As Mitchell points out, 'Thatcher used the term "Victorian values" as a measure against which to identify the social ills of her milieu – a regulated economy, welfare dependency and the decline of the family', and to assert 'traditional and naturalized boundaries between normalcy and deviancy, morality and perversity' (2010, 48). By choosing to depict issues with Thatcherism in a Victorian guise, Newman not only links Dracula's monstrous government with Victorian England in the mind of the reader. He also parodies the monstrousness of 1980s Britain, and of our own contemporary culture, both of which still vilify people with non-traditional sexual identities.

Anno Dracula is thus a text in which 'good' vampires are politically left-wing, in the sense of promoting a certain degree of class mobility, a welfare state, and sexual freedom. Almost all these vampires were 'born' and socialized in the West, and embody the kind of British values Newman himself advocates (an idea I will return to shortly). 'Bad' vampires, on the other hand, are caricatures of the neoliberal subject. They are hypocritical and intolerant of racial, sexual, and political difference. They are at once selfish and parasitic, and their devotion to neoliberalism's 'competitive individualism', here likened to Darwinian notions that 'only the fit shall survive', is portrayed as a kind of barbarism (Newman 2011, 294; Hassler-Forest 2016, 117).

Some physical associations with monstrosity do remain monstrous in Newman's novel. In *Anno Dracula* the Count (now the Prince Consort) retains the 'solicitousness' and 'surprisingly unaccented and mild English' of Stoker's novel (Newman 2011, 414, 411–12; see also Stoker [1897] 1997, 22), but he is also the same 'terrible monster' Dracula describes ([1897] 1997, 197). His true form is revealed in *Anno Dracula* to be fluid and animalistic, with a face in which 'red eyes and wolf teeth were fixed, but around them, under the rough cheeks, was a constantly shifting shape; sometimes a hairy, wet snout, sometimes a thin, polished skull' (Newman 2011, 412). This link between the vampire and the wolf is an amplified reference to Stoker's novel, where Dracula displays a strange affinity for the wild wolves he terms the 'children of the night' (Stoker [1897] 1997, 24. See also 19–20). As Bird argues, the animal is a figure that is allowed to remain traditionally monstrous in *Anno Dracula* (2014, 21). This is demonstrated, among other ways, by the ability of Dracula and his vampiric children to take on the form of animals, with various (and variously grotesque) degrees of success. Given Newman's focus on problems of social justice, it is arguably unsurprising that the human/animal distinction remains monstrous. In displacing monstrosity from Othered races and sexualities onto immorality and social Darwinism, animals offer a tempting metaphor for the conservative 'survival of the fittest' political philosophy Newman finds so distasteful (Brantlinger 1988, 228).

Reflecting this philosophy, even some of the novel's villains are classed as victims of society rather than as monsters. *Anno Dracula's* most deeply disturbed character is Dr John 'Jack' Seward, who is revealed to be the serial killer Jack the Ripper. Seward is the only character from Stoker's novel to initially resist Dracula's new regime. Mina Harker and Arthur Holmwood have embraced immortality, and serve the new, vampiric Prince Consort. Professor Abraham Van Helsing and Jonathan Harker have been executed, both for the murder of Lucy Westenra and for conspiracy against the crown. Emotionally broken, Seward has been allowed to keep his freedom, and manages Toynbee Hall along with Geneviève, though even he cannot escape Dracula's influence forever. In *Anno Dracula*, Seward is haunted, and slowly driven mad, by the events of *Dracula* and the Count's subsequent reign in Britain. Seward comes to view his actions in Stoker's novel as erroneous, noting: 'If I had known that vampirism was primarily a physical condition and not a spiritual one, Lucy might be un-dead still' (Newman 2011, 115). This thought only serves to drive him further into despair. Consumed with feelings of guilt for his part in Lucy Westenra's death, he begins murdering vampire prostitutes (who he imagines resemble his dead lover) under the moniker Silver Knife, trying to convince himself that it is the right thing to do after all.

Despite his monstrous actions, however, even Seward is ultimately held up as the natural product of a monstrous and indifferent system that breaks people, and then provides inadequate care for those who are broken. Early in the novel, Geneviève dismisses the outward signs of his inner turmoil – 'face lined' and 'hair streaked grey' although he is young – as the mark of a traumatized survivor rather than a monster, noting that many 'who'd lived through the changes were like him, older than their years' (Newman 2011, 26). Seward is also given the opportunity to justify his actions (and demonstrate his descent into madness) through his first-person narrative account, which opens *Anno Dracula* and continues throughout the novel. The rest of the novel is written in a more impersonal third person. Although Seward is eventually killed by Geneviève and Beauregard for his actions, it is described more as a mercy killing than an act of justice. Geneviève states to Beauregard that Seward was mentally ill, and therefore 'not responsible' for his actions (Newman 2011, 395). When Beauregard asks who *is* responsible, she blames Dracula, the master of the system, and the 'thing who drove him mad' (2011, 395).

One monster is a villain, but a monstrous individual in a nation or community of monsters is a new norm. Who, then, are the true villains? Like the Thatcherist reasoning it seeks to declaim, *Anno Dracula* still excludes one group of people by promoting another – specifically, those with the Western mindset of individualism, progressive civilization, and tolerance of difference. Ironically, the monsters in *Anno Dracula* are those who refuse to accept certain physical and social forms traditionally defined as 'monstrous'. The novel demonstrates that the mark of a true monster is one who imposes a regressive uniformity, but in doing so it imposes its own standard of uniformity upon its characters. British values are, ultimately, still the best values. The result is that a story of inclusion becomes one of postmodern exclusion, where everything is acceptable – except intolerance (see Sardar 1998).

As Bird also points out, despite Newman's aim of decrying the 'Victorian Values' of 1980s Thatcherism, *Anno Dracula*'s approach to Victorian London has exclusionary side effects. Drawing on Elizabeth Ho's work in *Neo-Victorianism and the Memory of Empire*, Bird suggests that despite the way that *Anno Dracula* draws attention to the '"dark spots" which narratives of the Victorian past tend to "gloss over", there are also moments when the novel risks re-inscribing the same nineteenth-century discourses it seeks to critique' (Ho 2012, 27; quoted in Bird 2014, 19). *Anno Dracula* notably falls short of its progressive ideals in its use of racial slur and stereotype to set the stage, as it were, of Victorian London. This racism is meant to caricature Thatcher's government rather than the Victorians. Because of the setting, however, what might otherwise have only been a subversive story about biocapital and the welfare state also becomes a metaphor for the supremacy of certain bloodlines, cultures, religions over others. This is a problem I will also return to in the following chapter, on ironic representations of history and historical fictions.

As an example of this problem in *Anno Dracula*, Bird takes the novel's portrayal of Dr Moreau, from the 1896 H.G. Wells novel *The Island of Doctor Moreau*:

Newman's use of H.G. Wells's character Dr Moreau is a good example of this problem. On the one hand, the disgust displayed by Beauregard and Geneviève towards Moreau's belief in the disposable nature of certain lives considered to be closer to animal existence (especially as concerns non-white peoples) suggests that Newman includes Moreau as a means of critiquing the (bio)political implications of nineteenth-century theories of degeneration and atavism. On the other hand, the terms Geneviève uses to criticise Moreau include 'ape-like' and 'cave-dweller'. (Newman 2011, 219, 224; in Bird 2014, 19)

In other words, Geneviève's critique of Dr Moreau relies on the same binaries ('human/animal' and 'civilized/savage') that Dr Moreau's do – a fact underscored by Geneviève's 'distance from the atavistic, shape-shifting, animal–vampire hybrids of Dracula's line' (Bird 2014, 19). The conventionally lovely, blonde, and nymph-like Geneviève, as a vampire 'of the pure bloodline of Chandagnac' (Newman 2011, 83–4), is ultimately a figure of Moreau's Darwinian evolutionary model, and not representative of any category of the self-made individual. For Bird, *Anno Dracula*'s theories about the disposability of life thus ultimately rely on the same system of distinction and 'originary violence of exclusion' that Thatcher's did (2014, 21). Of course, the way *Anno Dracula* frames all of its characters as monstrous – albeit in very different ways – does nuance this position. There are no real heroes in the novel, just as there are few wholly monstrous villains. In *The League of Extraordinary Gentlemen*, the moral and physical Otherness of heroic historical monsters is more pronounced.

The empire strikes back: Victorian monsters and *The League of Extraordinary Gentlemen*

Alan Moore and Kevin O'Neill's *The League of Extraordinary Gentlemen* is much like *Anno Dracula* in its criticisms of neoliberal politics. Although Moore and O'Neill's intentions for *League* were not explicitly political like Newman's (Nevins 2004, 254), when compared with *Anno Dracula* and *Penny Dreadful*, in its visual representation of otherness the series is perhaps the most direct example of Frankenfiction's monstrous sociopolitics. *League*'s monsters are not representative of Britain or the West, but rather of Britain's Others, and the negative effects of British imperial influence. These monsters also refuse to integrate, or to mitigate their apparent monstrosity. Throughout the *League* story arc, they remain essentially Other.

The *League* comics themselves are resolutely lowbrow in their approach to high culture, 'pulling down these snobbish barriers between genres, different levels of literature' (Nevins 2004, 254). In part, of course, this is due to the comics medium in which they appeared, which is not traditionally considered literary. First released as a six-issue limited series from March 1999 through September 2000, with America's Best Comics (an imprint of DC Comics) in the United States and Vertigo (another, specifically adult imprint of DC) in the UK, *League* chronicles the exploits of the titular League of Extraordinary Gentlemen.[4] The first League we encounter is initiated in 1898 by Campion Bond, an MI5 agent, to deal with the British Empire's more unusual problems. It is implied that such groups existed before this time, however. In the first volume of the comics series, the 1898 League must stop a plot concocted by MI5's M, who is revealed to be Professor Moriarty from the Sherlock Holmes adventures. In the second volume (published 2002–3), they fend off an attack by the Martian Molluscs from H.G. Wells's *The War of the Worlds* (1897).

Like *Anno Dracula*, *League* gives a Victorian (and, in later volumes, a more broadly historical) twist to the comic book trope of superhero teams. It features a rotating crew of superhuman 'heroes' – in this case more aptly described as monsters or anti-heroes – from Western literature. Volumes I and II take place in nineteenth-century London, and recount the formation and struggles of a League led by *Dracula*'s Wilhelmina Murray. In contrast to *Anno Dracula*, the events of Stoker's novel remain intact in Moore and O'Neill's timeline, though Dracula himself never makes a physical appearance in *League*. As in *Dracula*, Mina also becomes the guiding force behind a new 'Crew of Light' (Craft 1997, 445). Literally and metaphorically scarred by her experiences, Murray has survived her encounter with the Count, become divorced from her husband, and taken a job with British Intelligence. She has been working there for some time when she is asked to assemble a group (one character calls it a 'menagerie', echoing *Anno Dracula*'s animalistic imagery) of extraordinary people who can 'thwart a plot against the Empire' (Moore and O'Neill 2000, issues 1 and 3). In the same trend as *Anno Dracula*, it is from within the Empire, not outside it, that threats emerge. Despite refuting their function as political texts, Moore has repeatedly argued that Volumes I and II of *League* are a parody of Victorian attitudes towards otherness, and of a present-day culture that still labours under many of the same social problems (Nevins 2003, 229–30, 2004, 250, 253–5). Like *Anno Dracula*, then, *League* adopts late-twentieth-century criticism's reading of the monster as broadly misunderstood, and of differences that are social as well as physical. Conservative, dehumanizing social policies and prejudices are the comic's only consistently monstrous force.

The monsters found in *The League of Extraordinary Gentlemen* are distinct from *Anno Dracula*'s in that they explicitly draw on the well-established comic book traditions of both the anti-hero and the superhero team, in addition to the tradition of the Gothic villain. Although anti-heroes are present in most contemporary Western comics (and have also populated Japanese *manga* for some time), the shift from tales of heroes to tales of anti-heroes can perhaps be traced most clearly in the American comic book, where the incredibly popular superhero teams of the 1960s and '70s (first appearing in the '40s) were replaced by the anti-hero teams of the 1980s and '90s (Weinstock 2013, 279). It was as part of this late twentieth-century trend that the first issue of *The League of Extraordinary Gentlemen* was released in March 1999. Comic book fans have long been accustomed to the idea of identifying with the unapologetic villain, or rooting for the monstrous anti-hero, meaning the monsters and monstrous others in *League* do not require the naturalizing, 'nonsensical origins' Weinstock describes, and which *Anno Dracula* more explicitly provides in its exploration of Geneviève's history as a fifteenth-century nurse and child soldier under the saintly Joan of Arc (2013, 276).

League can be read as a pastiche of the superhero comic, in that it takes a well-established pattern in the industry and uses it to perform a sensationalized social critique. Superhero team narratives have existed since the early days of the American comic book industry, and the transposition of superhuman characters into alternate timelines or time periods is far from unheard of in comics (Kukkonen 2010; Ndalianis 2009). In Marvel's *1602* series, for example, well-known superheroes are transposed into the Elizabethan era. Likewise, borrowing or 'cloning' characters from other works occurs so frequently as to be unremarkable, and is often a way for major distributors like Marvel or DC comics to manoeuvre around complex copyright and intellectual property laws (Wolf-Meyer 2003, 504). Although *League* borrows its characters and plotlines from classic novels rather than other comic books, it fits into a much more established tradition of these kinds of appropriation than a novel like *Anno Dracula,* or a television programme like *Penny Dreadful.* Consequently, *League* can often afford to be more direct about its own monstrosity and intertextuality than these other texts might.

Unlike Kim Newman and John Logan (*Penny Dreadful*'s showrunner), Moore received no formal academic training before launching his comic book career, but read voraciously and 'omnivorously' from a young age (Khoury 2003, 16). From several of his many interviews, it is also clear that he has come into contact with various academic theories of monstrosity. In one podcast, for example, he explains how monsters in popular culture can be used to assess a nation's fears and anxieties at a particular point in time, citing readings of the classic Japanese horror film *Godzilla* (1954) as a metaphor for nuclear power (Pip 2014). Although it is unclear whether Moore read one of the early academic articles on the subject (Noriega 1987 and Wharton 1974 are two of the earlier scholarly articles to take this approach) or first encountered the idea in another, more popularized form, he has certainly conducted his own research into the symbolism and cultural significance of the monster. In a 2004 interview, Moore speculated on the effect of viewing nineteenth-century monsters from a twenty-first-century perspective, suggesting:

> It kind of reinvests those ideas with some of the power that they originally had, which has been worn down through a lot of our successive reinterpretations of them over the intervening century. (Nevins 2004, 256)

O'Neill, too, was an avid fan of film and literary horror long before he collaborated with Moore on *League* (see Ó Méalóid 2011; Meylikhov 2014). When Moore and O'Neill assemble their League of Extraordinary Gentlemen, then, we can assume that they knowingly engage with many of the themes from these various literary and academic texts as they transform their classic monsters into comic book heroes.

Dracula may be absent from *League*, but the series features many other monstrous characters from the pages of nineteenth-century fiction. The ironically labelled 'gentlemen' Murray assembles to join her in the League are Prince Dakkar (Captain Nemo), Allan Quatermain, Dr Henry Jekyll/Mr Edward Hyde, and Hawley Griffin (the 'Invisible Man') – drawn from the work of Jules Verne, H. Rider Haggard, Robert Louis Stevenson, and H.G. Wells, respectively.[5] Together, they represent the kinds of people the British Empire classified as monsters – some for their actions, some for their backgrounds. Nemo is an Indian pirate with a hatred for British colonial oppressors, Quatermain is an elderly opium addict long past his days of glory as an imperialist explorer, and Griffin is an invisible sociopath and a serial rapist. Dr Jekyll is an infirm and emotionally vulnerable coward, and his alter ego Hyde possesses nearly every stereotypically monstrous characteristic imaginable. Hyde is physically large and animalistic, as well as being vulgar, lecherous, violent, and bigoted. His skin tone is even distinctly brown, in contrast to Jekyll's sickly white, though this artistic decision may be best attributed to Ben Dimagmaliw, the colourist for *The League of Extraordinary Gentlemen* series, rather than to Moore or O'Neill. Like *Anno Dracula*, however, *League* interrogates the 'true' sources of its characters' monstrosity. As Hyde explains, it is precisely Jekyll's erroneous desire to drive out his 'baser' urges that created him in the first place. Hyde recounts how at first, Jekyll was the larger and stronger of the two, but their separation marked his downfall. 'Without me, you see, Jekyll has no drives', says Hyde, 'and without him, I have no restraints' (Moore and O'Neill 2003, issue 5).

If we classify *League* as a superhero narrative, then, the team is ironically unheroic. The League's lone female member, Mina Murray, is both a 'fallen woman' and a 'New Woman' – in many ways a conflation of Mina and Lucy from Stoker's novel, but also an increasingly familiar example of the popular action heroine (Nevins 2003, 163). Having survived Dracula, she is unafraid of the lesser monsters she commands in the League, and the monsters they confront outside of it. Each member of the League is a 'monster' to Victorian society in his or her own right, whether physically, morally, or sexually. Moore and O'Neill's combination of monsters is more physically and culturally diverse than Newman's, whose heroes are exclusively white, upper-class Westerners. The comic's diversity is also literally more visible than any that might be present in *Anno Dracula*, as the visuality of the medium makes differences in gender, skin tone, and national heritage immediately plain to the reader (see Figure 2.1). Moore and O'Neill's choice to present foreign or non-human languages in speech bubbles without translation is another alienating tactic the comic employs very effectively. Although Moore may claim that the comic does not set out to make a political statement, then, visually speaking its politics are relatively progressive – especially in the largely male, white, and Western comic book industry (see Cocca 2016, 5; Domsch 2012, 114; Singer 2002, 107).

As the above description indicates, of course, the members of the League are morally as well as physically monstrous, again marking them as socially Other. There are several exceptions to this rule. Although her gender and her past trauma categorize Murray as monstrous to the other characters in the comic, as in *Dracula* she serves as the League's moral and political compass. Overall, however, *League*'s monsters are less ambiguous, and occupy less of a moral grey area than do *Anno Dracula*'s. They are established social outcasts, and embrace their own differences and vices. Often, the monsters they fight are only coincidentally their enemies. In *Volume II*, Hyde expresses his admiration for the pure, senseless destruction the Martian Molluscs have unleashed. In issue 4 of *Volume I*, Nemo's ship is visually compared with villain Fu Manchu's underground lair, and the Indian pirate serves as a narrative parallel to the Chinese drug lord.[6] Although Fu Manchu is clearly established as a moral

Figure 2.1 Cover image from *The League of Extraordinary Gentlemen Vol. I* (2000 paperback edition), © Alan Moore and Kevin O'Neill. Permission given by Tony Bennett at Knockabout Comics. Scan by the author.

and physical monster, who has reptilian pupils and practices ghoulish forms of torture, at the end of the first volume his forces can also be found fighting against Moriarty, if not strictly *with* the League.

With the exception of Murray, the members of the League fight for selfish reasons – money, power, love of violence, or love for Murray herself – rather than any grander moral or national obligation. In many ways, then, *League* confirms Victorian Britain's assessment that these characters are monsters. This is also an important part of their function within the narrative. As Sebastian Domsch argues, the series itself suggests that 'every Empire needs a demonic other to secure the integrity of its identity and to hide its own inherent monstrosity' (2012, 119). In an act of seeming self-sacrifice, *League*'s monsters are bad so others can be good. As a superhero narrative, however, it does not draw the same conclusions from this identification as we might expect. As the focus of a superhero comic, these monsters are positioned as heroic (and thus good) by default. Ultimately, *League* suggests that, as in *Anno Dracula*, the difference between a 'good' monster and a 'bad' one lies not in physical otherness (or in this case, even moral otherness), but simply in one's perspective. This not only makes *League* less overtly progressive or satirical than *Anno Dracula*, but also sidesteps the novel's exclusionary politics.

Although *League* may not be intended as particularly subversive or revolutionary, it often successfully avoids romanticizing or exoticizing otherness – something *Anno Dracula*, *Penny Dreadful*, and even *Athena Club* are sometimes guilty of. *League*'s representational politics are not flawless, however. Like *Anno Dracula*, *The League of Extraordinary Gentlemen* harnesses some of the more brutal, chauvinistic, and racist images of the times in order to satirize and sensationalize them. For the most part, it does this very evenly; depictions of ethnic minorities as slow, ugly, brutal, or animalistic are balanced by similar depictions of the English, and the use of racial slurs like 'chinaman' or 'darkie', when they appear, are almost always ironic references to presumed Victorian nomenclature, rather than expressions of hate or condemnation. In fact, these slurs are generally spoken by the heroes themselves, either about each other or about their adversaries. In *Volume I*, Prince Dakkar refers to the Egyptians as 'a Mohammedan rabble' – an explicitly ironic statement delivered by a bearded man in a turban, who is descended from Muslim kings. Likewise, when Hyde informs Mina in *Volume II* that he is not averse to companionship, it is simply 'the darkies, opium-sots and snickering lunatics' he detests (i.e. all the other members of the League), his own fitness for many of these labels has already been firmly established in the story (Moore and O'Neill 2003, issue 2). Of course, to some extent the presence or absence of irony is determined by the audience. I will expand on this issue in the following chapter.

Like *League*'s engagement with race, its depictions of women, though scarce and often problematic, cover a wide spectrum. As in Stoker's novel, Mina Murray is the cornerstone of the group, though in this version she is neither domesticated nor punished for her boldness. Murray is nearly always the character who takes the initiative, assembles the plans, and acts when others are still debating or fumbling for solutions. Despite the series' strong female lead, and its initially general audience,[7] however, *The League of Extraordinary Gentlemen* does not escape the stereotypical sexualization of women that still permeates the mainstream comics, or the sexual violence that too often features as a plot device (S. Scott 2013; Simone 1999; Tondro 2011, 4). Sexual assault features frequently as a threat to Murray, and to other women and men throughout the *League* series (see Nevins 2004, 273 for reference). It is implied that a prolonged period of violation at the hands of Dracula is the cause of both Murray's isolation from society and her inner strength. Although many superheroes in comics possess a tragic past, the fact that Murray's power stems from her status as a victim reinforces a stereotype in the genre in which women can only find meaning through men. As the sole female member of the League for the first two volumes, she is also the default target of most romantic tension, and is the object of sexual actions or words from every other member of the League at one point or another, excepting Captain Nemo.

Despite these by-products of its Victorian context and comic book medium, however, *League* offers a compelling narrative of how a group with few commonalities and conflicting interests can be mobilized to combat the seemingly overwhelming forces of imperialism and colonialism. If *League*'s monsters can be said to serve as a metaphor for either a Victorian or a twenty-first-century body politic, the image they convey is resoundingly multicultural – both in terms of the series' heroes and themes, and in its crowd scenes and background art. This arguably represents a much greater and more urgent challenge, and one more in line with our contemporary sociopolitical climate, than the exclusively progressive society promoted in *Anno Dracula*. *League*'s heroic monsters are re-politicized not because they are all politically progressive, but because, despite their vast differences, they all stand together. Without its monsters and monstrous Others, the series seems to argue, Britain would have been doomed long ago.

'We are all monsters': Reclaiming privilege in *Penny Dreadful*

Penny Dreadful represents yet another politically inflected model of monstrous identity and political community. Of the three texts so far, it displays the clearest engagement with scholarly discourses of monstrosity – in fact, showrunner John Logan drew directly on Cohen's 'Monster Culture' chapter for the series proposal, resulting in Cohen being featured in one of the show's video featurettes (Penny Dreadful 2014). This explicit engagement with academia informs and encourages *Penny Dreadful*'s framing as 'quality television', a meta-genre of programming popular since the 1990s, initially aimed at higher-income viewers and 'organized around hybrid texts that combined familiar television formats with themes and aesthetics drawn from more celebrated sources such as the Hollywood gangster film, romantic comedy, and European arthouse cinema' (Hassler-Forest 2014, 163). As Hassler-Forest argues, such programmes successfully incorporate 'the aesthetics of cinema on the one hand, and the narrative structure of the 19th-century realist novel on the other', attempting to market themselves as an alternative to television's traditionally lowbrow or morally conservative programming (2014, 163; see also Poore 2016, 66). The socially 'progressive' potential of quality television remains a complex issue, however (see Arthurs 2004, 35; Hassler-Forest 2014, 171). Like *Anno Dracula* and *League*, I argue that *Penny Dreadful* only represents a *relatively* progressive political approach to contemporary monstrosity, as compared to other popular texts.

Like the other Frankenfictions in this chapter, *Penny Dreadful*'s characters are either drawn from or inspired by classic literature. It borrows from its source texts thematically as well as superficially, acting as an extended adaptation of *Dracula*, *Frankenstein*, and *The Picture of Dorian Gray*. If these characters had known each other, runs the logic of *Penny Dreadful*, their stories might have ended differently, or taken on a different significance. Where *League* promotes monstrosity at large through the actions of its monstrous characters, in *Penny Dreadful* different kinds of monstrosity are valorized in different contexts, and it is only at the end of the series that it becomes clear which kind of monster the show ultimately advocates.

On a superficial level, *Penny Dreadful* bears much similarity to *League*, which initially provoked accusations of plagiarism from various fans and critics. Like *League*, the central character of *Penny Dreadful* is a strong woman with a dark past. Although Vanessa Ives is not Mina Murray (who also appears in the series), she bears a striking resemblance to Moore and O'Neill's character in both appearance and manner. Although she is not the official leader of the group that comes together over the course of the first season, she becomes the key unifying character across seasons two and three. Her struggle to reconcile her privileged, religious upbringing, which she values, with her monstrous supernatural abilities, which make her feel unique, important, and empowered, forms a central story arc in the series. Several other character types from *League* also re-appear in *Penny Dreadful*, including the colonial explorer, the American gunslinger, and Dorian Gray. The parallels between the two storyworlds are especially notable if one takes *League*'s 2003 film adaptation into account.

Ultimately, however, the two texts have dramatically different aesthetics. The cluttered and garish panels in *The League of Extraordinary Gentlemen* contrast sharply with *Penny Dreadful*'s austere and expansive sets and arthouse gore. Each text also has very different approaches to late-nineteenth-century monstrosity. Where race is central to *League*'s multicultural storyworld, *Penny Dreadful* takes an extended look at mainstream society's white, patriarchal structures. Moreover, the two texts employ opposite approaches to the idea of 'high' literature. *The League of Extraordinary Gentlemen* selects its texts primarily for their bawdy sense of adventure, often playing with the fact that we are still entertained by the same inappropriate things the Victorians were. *League* affects flowery language and extravagant settings only in order to tear down the boundary between high and low culture. In contrast, *Penny Dreadful*'s interpretation of the source material treats nineteenth-century Gothic novels as literary classics, embodiments of the authors' efforts to come to terms with their environment and their own sense of self. It then sets itself up as the successor to these acclaimed works of literature.

Writing about season one, Benjamin Poore suggests that '*Penny Dreadful* capitalizes on the fact that there is no single, agreed definition for what the Victorian penny dreadful was', in terms of both audience and content (2016, 63, 66). For this reason, Poore argues, the 'multiple meanings and ironies of the title *Penny Dreadful* precisely calibrate the series' cultural positioning between seriousness and self-awareness, between period-specificity and anachronism, between blending and trumping concepts of adaptation, and between televisual populism and critical and fan appeal' (2016, 77). Poore's article offers several insights into the politics of *Penny Dreadful*'s aesthetics, though he is more interested in the show's experimentation with genre and transgression than in its race or gender politics. In analysing the effect of its title, Poore suggests that it 'gives the show a kind of outlaw, rebellious power: this is the show they don't want you to watch, this is the show they'll try to shut down or brand obscene' (2016, 66). This is of course not the case, as Poore later points out. *Penny*

Dreadful is critically applauded for its handling of 'adult' content, not maligned for it, and in this regard it is far less socially and politically transgressive than other programmes currently on television (2016, 75). Both *League* and *Penny Dreadful* approach the Victorian canon with a certain sense of familiarity and affection, but from completely different angles. Essentially, *Penny Dreadful* takes a more conservative stance towards its source texts.

   Penny Dreadful is not as interested in historical detail as either *Anno Dracula* or *League*, and does not necessarily seek to imagine an alternate history, or to remain historically accurate. Instead, this mashup aims to be faithful to the nineteenth century's stylistic heritage. With the show, Logan – as creator, writer, and producer – set out to rehabilitate both horror and terror, telling a classic Gothic story in which these emotions are refocused from the monster onto the human. In one of the show's YouTube featurettes, Logan himself explains why this show is not really about fantastical monsters at all: 'Within all of us we have secrets, we have demons. We are all monsters' (2014). For Logan, *Penny Dreadful* is about the figurative monsters in each of us, and how this monstrous difference can encourage us to come together as both individuals and communities.

   Again separating it from *League* is the fact that *Penny Dreadful*'s monsters are not framed as superheroes. Instead, Logan directly engages with the traditional self/other binary, claiming in one interview that the show is an 'exciting way to play with the central duality of what it is to be man, what it is to be a monster, what it is to be woman' (Ryan 2014, para. 18). For Logan, the experience of monstrosity is also strongly linked to his own experience as a gay man (Thomas 2014; Thielman 2014). His statement in another interview that 'the thing that made me [...] monstrous to some people is also the thing that empowered me and gave me a sense of confidence and uniqueness and a drive toward individuality' could well be read as the central message of the series (June Thomas 2014, para. 5). This perspective on monstrosity and difference shows strongly in the show, which takes many opportunities to visualize queer experience, and to comment on monstrous identity and empowerment. Making an allusion to *The Picture of Dorian Gray*, Logan states:

> I wanted to write characters who felt they are different, yet have power in that difference. We all have secrets, portraits in the attic; it's about saying the real strength is in the forbidden – you must just be uniquely who you are. (Daniels 2015, para. 8)

In other words, the show's monsters are intended precisely to make audiences 'reevaluate our cultural assumptions about race, gender, sexuality, our perception of difference, our tolerance toward its expression', as Cohen indicates (Cohen 1996, 20). Like *Anno Dracula* or *League*, *Penny Dreadful* seeks to suggest that monstrosity is first and foremost the result of exclusionary systems, not inherent otherness or evil. This is done with varying degrees of success across the show's three seasons.

In *Penny Dreadful*, the lead team of characters is assembled by Sir Malcolm Murray, an Allan Quatermain-type character who spent his youth as a hunter, explorer, and soldier. Although not drawn directly from Stoker's *Dracula*, as his name might suggest, in *Penny Dreadful*'s first season he is engaged in a hunt for his daughter Mina, who has vanished under mysterious circumstances. Like *Anno Dracula*, then, *Penny Dreadful* imagines Stoker's novel from an alternative perspective. Murray enlists the help of his African manservant Sembene, Mina's childhood friend Vanessa Ives, the American gunslinger Ethan Chandler (a werewolf), and a young doctor named Victor Frankenstein, to track down his daughter and destroy the creature who abducted her. Other key literary characters introduced through parallel subplots include Dorian Gray, Frankenstein's Creature (called Caliban in season one and John Clare in season two), Brona Croft (resurrected in season two as Lily Frankenstein, a female Creature), and, in season three, Henry Jekyll. In this retelling Jekyll is a friend of Victor Frankenstein who is trying to prove he is worthy of his father's title – Lord Hyde.

As in *Anno Dracula* and *League*, each character in *Penny Dreadful* has a different 'curse' or potentially monstrous otherness that distinguishes them. In line with *Anno Dracula*, and with Weinstock's analysis of contemporary monsters, this is often an invisible, internal monstrosity rather than a physical one. In general, what separates the 'good' characters from the 'evil' ones in *Penny Dreadful* is their independence and self-knowledge, and how this relates to their morality. The show's heroic characters take their cues from their own consciences, which are expressly at odds with society's dictates. The vampires, witches, and overtly evil characters that populate the show are defined by their service to a greater master, and to hegemonic structures. They may be physically beautiful, and are often socially and politically powerful, but their dependence on an even higher system of power (in this case the devil), rather than each other or their own individual codes, marks them as the real monsters of *Penny Dreadful*'s first two seasons.

The Nightcomer witches of season two, led by the manipulative Evelyn Poole, stand in particular contrast to Joan Clayton – the Daywalker witch who trains Vanessa Ives – in this respect. As hermit, herbalist, and 'cut-wife' (abortionist),

Clayton chooses to live independently, on the margins of society. The villagers consider her to be monstrous, but she is marked as a grudging hero and pioneer of social justice by the show. Poole, in contrast, sells her services to Lucifer in exchange for personal power, status, and social influence. She is embraced by the society in which she lives, but which she secretly aims to destroy. In this season of *Penny Dreadful*, then, marginality actually seems to indicate goodness, whereas characters who are part of mainstream society are marked as evil. Again, this aligns with many of twenty-first-century culture's shifting definitions of the monster as 'everywhere and nowhere' (McNally 2012, 2), and allows the various metaphors of monstrosity in *Penny Dreadful*'s classic source texts to interact on a number of different levels.

In *Penny Dreadful*, as with the other texts in this chapter, the 'good' characters initially bond through their monstrosity, forming their own community that supersedes the society in which they live. As Murray puts it in the episode 'Resurrection', they effectively 'proceed as one', and fulfil various familial roles for each other (Walsh 2014). Problematically, it is relatively easy for them to do this because, barring their diverse sexual and gender identities, they are still largely homogeneous: white, upper class, and colonialist. The show's theme of fidelity through monstrosity only works because, in contrast with *League*, there is no real conflict between its good monsters and their agendas – they all have similar problems and similar desires. For the first two seasons of *Penny Dreadful*, then, the 'monster within' remains a rather indulgent metaphor for first-world problems, reflecting the twenty-first-century monster's outward invisibility, rather than its potential as a metaphor for the socially and legally marginalized.

Penny Dreadful is more interested in some aspects of Logan's 'central duality' of identity than it is in others (Logan 2014). The show liberally explores questions of identity insofar as sexuality is concerned, but whenever the show turns to issues of gender, race, or colonialism, the focus is inevitably on white, masculine guilt, inadvertently reproducing the power structures it seeks to undermine. With the exception of Vanessa Ives, all the main characters in the first two seasons who are not white men suffer violent deaths. This unfortunately echoes the treatment of such characters in popular culture more broadly. Even the show's discussion of gender and sexuality is 'paradoxical and problematic in terms of its depiction of queer desire and monstrous bodies' (Phillips 2017, n.p.), marked by the disposability of many of its LGBTQ characters. Although it continually introduces characters who could break this cycle, the show persistently falls back on the stereotype of a single strong – if sexually traumatized – white woman, rather than engaging in an intersectional approach to identity. Despite John Logan's repeated statements about the show's grounding in identity politics, then, the show's treatment of marginalized characters does not differentiate it from Showtime and Sky Atlantic's other programming.

In the third season the show takes steps to address this issue, with mixed success. In this season, the core group of characters is divided both geographically and morally. Dracula, the elusive villain of season one, journeys to London to seduce Vanessa Ives and help her unleash her dark potential, bringing about an apocalyptic 'eternal night'. Ethan Chandler is transported back to America on criminal charges, only to be broken free by Kaetaney, an Apache warrior whose tribe he murdered as a young soldier. Kaetaney transmitted the werewolf curse to Ethan in revenge. Dorian Gray's character becomes a villainous metaphor for Western decadence and privileged masculinity, aligning him with the show's 'evil', hegemonic characters. Over the course of this final season, each character is forced to question the nature of their own monstrosity, as well as the monstrosity of the people they considered to be friends, family, enemies, or lovers in previous episodes. They must decide whether this monstrosity is something to be embraced, tolerated, or eradicated. These are issues immediately relevant to the twenty-first century, but which nevertheless find a natural reflection in the Gothic spaces and characters of *fin-de-siècle* London. What emerges from this unique adaptation of classic monster literature is a battle between mainstream, socially accepted monstrosity – white privilege and male guilt – and the more marginalized monstrosities of post-colonialism and feminism.

The show's portrayal of Henry Jekyll and his relationship with Victor Frankenstein is one key contributor to the third season's extended interrogation of social monstrosity, and its argument that the only path to freedom and empowerment comes through embracing one's marginality. Henry Jekyll's biological father is a white English Lord, who abandoned his Indian mother. The show makes sure audiences are aware that Henry's race is an issue here: in the scene where he is introduced London bystanders shout racist slurs in his direction (D. Thomas 2016a). Henry is desperate to prove himself and become the future Lord Hyde, despite the racial and class biases against him. Jekyll feels monstrous because of his disadvantaged background, but those who know Stevenson's narrative will recognize Lord Hyde (and Jekyll's efforts to become him) as the 'true' monster, even though the race and class of these characters have been flipped. Frankenstein's pain, in contrast, has less to do with his upbringing than with his own privileged choices. In the episode 'This World is Our Hell', Henry's motivation for his creations is to change himself so he will be accepted by others, where Victor Frankenstein wants others to accept him as he is. The show fails to do much more with this character dynamic, however. At the end of the series Henry Jekyll becomes Lord Hyde, and Victor Frankenstein is likewise subsumed back into familiar hegemonic structures of patriarchy and class privilege.

In the final season of *Penny Dreadful*, the show also moves from its singular focus on Vanessa Ives to a broader cast of female characters. Although this process begins with the addition of Lily Frankenstein and Hecate Poole, who manage to survive the season two finale, the second season's redemptive arc is most concerned with Vanessa Ives, Malcolm Murray, Victor Frankenstein, and Ethan Chandler. Hecate becomes one of Ethan's guides and mentors in season three. Lily, whom Victor Frankenstein initially creates as a partner for Caliban, performs the role of an ideal woman until the very end of the second season. She serves mainly to create conflict between these two men. In the third season, with the addition of Catriona Hartdegen (literally 'hard dagger'; an analogue of Van Helsing), Justine (no relation to *Frankenstein*), and Dr Florence Seward (an alienist who treats Vanessa's depression), *Penny Dreadful* attempts to become a metaphor for the monstrous power of patriarchal society through its engagement with various historical images of the monstrous feminine. It is through the characters of Vanessa and Lily, and through the parallels to *Dracula* and *Frankenstein* they embody, that the show is most effectively able to illustrate how certain kinds of historical monstrosity have been co-opted by twenty-first-century popular culture.

Lily Frankenstein's body is the reanimated corpse of Brona Croft, an Irish prostitute whose life was marked by sexual and emotional violence, and whose infant daughter perished as a result of this violence. She uses this identity to manipulate the men around her, but does not seem to want equality, or even redemption. Instead, she wants destruction and mastery, assembling an army of battered women and sending them out to enact revenge on the men who abused them (or enabled their abuse). While she often performs an idealized femininity, then, in *Penny Dreadful* it is not her femininity that is portrayed as truly monstrous – it is her feminism.

Lily's monstrous feminism is made explicit in the season three episode 'No Beast So Fierce', where she teaches her army of women about the fate that awaits women who fight back:

> We are not women who crawl. We are not women who kneel. And for this we will be branded radicals. Revolutionists. Women who are strong, and refuse to be degraded, and choose to protect themselves, are called monsters. That is the world's crime, not ours. (Cabezas 2016b)

Strong women who fight for their human rights are monsters in Lily's mind, reinforcing the series' message that the 'good' monsters are those who resist hegemonic structures. Lily counters the violence and oppression that was inflicted upon her to destroy not just the men who wronged her, but the society that enabled them. Ironically, however, the show does not align Lily with the Victorian feminist movement. In the episode 'Good and Evil Braided Be', Lily and Justine watch as a protesting group of suffragettes is detained by the police. Justine suggests that they and Lily are similar, but Lily dismisses this comparison on the grounds that the suffragettes are too unambitious (they want equality, not mastery) and too obvious:

> [T]hey're all so awfully clamorous. All this marching around in public and waving placards. That's not it. How do you accomplish anything in this life? By craft. By stealth. By poison. By the throat quietly slit in the dead of the night. By the careful and silent accumulation of power. (D. Thomas 2016c)

Lily advocates fighting a patriarchal society in precisely the way it expects: with craft and guile, in the dark and private spaces that have been a woman's traditional domain, and in which no one has thought to look before. By abusing her militant feminism rather than attempting to redefine or repackage it to appeal to the mainstream, Lily effectively becomes *Penny Dreadful's* most socially disruptive monster. Lily's monstrous triumph is never recognized on screen, however. Dorian Gray and Lily Frankenstein become immortal lovers, but Dorian is driven only by hedonism. Bored and annoyed by the 'familiar' politics and hard work of revolution after several lifetimes of experimentation, Dorian betrays Lily to Victor Frankenstein and Henry Jekyll, who are working on a serum meant to transform social deviants like herself into model citizens – from 'devils' into 'angels' (Cabezas 2016c; D. Thomas 2016b). Although she escapes in the end, this represents the end of her character arc on the series.

Writing on cinematic horror, Barbara Creed describes the way that women have historically been 'constructed as "biological freaks" whose bodies represent a fearful and threatening form of sexuality' (1993, 6). From a feminist and psychoanalytic perspective, she outlines five guises of the monstrous feminine: 'the archaic mother; the monstrous womb; the witch; the vampire; and the possessed woman' (1993, 7). These active representations of women in popular horror, she argues, 'challenge the view that the male spectator is almost always situated in an active, sadistic position and the female spectator in a passive, masochistic one' (1993, 7). Like Cohen, Creed does not argue that such representations are always empowering, however, and *Penny Dreadful's* third season aptly illustrates how narratives of monstrosity can send messages that are neither transgressive nor conservative. *Penny Dreadful*'s monsters can be read through the oppositional discourse of hegemonic and resistant monstrosity that Logan constructs, building on Cohen's discussions of marginality and monstrous otherness. In the final episodes, we are shown what happens when characters either reject or embrace a discourse of empowerment through marginal monstrosity.

Vanessa Ives comes to embody all five guises of the monstrous-feminine by the end of the third season. She is possessed by a powerful female spirit, the reincarnated mother of all monsters who will give birth to an eternal night (Cabezas 2016c). She is also a witch in many different conceptions of the label, adept in the folk medicines and charms of pre-modern society, able to read people's futures and commune with spirits, and fluent in the devil's language: the magic of murder and destruction. Once she accepts Dracula's bite in 'Ebb Tide' (Cabezas 2016c), she also takes on the bodily attributes of a vampire. In 'The Blessed Dark', season three's ninth and final episode, *Penny Dreadful* concludes Vanessa's story in ways that are both unexpected and disturbingly familiar. Despite the power her monstrosity gives her to disrupt the established social order, and the show's previous emphasis on this kind of monstrosity as a force for good, Vanessa gives it up (along with her life) to preserve the status quo. Light triumphs over darkness (Cabezas 2016d). Rather than embracing her monstrosity, her final character arc is thus resoundingly conservative.

The fact that the show is involved in a sustained intertextual relationship with Stoker's *Dracula* only strengthens this conservative reading of Vanessa's story, and the show's ultimate message about monstrosity. If we compare Logan's story to Stoker's, there are many parallels. Writing about the scene in Stoker's *Dracula* where the Crew of Light (Van Helsing, Quincey, Arthur, and Jonathan) drive a stake through Lucy Westenra's heart, Christopher Craft points out the heteronormative impulse of this act. It stands, he writes:

> [I]n the service of a tradition of 'good women whose lives and whose truths may make good lesson [*sic*] for the children that are to be'. In the name of those good women and future children (very much the same children whose throats Lucy is now penetrating), Van Helsing will repeat, with an added emphasis, his assertion that penetration is a masculine prerogative. His logic of corrective penetration demands an escalation, as the failure of the hypodermic needle necessitates the stake. A women is better still than mobile, better dead than sexual. (Craft 1997, 451–2)

With Lucy's death, the power of penetration (and of patriarchy) is reasserted, pointing to the salvation of Mina Harker and final triumph against Dracula at the novel's end.

Rather than explore the 'Blessed Dark' of the episode's title (Cabezas 2016d), Vanessa chooses Lucy Westenra's fate instead. She dies, virginal in a white gown, penetrated by a bullet from Ethan's gun to undo her penetration at the hands of Dracula (see Figure 2.2). After her death, Ethan, Malcolm, Victor, and Caliban lament her passing, acknowledging that her death was necessary for their salvation. While she shares Lucy's fate, then, she also shares Mina's role as an ideal woman. At the end of Stoker's novel, Van Helsing frames Mina Harker as a sacrificial object. Her purity and goodness provide the proof for the preceding narrative, the reason for its happy conclusion, and the assurance of future triumph over evil. He proclaims: 'Already [her son] knows her sweetness and loving care. Later on he will understand how some men so loved her, that they did dare much for her sake' (Stoker [1897] 1997, 327). Van Helsing's words could just as easily be applied to *Penny Dreadful*, and to Vanessa Ives. Like Mina, Vanessa's monstrosity (or monstrous femininity) is usurped by her sacrificial goodness (or traditional femininity). In the context of the show's meta-plot, and the battle against Dracula, this makes Vanessa heroic, but it also contradicts the show's premise of solidarity in monstrosity and weakens the political symbolism of the monster. In essence, it places Vanessa within

Figure 2.2 Screenshot from 'The Blessed Dark' (*Penny Dreadful* season 3 finale), © 2016 Showtime/Sky.

the binary, restrictive, 'angel/monster image' Sandra Gilbert and Susan Gubar describe in their feminist study of Victorian literature (2000, 17).

The failed feminism of the series is reinforced by the fact that Dracula is not killed in the season finale of *Penny Dreadful*, although his plans are thwarted. He simply fades away. Under other circumstances his impotence might be read as revolutionary, but here he has already served his purpose by seducing the heroine. Dracula's masculine, upper-class monstrosity is not the real threat (or the real source of empowerment) in *Penny Dreadful*. It is female monsters, queer monsters, brown monsters, and other socially disruptive figures who apparently need to be driven out. Vanessa's monstrosity is acceptable only if its difference is not too extreme, and does not challenge the status quo too radically. Lily is allowed to escape and survive her own story arc, but the show does not devote much time to this victory. She is also only allowed to escape once she reveals her feminine role as a mother, though Lily's child is dead – the victim of patriarchal institutions. Motherhood is still a less comfortable identity for Lily than it was for *Dracula*'s Mina, whose 'sweetness and loving care' inspires men to 'dare so much' (Stoker [1897] 1997, 327).

In the introduction to their edited collection *Neo-Victorian Gothic*, Marie-Luise Kohlke and Christian Gutleben ask: 'How can the Gothic go on celebrating otherness as it becomes increasingly homogenized?' (2012, 2). Season three of *Penny Dreadful* is an extended, if incomplete, answer to this question. Although the answer sometimes seems to be 'embrace your sins' (Cabezas 2016a), i.e. recognize and weaponize your social monstrosity, this position is never fully realized in the series. Most of *Penny Dreadful*'s monstrous characters are punished for their unconventional otherness. At worst they are killed, at best they are marginalized, and only a few are able to embrace that marginality to find empowerment. Despite its self-stated interest in monstrous identity politics, then, *Penny Dreadful* is ultimately the most conservative mashup in this chapter.

'Monstrum sum': Intersectional monstrosity in *The Extraordinary Adventures of the Athena Club*

Where the previous three texts used the potential of monstrous community to re-politicize popular identity politics, and effectively advocate for a multicultural society, Theodora Goss's *Athena Club* series (2017–19) arguably offers the best model for doing so. Set at the turn of the twentieth century, the series chronicles the adventures of the daughters of famous 'mad scientists' from nineteenth-century literature, and their eventual formation of the Athena Club to help women like themselves. Main characters include Mary Jekyll (the invented daughter of Henry Jekyll from Robert Louis Stevenson's *Strange Case of Dr Jekyll and Mr Hyde*, 1886), Diana Hyde (invented daughter of Jekyll's alter ego Edward Hyde), Catherine Moreau (the puma woman from H.G. Wells's *The Island of Doctor Moreau*, 1896), Justine Frankenstein (a version of the female creature from *Frankenstein*), Beatrice Rappaccini (from Nathaniel Hawthorne's 1844 short story 'Rappaccini's Daughter'), and later Lucinda Van Helsing (the invented daughter of *Dracula*'s Abraham Van Helsing). The books draw supporting characters from a range of late Victorian fiction, including *Dracula*, Arthur Conan Doyle's *Sherlock Holmes* stories (1887–1927), and Joseph Sheridan Le Fanu's *Carmilla* (1871). Several real historical figures, including Sigmund Freud, also appear as supporting characters in the series.

All of the Athena Club's members are self-declared monsters, in ways familiar from the previous case studies in this chapter – they have been 'separated from humanity' or society (Goss 2017, 171), in most cases by their scientist fathers. Each has been 'affected by experiments of various sorts', from which she 'will never entirely recover', and which 'have altered her physically and psychologically' (Goss 2018, 676). Like the other case studies in this chapter, the *Athena Club* series also plays with the distinction between physical and social monstrosity. In *The Strange Case of the Alchemist's Daughter* (2017), for example, it is suggested that as the Athena Club works 'to stop the malicious machinations' of the Société des Alchimistes, their fathers' secret organization, 'it is time for the monsters to triumph over the monstrous' (Goss 2017, jacket blurb). Although physical norms may render these women monstrous to some, the 'true' monsters are the men who created and experimented on them, and the society that allowed it.

For the women themselves, monstrosity can mean many things. Beatrice Rappaccini is a Gothic femme fatale, an Italian beauty whose touch is poisonous to other living things. She considers herself a monster because of her isolation, which hinders her from exercising her educated mind and her passion for social justice. For Justine Frankenstein and Catherine Moreau, monstrosity revolves around their 'unnatural' construction. One is built from the dead body of Justine Moritz, the other surgically transgresses the animal boundaries between feline and human. Both have been forcibly socialized into the roles of adult women, and it is their traumatic entry to these social systems that is the source of their monstrosity. When the two characters first meet, Catherine reveals her surgery scars and tells Justine 'I, too, am made. I, too, am a monster. *Monstrum sum*' (Goss 2017, 358). The Latin reference, meaning 'I am a monster', echoes René Descartes's humanist proposition *cogito, ergo sum*: 'I think, therefore I am'. Unlike Descartes's ideal man, the fact that these women are at all 'rational' and 'capable of reasoned thought' makes them monstrous (Goss 2017, 344).

Mary Jekyll and Diana Hyde present a different example of monstrosity. They are physically unremarkable and socially 'normal', but psychologically they are the mis-matched by-product of their father's own split personality. Mary was conceived by the Henry Jekyll personality and raised as a lady. Diana was conceived by the Edward Hyde personality and raised in an orphanage. Nurture compounds the traits instilled by nature for both characters. Mary is perfectly socialized and rational but lacks healthy emotional expression – of all the Athena Club's female monsters, she is best able to pass within polite society. Diana is passionate, creative, and impulsive, and impossible to integrate into Mary's upper-class world. She is the perfect picture of the Victorian urchin, however. As the series' fictional version of Sigmund Freud points out to Mary, 'it seemed to me that [Diana] was perfectly well-adjusted, that her actions made sense and would not be blamable, in a society different from ours. It seemed to me that it was our society which was at fault, rather than your sister' (Goss 2018, 234). Like *Penny Dreadful*, *Athena Club*'s focus is often on larger social systems of oppression, not on individual monstrosity. Clothing, education (or lack thereof), etiquette, and the institutions for regulating madness and medicine are all tried as culprits of women's literal and metaphorical monstrosity.

In contrast with *Penny Dreadful*, however, in the *Athena Club* series it is the characters who *do* claim wider social responsibility, rather than renouncing it, who are on the side of good. The series also takes a more consistently feminist perspective, referencing the history of women's liberation and the 'New Woman' (Goss 2018, 539) as well as twenty-first-century preferences for outspoken and physically adventurous women. Beatrice is an advocate of Rational Dress (Goss 2017, 192), a middle-class feminist movement in the late nineteenth century. Both Beatrice and Mrs Poole (the Athena Club's housekeeper) attend women's suffrage rallies (Goss 2018, 16). Justine, Mary, and Catherine each take up regular work outside of the home, and all the members of the Athena Club advocate a woman's right to be educated and autonomous. The patriarchy has made the women of the Athena Club monstrous – once literally, through their fathers' experiments, once metaphorically, through their socialization into Victorian society. Interestingly, each woman in the series has her own preferences and reservations about feminist politics. Although she is an advocate of women's voting rights, for instance, Mrs Poole objects to Catherine's writing career: 'Gallivanting around Europe is one thing, but writing about it ... It's not ladylike, is all I say' (Goss 2018, 16).

Kimberle Crenshaw uses the term 'intersectional' to describe how 'the intersection of racism and sexism', and in this case also classism, function together 'in ways that cannot be captured wholly by looking at the race or gender [or class] dimensions of those experiences separately' (Crenshaw 1991, 1244). The Athena Club's members are women from different places, cultures, and social classes, with differing backgrounds and often-intersectional identities. Mary and Beatrice come from relative privilege, but Justine, Catherine, and Diana are working-class women. As Diana sarcastically remarks on infiltrating a Viennese madhouse:

> So this was what madwomen did in the afternoons – sat around and read fashion magazines, or drew silly pictures? It did not seem so different from what most women did in their ordinary lives. Wealthy women, that is. Poor women had better things to do than draw, or read magazines, or go mad! (Goss 2018, 279)

Here and elsewhere, the novel draws attention to the different systems of oppression that impact women of differing social classes, and reminds us that our twenty-first-century idea of the historical woman is often dominated by images of upper-class privilege.

Catherine is a woman of colour, as are many of the series' supporting characters. The majority of the Athena Club's members are immigrants to Britain. As the second book of the series, *European Travel for the Monstrous Gentlewoman* (2018), points out, this puts them at a disadvantage among the English, who often incorrectly assume other countries are 'uncivilized' (Goss 2018, 598). Native Londoners are also assumed to be foreign because of their skin tones. For instance, one of Catherine's fellow circus performers is Madam Zora from the 'Mysterious East', with 'skin [...] as brown as Catherine's', 'dark brown eyes outlined with a great deal of kohl', and an 'undefinable' accent (2018, 215–16). Mary initially mistakes her for a foreigner, until it becomes clear that the 'East' from which Madam Zora hails is in fact Hackney, and her accent is 'the voice of London, inflected by the East End' (2018, 216).

Crucially, none of the women in the *Athena Club* series stands in for all women, nor do they always agree with each other on the correct ethics or course of action in a particular situation. And often women who might be expected to band together on one issue are divided by another part of their identity or experience. Although Catherine and Zora are both 'brown girls'

(2018, 361), and Zora expects Catherine and herself to become friends, for example, Catherine's mistrust of people keeps them at odds for most of the story. Another conflict in the series is between the Athena Club and a fellow monstrous woman, Ayesha the president of the Société des Alchimistes. This conflict also demonstrates the effectiveness of the Club's monstrous community. Ayesha refuses to ban the society's experiments in transmutation, because in her estimation the ends justify the means – even though these women were experimented on against their will (2018, 670–1). Despite their firm disagreement with her decision, the Athena Club are able to work together to find a democratic solution, and convince Ayesha establish an ethics committee that will protect future experimental subjects from suffering as they did. These monstrous women work within the system when they can, but are also willing to tear it down when they must. And as Mary notes, even though the women of the Athena Club can accomplish great things together, they do not always do so without conflict: 'They were all stronger together. Less amicable, but stronger' (2018, 591). In the *Athena Club*, the price of strength and diversity is often disagreement and discord, but it is framed as a price worth paying.

The manner in which the *Athena Club* series is written reinforces this dynamic. A large part of the story is narrated from the perspective of Mary Jekyll, a white, upper-class woman. Rather than making her 'special' through this narration, however, the novels make clear that Mary is simply 'the easiest to write about' because she is the most familiar to readers (2018, 439). Rather than being a particular compliment to Mary, this is a comment on the failing of contemporary readers, who allegedly 'would fall asleep' if the author 'wrote down all the things Justine thinks about – seventeenth-century peasants' revolts and the rights of man, and whatever Voltaire said' (2018, 439). Justine is quite a conservative humanist thinker, but is certainly not more boring than the others when her time for narration does come. Likewise, though Mary offers the central point of view, the novel is actually 'written' by Catherine, a prolific author of novels, and official chronicler of the Club's adventures. Catherine's authorial perspective is made explicit at numerous points throughout the books, often in her romanticized descriptions of events (something the hyperrational Mary would be incapable of), more occasionally in an author's note (2017, 20) or direct shift to the first person (2018, 672). Catherine's authorship also allows her, as a 'brown' colonial subject (2017, 297), to speak to issues of race and oppression in ways neither Mary, nor Theodora Goss herself can. Where Mary and other women are hesitant to embrace the title of 'monster', Catherine owns the term for herself (2017, 358, 2018, 698).

The narration is also fragmented on another level, as the books frequently diverge into chapters narrated *to* Mary rather than *by* her. This allows other people to give their own accounts of their histories and origins in their own voices. The novels also include direct interjections from all the members of the Athena Club, whom Catherine has allowed to read the draft manuscript. Through these interjections other characters offer comments and additions to the story, or, more often, disagree with Catherine on facts or perspectives in her narrative, reminding her of their own agency: 'We are not your characters, but fellow members of the Athena Club' (2018, 88). More so than the other Frankenfictions in this chapter, then, the 'monstrous' format of the *Athena Club* series reflects its monstrous characters. As Justine Frankenstein suggests, the form of the books is 'different. As though it's been stitched together of various parts. Like my father's monsters'. To this Catherine replies, 'we're different. I have to tell the story in a way that fits who we are' (2017, 206).

The *Athena Club* series represents an intentionally less rational, less structured, and less traditionally 'historical' mode of historical accuracy. As Justine writes, it is 'not simply a story of our adventures. It's a story about us – our emotions and relationships' (2018, 622). While the books comment on historical institutions and events, then, their main interest is in conveying personal, *feminist* histories, emotions, and experiences: past and present, and always plural. That there are so many examples of diverse communities in the *Athena Club* novels, and so many women in the series with their own voices and opinions, helps *Athena Club* avoid many of the representational issues found in *Anno Dracula*, *The League of Extraordinary Gentlemen*, and *Penny Dreadful*. *The Extraordinary Adventures of the Athena Club* is clearly indebted to these earlier texts, acknowledging the pattern in which so-called monsters end up being predominantly white and male, easily absorbed into mainstream popular culture. The word 'Extraordinary' in the series title also echoes Moore and O'Neill's *League* comics. But rather than taking a direct interest in the now-familiar monsters (Dracula, Frankenstein's creature, Mr Hyde), as earlier team mashups do, *Athena Club* focuses on the real Others of the story – monstrous women who are present on the periphery or in the margins of these well-known fictions, but are never given a satisfactory voice.

Like the other monster mashups in this chapter, Goss's work also speaks back explicitly to older fictional traditions, and to critical theories of the monstrous. Goss holds a PhD in Victorian monsters (Goss 2012), and this body of academic knowledge is readily visible in the *Athena Club* series' many literary and critical references. Justine is very knowledgeable about continental philosophy and

Romantic poetry. Beatrice is well versed in Freudian theory, as demonstrated in her interpretation of Justine's dreams:

> BEATRICE: The lake is a symbol of the feminine. Perhaps it represents your mother, and the rain coming down represents the male principle that disturbs the female? Rain is often a symbol of the father, and the storm clouds are of course associated with the father-god Zeus. So your father, Frankenstein, who sought to be a god, disturbed the feminine principle of creation, and what emerged was you, as you are now – a stranger to that other Justine. (Goss 2018, 239)

At one point in the series Goss even makes an apparent reference to her own PhD thesis, titled 'The Monster in the Mirror: Late Victorian Gothic and Anthropology'. Near the very beginning of *Alchemist's Daughter* Catherine (who tends to otherwise scoff at critical discourse) writes: 'I have paused to show you Mary staring into the mirror because this is a story about monsters. All stories about monsters contain a scene in which the monster sees himself in a mirror' (2017, 4). Many characters in the novels are avid readers (and, in Catherine's case, writers) of popular fiction themselves. At one point Mary comments that she feels like she is 'entering the Castle of Otranto' (2017, 44), and Diana is thrilled to discover that vampires exist, just as she has read in her penny bloods (2018, 420). When Diana comments on the obsession the Société des Alchimistes seems to have with madhouses, Mary references Gothic theories of doubleness: 'We have often been told, by criminologists such as Lombroso, that genius and madness are closely related. Perhaps they see, in these madmen, a dark reflection of themselves' (2018, 132).

Athena Club's extensive engagement with Gothic fiction and criticism brings us back to Adrienne Rich's assertion that we 'need to know the writing of the past, and know it differently than we have ever known it; not to pass on a tradition but to break its hold over us' (1972, 19). Where Rich's aim is to describe real women in the twentieth-century writing themselves and their art into classic literary history, Goss explores the twenty-first-century importance of writing women back into our popular, marginal, and monstrous narratives as well. Through this exploration, she also delivers a powerful example of how monster mashup can productively re-ignite discussions of identity politics in the popular sphere.

The promises of monsters

The case studies in this chapter reveal an interesting pattern. *Anno Dracula, The League of Extraordinary Gentlemen, Penny Dreadful,* and *The Extraordinary*

Adventures of the Athena Club each have their own form and genre. Each also has its own politics of the monstrous, though they share the aim to transform the popular monster into a sociopolitical metaphor for a multicultural and intersectional Britain – and a multicultural and intersectional world. They do so by adapting old monsters as well as new ones, by ensuring that more than one kind of 'monstrous' difference is represented in their narratives, and by reminding audiences that the monster was – and still is – a marker of 'cultural, political, racial, economic, [and] sexual' difference (Cohen 1996, 7). Like the Creature of Shelley's novel, they direct the myths and belief structures of Western civilization back at the culture that created them.

Of course, each of these texts is primarily designed to entertain, not just to serve as an object of activism or criticism. And because they expand upon existing stories and characters rather than forging more 'original' ones, the monsters of Frankenfiction will never represent a canonical definition of the monstrous. The very depiction of collective otherness that these texts offer can more readily open them to such uses, however. As I have argued, to be a monster in fiction (or in society) is no longer necessarily marginal or transgressive. Frankenfiction is only able to depict 'actual', politically productive monstrosity when it combines multiple monstrous narratives. By presenting a world of difference in which fantastical monsters are as diverse as real-world individuals, texts like *Penny Dreadful, League, Anno Dracula*, and *Athena Club* remind us that even when the monster is the privileged subject of its own narrative, there are still monsters – like us, but still Other – on the margins. This kind of marginalized subjectivity offers its own political promise as well. As feminist critic Judith Butler writes in *Undoing Gender*:

> [We must] underscore the value of being beside oneself, of being a porous boundary, given over to others, finding oneself in a trajectory of desire in which one is taken out of oneself, and resituated irreversibly in a field of others in which one is not the presumptive center. (Butler 2004, 25)

This monstrous view of identity decentres the subject, placing it alongside the other rather than against the other, and potentially allowing for a less inherently exclusionary politics of identity. By being alongside others, both subjectively and physically, we are constantly forced to negotiate the presupposed primacy and wholeness of that same subject position. Frankenfiction thus invites us to desire the monster, but also makes sure we understand that the monster is multiple, and brings conflict to established systems of identity. Desiring the monster means accepting its inherent otherness and fragmentation, not just a singular, glamorized view of monstrosity.

This characteristic also gives Frankenfiction great promise as a genre. As Hassler-Forest writes of twenty-first-century storyworlds:

> [I]n a context where even the most subversive counternarratives can be effortlessly appropriated and recycled within the very system they attack, the important work of imagining alternatives and creating productive resistance expands to the larger sphere of world-building. (Hassler-Forest 2016, 175)

In other words, it is not enough to write subversive stories. These can be (and are) easily appropriated, adapted, and remixed by the mainstream culture they claim to defy, often at the expense of the narrative's initially subversive impulse. What a narrative can do, and what these Frankenfictions attempt to do, is show audiences that even when monstrosity and transgression are entertaining, and even when a particular monster has become accepted and beloved, that monster could only come into being in a world where some people are excluded from the categories of the normal and the human. They make the monster seem like a natural part of history – not just because they make history fantastical, but because through their adaptations of specific figures they reveal fantasy's historical politics.

In this chapter, I discussed the politics of fantasy, arguing that some works of Frankenfiction use the theme of monstrosity to engage (albeit indirectly) with sociopolitical issues. Despite the entertaining function and the mainstream positioning of *Anno Dracula, League, Penny Dreadful,* and *Athena Club,* their approach to the stories and characters they appropriate is comparatively politicized. In the next chapter, I will step back to examine the irony of this popular-political approach, and consider the politics of parodying one kind of monstrosity (social) through another (fantastical). This is not always done with the aim of disclosing a deeper, historical significance. In some Frankenfictions, like the novel-as-mash-up, parody simply serves to interrogate twenty-first-century popular culture's methods of engaging with the past.

Notes

1   Count Dracula and Mina Harker are taken from *Dracula,* and Daniel Dravot from Rudyard Kipling's short story 'The Man Who Would Be King' (1888). Lord Ruthven comes from *The Vampyre* (1819), by John William Polidori, and Count Vardalek is a character in 'The True Story of a Vampire' (1894), a short story by Count Eric Stanislaus Stenbock. Newman describes the process of writing Kate Reed, one of *Anno Dracula*'s vampire characters (later an undead journalist): 'in Stoker's original

outline for *Dracula*, she would have been a friend of Mina Harker's – but he cut her from the book; I now feel quite proprietorial about her' (2013, para. 5).

2   This is a Marxist metaphor that itself dates back to the nineteenth century. Consider Karl Marx's explicitly political use of the vampire as a metaphor in *Capital*: 'Capital is dead labour which, vampire-like, lives only by sucking living labour', and it has a 'vampire thirst for the living blood of labour'. Finally, Marx describes how 'the vampire will not let go "while there remains a single muscle, sinew or drop of blood to be exploited"' (Marx 1976, 342, 357, 416).

3   I classify *Anno Dracula* retroactively as a neo-Victorian novel, despite the fact that when it was first published by Simon & Schuster in 1992, the term 'neo-Victorian' was not in use by either scholars or the publishing community, and was thus not attached to the work in any meaningful sense. After its initial publication, *Anno Dracula* fell out of print for nearly a decade before the 2011 edition from Titan Books signalled renewed interest in the themes and genres it introduced. Titan also repackaged the novel to appeal to readers of contemporary steampunk and neo-Victorian fiction. It is this self-aware edition of *Anno Dracula*, with an entirely new series of authorial notes, alternate endings, and other 'bonus materials to sweeten the package', that offers the most interesting perspective on the novel's context, and on its monsters (Botelho 2012).

4   Later volumes – *The Black Dossier* in 2007 and a *Volume III* trilogy between 2009 and 2012 – were bundled as graphic novels straight away, skipping the usual issue-based release. These followed a changing League through the twentieth century and into the twenty-first. The hardcover spinoff trilogy *Nemo* (2013–15) tells the story of Janni Dakkar, daughter of original *League* member Captain Nemo, and the heir to his ship and title. The fourth and final volume, *The Tempest* (2018–19), returned to the six-issue miniseries format.

5   Prince Dakkar is a character in Jules Verne's *Twenty Thousand Leagues Under the Sea* (1870), Allan Quatermain is the protagonist of *King Solomon's Mines* (1885) by H. Rider Haggard, Dr Henry Jekyll/Mr Edward Hyde feature in Robert Louis Stevenson's 1886 novella *Strange Case of Dr Jekyll and Mr Hyde*, and Hawley Griffin is an amalgam of Dr Griffin from H.G. Wells's *The Invisible Man* (1897), and Dr Hawley Crippen, 'one of the most notorious of England's pre-WWI murderers' (Nevins 2003, 54).

6   Fu Manchu is a character from the novels of Sax Rohmer. This character is not in the public domain, however, and so for copyright reasons, he is referred to as 'The Doctor' throughout *League* Volume I.

7   Although reprints and subsequent volumes would be issued by Vertigo, DC's imprint for 'mature readers', the first three volumes were released by the general imprint America's Best Comics in the United States. When released in the UK, *League* was published under the Vertigo imprint.

3

Mashing Up the Joke

It was not joy only that possessed me; I felt my flesh tingle with excess of sensitiveness, and my pulse beat rapidly. I was unable to remain for a single instant in the same place; I jumped over the chairs, clapped my hands, and laughed aloud. Clerval at first attributed my unusual spirits to joy on his arrival, but when he observed me more attentively, he saw a wildness in my eyes for which he could not account, and my loud, unrestrained, heartless laughter frightened and astonished him.

(Shelley [1831] 2015, 53)

There is precious little joy in *Frankenstein*. In the passage above, Henry Clerval mistakes Victor Frankenstein's laughter as a sign of good spirits, but is soon corrected. Victor's recent activities – specifically, giving life to the creature – have produced hysteria, not humour. In Frankenfiction, however, humour and enjoyment play a central role, not least in the way such texts engage with classic texts and genres. In the previous chapter, I explored one of the ways in which Frankenfiction, through a discourse of monsters and the monstrous, adapts and remixes the textual past. I framed this discussion in light of how Frankenfictions appropriate certain characters and narrative themes. In this chapter, I will use the example of the novel-as-mashup (*Pride and Prejudice and Zombies, Jane Slayre*, and other cut-and-paste novels) to talk about how Frankenfiction engages with the broader structures, genres, and textual conventions of earlier fictions. This is often done through parody.

As with the other concepts I have introduced, 'parody' is a term that has frequently been contested and redefined. In many ways, it overlaps with both 'adaptation' and 'remix', and some critics use the terms interchangeably when talking about the way certain texts (like mashup) reference others. For Linda Hutcheon, parody and adaptation certainly seem to be related categories. Hutcheon defines parody as 'a form of imitation, but imitation characterized by ironic inversion, not always at the expense of the parodied text' (1985, 6).

Elsewhere, this is simply reiterated as 'repetition with distance' (1985, 32). So far this aptly describes the Frankenfictions I have discussed in this book. *Anno Dracula, The League of Extraordinary Gentlemen, Penny Dreadful,* and *The Extraordinary Adventures of the Athena Club* all repeat the characters and themes of nineteenth-century fiction, but in different contexts and combinations. Here Frankenfiction's repetition is automatically ironic: its status as fantastical fiction, and particularly its use of fantastical monsters, ensures that we cannot take its depictions of the past (or past texts) at face value.

For Hutcheon, parody is paradoxically both inclusive and exclusive, imitating a particular text at a basic level while also setting itself apart from that text on an ironic level – that is, in a way that distances its content from its context. She argues: 'While the act and form of parody are those of incorporation, its function is one of separation and contrast. Unlike imitation, quotation, or even allusion, parody requires that critical ironic distance' (1985, 34). In other words, its use of the text it appropriates is automatically re-visionary and re-interpretive, since it reproduces the text imperfectly and ironically, whether at a formal level or a narrative one. This makes the question of whether *Bridget Jones's Diary* is a better adaptation of *Pride and Prejudice* than *Pride and Prejudice and Zombies* moot. Each reinterprets *Pride and Prejudice* ironically, through re-vision and difference. As Thomas Leitch points out, this approach potentially makes parody synonymous with adaptation, and indeed Hutcheon's theorization of adaptation as 'repetition without replication' strongly echoes her definition of parody (Leitch 2012, 95, 102; Hutcheon 2013, 7). An adaptation is, by definition, not a replica but a 'repetition with distance', whether that distance is temporal, generic, or otherwise (Hutcheon 1985, 32). Like adaptation, parody is also capable of being read as a 'formal entity or product', a 'process of creation', and/ or a 'process of reception' (Hutcheon 2013, 7–8).

For remix and remix studies, on the other hand, parody is clearly one appropriative attitude among many. Remix parodies certainly do exist (consider Hawcroft 2011; da Silva and Garcia 2012), but in a work where 'the sources of origin may still be identifiable yet not perceived as the original version' (Sonvilla-Weiss 2010, 9), for Hutcheon we are arguably missing an important aspect of parody's (and adaptation's) imitative nature: the ironic distance between presentation and meaning, which paradoxically requires a certain intimacy with the 'original' text on one level or another. We might compare this aspect to the distinction between revision and recycling. Where a parody or adaptation sees the appropriated text as inherently valuable and worthy of comment or revision, remix may simply see the appropriated text as raw material to be recycled into something new. Remix's extension beyond the narrative mode also makes it difficult to claim as parody, suggesting that parody is often considered as a textual, if not necessarily literary mode. In Stefan Sonvilla-Weiss's description of Google Maps, for instance, in which 'different services are over-layered so as to provide for the user parallel accessible services' (2010, 9), the term 'parody' may be applicable but seems ill-fitting. In such cases, remix lacks the narrativity, the sense of intimacy, and the 'critical ironic distance' that Hutcheon deems essential to parody (Hutcheon 1985, 34).

For Hutcheon (and for myself), irony is a key component of both adaptation and parody, and something that potentially separates these terms from remix. In this case irony is most clearly the product of expectations: audiences react to an adaptation or parody based on the way it is constructed and positioned among other texts, and whether or not it fits in with the texts it references. Irony is also made possible by the way adaptation and parody, as genres in their own right, traditionally invite audiences to make such comparisons. When a reader or viewer notices a difference between the text and its reference, expectations are challenged, and irony is produced. Not every adaptation or parody is necessarily ironic to the same degree, but all contain ironic potential.

Of course, complications arise from the fact that irony can be understood in a number of different and contradictory ways. Ostensibly, irony appears simple enough to define. As Claire Colebrook writes, 'irony has a frequent and common definition; saying what is contrary to what is meant' (2004, 1). As she points out, however, irony is also an immensely broad concept, employed across a wide range of comic and intertextual discourses. In everyday speech, irony is generally interpreted as a disingenuous or insincere act – by its most basic definition irony cannot suggest 'a *congruence* between avowal and actual feeling', as does sincerity (Trilling 1972, 2, my italics). As Jacob Golomb argues, the 'ethos of honesty and sincerity is diametrically opposed to irony' (1995, 28). Even when irony is understood and accepted, it is the speaker's *insincerity* about what is literally being said that is appreciated by the listener, not the statement itself. Hutcheon conceptualizes this 'edge' to ironic communication as follows:

> [T]he 'ironic' meaning is inclusive and relational: the said and the unsaid coexist for the interpreter, and each has meaning in relation to the other because they literally 'interact' (Burke 1969a, 512) to create the real 'ironic' meaning. The 'ironic' meaning [...] undermines stated meaning by removing the semantic security of 'one signifier: one signified' and by revealing the complex inclusive, relational and differential nature of ironic meaning-making. (Hutcheon 1994, 12–13)

This is in contrast to a 'sincere' utterance, intended to reinforce semantic security. If a listener interprets the sincere statement other than it was directly said, they have misunderstood. Sincerity relies on the semantic system uncritically, while irony exploits its complexities and inadequacies. The distinction between the two is rarely straightforward, and takes place in the process of interaction between texts, their initiators, and their receivers.

In verbal irony, one says the opposite of what one means in order to critique a particular act or state of affairs. This is often done in a mocking or antagonistic way, but one which might pass over the heads of those who think differently. For instance, one reviewer's assessment that Sam Riley's performance of Mr Darcy in *Pride + Prejudice + Zombies* (2016) 'seems to hint that he'd be more at home at a Marilyn Manson concert than felling the undead at Pemberley' implies that Marilyn Manson fans are 'awkward and maladjusted' (Gilbert 2016, para. 7). Fans of Marilyn Manson may miss the irony, as might fans of Mr Darcy who see the character's awkwardness as appropriate and attractive. Textual irony in art and literature functions similarly, but in a different context. This is partly because in one sense all art is parodic, mediating reality, history, or human experience 'with [ironic] distance'. This is certainly true within the context of post-structuralist criticism. Committing a story to print or visual media is automatically committing to a particular version of that story, making it inherently inaccurate or incomplete. Paradoxically, however, art's ironic, mediated approach to reality is often considered to be more truthful or 'authentic' than the reality it describes. In this reasoning, sometimes saying what one means is incompatible with saying what is true, and to outline the truth one must resort to its ironic counter-image. Where sincerity entails saying or presenting what one means directly, in art irony is often *paradoxically* (or ironically) sincere, in that it describes something in imperfect or knowingly inaccurate ways in order to suggest how it might really be. This ironic 'sincerity' is more commonly framed as authenticity.

Again, 'authenticity' is a contentious label, particularly in art. Lionel Trilling's description of the term in this context is still the most cited, though he too is hesitant to settle on a single definition. When he does, it is seemingly self-contradictory. Authenticity, Trilling argues, suggests:

> [A] more strenuous moral experience than 'sincerity' does, a more exigent conception of the self and what being true to it consists in, a wider reference to the universe and man's place in it, and *a less acceptant and genial view of the social circumstances of life*. At the behest of the criterion of authenticity, much

that was once thought to make up the very fabric of culture has come to seem of little account, mere fantasy or ritual, or downright falsification. Conversely, much that culture traditionally condemned and sought to exclude is accorded a considerable moral authority by reason of the authenticity claimed for it, for example, disorder, violence, unreason. *The concept of authenticity can deny art itself, yet at the same time it figures as the dark source of art.* (Trilling 1972, 11, my emphasis)

Artistic irony's position is thus a contrary one, the 'dark source of art' revealing how the artist thinks life is or should be, at the expense of what it is now *assumed* to be. Authenticity is 'implicitly a polemical concept, fulfilling its nature by dealing aggressively with received and habitual opinion, aesthetic opinion in the first instance, social and political opinion in the next' (Trilling 1972, 94). This is arguably what the texts in the previous chapter are doing when they insert monsters into historical contexts. Our world is not populated with fantastical monsters, but these monsters serve as metaphors that make real-world categories of otherness visible. They 'deal aggressively' with the assumption that monsters are apolitical in the twenty-first-century mediascape. In this, despite their status as ironic or parodic texts on a formal level, they can be seen as 'authentic' works of fiction – works with countercultural significance or value.

For Trilling, the idea that art, through irony, is able to be more honest about reality than reality itself is summarized in Oscar Wilde's well-known maxim: 'Man is least himself when he talks in his own person. Give him a mask and he will tell you the truth' (cited in Trilling 1972, 119). Through the mask of ironic pretence, art is theoretically able to gesture towards an underlying truth. As Trilling notes, the etymology of irony also 'associates it directly with the idea of a mask, for it derives from the Greek word for a dissembler' (1972, 120).

Of course, socially 'authentic', countercultural irony is not the only formal technique art (or parody) employs, or through which it can reveal meaning. As I have already suggested, the idea that art must take up a pose that is 'less acceptant and genial' of social circumstances would arguably exclude remix, which is often more concerned with remediations of other texts than with mediating social circumstances. The idea that all art must be aggressively ironic also fails to consider irony that is not intentional, but situational. As Hutcheon points out, irony can also be created by the reader, disrupting 'the neat theories where the interpreter's task is simply one of decoding or reconstructing some "real" meaning (usually named as the "ironic" one)' (1994, 11). 'Authentic' art criticism also ignores the irony that emerges simply through the act of mediation.

As I discuss in the following chapter, a photograph may capture events as they occur, but the photographer's position is never neutral, and with the passage of time distance also opens up between image and reality.

Trilling problematizes an exclusively 'authentic' view of art by suggesting that it forms the basis for our narrow definition of high or 'serious art, by which we mean such art as stands, overtly or by implication, in an adversary relation to the dominant culture' (1972, 67). In this view, 'serious' art can be *ironically* authentic, but never sincere. Sincerity implies a mainstream and uncritical position of the dominant culture that goes against our modern (and postmodern) understanding of artistic expression and power (1972, 7). As I will discuss shortly, this is precisely the distinction that gave rise to camp art in the 1960s, and ultimately to Frankenfiction.

So far, then, I have established that 'authentic' or oppositional irony (as a kind of artistic parody of consensus reality) is a more familiar concept in adaptation than in remix. In the context of parody, we might consider 'authentic' irony to be synonymous with satire. Satire is a parodic form that always uses ironic distance 'to make a *negative* statement about that which is satirized' (Hutcheon 1985, 44, emphasis mine). For Hutcheon, satire suggests a 'kind of encoded anger, communicated to the decoder through invective' which is intended to discredit or destroy its target (1985, 56). This antagonistic stance also makes satire more overtly political than parody, at least in the context of its initial production. As Hutcheon argues, referencing Edward and Lillian Bloom, there is an 'implied idealism' in satire's destructive humour, as it is often 'unabashedly didactic and seriously committed to a hope in its own power to effect change' (Bloom and Bloom 1979, 16; Hutcheon 1985, 56). This is perhaps a strong argument to make about Frankenfictions, which are often commercial, mainstream products, though, as I will discuss, the texts Frankenfictions parody often fit this description. All parody is ironic, in the sense of acknowledging itself as mediated, and not a direct representation of reality, but satirical irony has the secondary goal of revealing the 'authentic': standing in opposition to mainstream conceptions of reality. Of course, as Hutcheon suggests, there can also be substantial overlap between parody and satire. Both use irony to create distance, though the object of their irony is necessarily distinct. One text can parody another on a formal level, while also satirizing the reality communicated through that text at the narrative level, for instance. *The League of Extraordinary Gentlemen* is parodic in the way it includes captions in the style of *The Boy's Own Paper* (1879–1967) to indicate the end of a serialized issue, and satirical in the sense that it also mocks the racist, sexist, and imperialist attitudes the *Paper* presented.

Camp as sincere parody

Under the blanket of parody, there is also camp, which runs counter to satire. In their study *Making Camp: Rhetorics of Transgression in U.S. Popular Culture*, Helene A. Shugart and Catherine Egley Waggoner suggest that a camp 'aesthetic' can be 'understood at the most basic level as over-the-top, playful, and parodic' (2008, 4). Camp is also a kind of parody, then, but it is one that fits more comfortably within remix studies than it does with adaptation. Rather than re-imagining or revising through oppositional irony, camp recycles and layers, exploring the hermeneutical irony in 'the coexistence of two codes in the same message' (Ben-Porat 1979, 247). For instance, Dan Hillier (whose work I will discuss in the following chapter) uses Victorian illustrations in his art that, when recombined on his computer, can 'say' something quite different than they did in their original context. This is not a critical or antagonistic move, but it still serves to underline the ways even seemingly authentic, straightforward, or realist art represents reality in a specific way.

While there have been numerous studies of the camp aesthetic over the past fifty years, most refer back to Susan Sontag's 1964 definition. Sontag's collection of notes describes camp as 'a sensibility that, among other things, converts the serious into the frivolous' by reproducing it too accurately (1999, 53–4). Camp, Shugart and Waggoner expand, occupies:

> [A]n ambiguous and arguably liminal space in the contemporary mediascape: that is, camp itself constitutes an appropriation of contemporary media aesthetics, practices, and tactics, even as they might have been and continue to be appropriated in contemporary media fare. Indeed, camp sensibilities are highly compatible with – complementary to – these sensibilities, turning as they both do, in large measure, on parody, irony, an emphasis on aesthetics, and incoherence. (Shugart and Waggoner 2008, 10–11)

In their definition, camp is parody in the sense that it repeats with distance, but its irony or play distances through overperformance rather than opposition. Crucially, camp emerged in a mediascape in which 'parody, irony, an emphasis on aesthetics, and incoherence' had become the dominant media practice. As Kristin Horn puts it, camp 'therefore both *results* from a more complex relation to popular culture, which stresses its incongruities and undermines its so-called truths and norms, and it *creates* a more complex relation to popular culture that combines critical awareness and affect' (2017, 254, original italics). In this it is distinct from kitsch, which must be enjoyed ironically, with the full knowledge that the object of enjoyment is awful in comparison to 'real' art. Camp involves a voluntary shift in sensibilities, demonstrating the value in the marginal, unpopular, clichéd, or outmoded, and creating 'spaces of alternative identification and pleasure' that are neither fully absorbed into popular culture or in direct opposition to it (2017, 254).

Camp is also traditionally a queer mode of discourse, and for Horn camp explicitly 'offers an answer to the question of how queer subjects can participate in the mainstream media landscape without having to lose or deny their identity' (2017, 4). Moe Meyer (in my opinion justly) accuses Sontag of erasing homosexuality from camp to make it more marketable to mainstream audiences, 'its homosexual connotations downplayed, sanitised, and made safe for public consumption' (1994, 7). This is certainly not my intention in this chapter. Instead, in addition to camp's explicitly sexual queer connotations, I want to draw attention to the way the term queer 'does not invest just gender, but semiotic structures at large, the signs of domination moving in concert with sexual and non-sexual hierarchies, and the constitution of self-alleged naturality and univocity of the sign' (Cleto 1999, 19). Queerness is a value, originating in notions of sexual identity, that becomes a vital part of subcultural resistance as Western mainstream capitalist culture continues to expand its borders. For Fabio Cleto, camp 'works on the *crisis* of codes and signs, and through these, of the cultural hierarchies that are inscribed in all "naturality of signs"' (1999, 19). Camp denaturalizes the 'natural', potentially transforming the dominant discourse from within. As Horn suggests, camp represents 'the acknowledgment that popular culture cannot be radical in the sense of being anti-capitalist', but does not 'exclude the notion that it is still capable of transporting other forms of resistance within the limitations of a capitalistic framework and market logic' (2017, 6).

Where satire demolishes, camp rehabilitates (Sedgwick 2003, 149–50; Horn 2017, 254). In the context of Frankenfiction, camp rejects (post)modernism's emphasis on an authenticating irony, instead presenting itself as ironically authentic – in the sense of being surprisingly incongruous, rather than intentionally antagonistic. An example of this tactic can be seen in *Penny Dreadful's* use of Romantic poetry. Although melodramatic meditations on nature, beauty, and the uniqueness of the human spirit might seem extremely out of place in a sexually and violently explicit adult drama, *Penny Dreadful* regularly utilizes poems by Wordsworth, Keats, Blake, and others, sometimes read out in their entirety on screen by characters in moments of emotional anguish. These moments are campy, in that they are unexpectedly sincere and unfashionably political. The show's reimagining of the popular penny dreadful as a high-concept television drama also straddles the line between camp and more serious, psychological horror (see Poore 2016, 66).

Camp is thus 'the inversion of taste in favor of the neglected, the other, the marginalized' (Horn 2017, 4). This sometimes – but not always – provokes a re-evaluation of the appropriated object or aesthetic. This is a re-evaluation that necessarily takes place paratextually, outside of the narrative: camp is ironic, but on a contextual or situational level (at which it is absurd) rather than a formal or narrative one (at which it embraces cultural norms). It is also rarely antagonistic or satirical. As Sontag argues, when a parody 'reveals (even sporadically) a contempt for one's themes and one's materials [...] the results are forced and heavy-handed, rarely Camp' (1999, 58). Instead, camp involves 'relating in a new way (namely in a distancing manner) to what is usually considered a serious matter (notions of personal authenticity and originality, the heteronormativity of relationships and gender identity, etc.) and conversely arriving at a more complex idea of what it is worth being serious about' (Horn 2017, 253–4).

Frankenfiction contains examples of both satire and camp. The texts I discussed in the second chapter – *Anno Dracula*, *The League of Extraordinary Gentlemen*, *Penny Dreadful*, and *The Extraordinary Adventures of the Athena Club* – operate most 'authentically' or oppositionally, within the realm of satire. Although they appropriate literary characters and historical figures, they do so to satirically comment on 'mores, attitudes, types, social structures, [and] prejudices' (Ben-Porat 1979, 247–8), rather than to parodically encourage their audience to relate to specific texts or (staged) historical moments. The visual artists I introduce in the following chapter are more readily identified as camp. Their juxtapositions of historical images with the aesthetics of popular art reject 'both the harmonies of traditional seriousness, and the risks of fully identifying with extreme states of feeling' (Sontag 1999, 62). They demonstrate how an object can mean something quite serious or straightforward at one point in time, and quite the opposite in another.

In one form of Frankenfiction, the literary novel-as-mashup, the text oscillates between camp and satire, parodying multiple things simultaneously. Carolyn Kellogg sees the novel-as-mashup as distinct from other postmodern literary experiments, which already recycle characters, settings, or plot points from existing works (2009, para. 3). Instead, the novel-as-mashup appropriates an author's actual words and sentences in their entirety, making minor changes throughout the text to create a new, though fundamentally similar, story. This serves as a tongue-in-cheek satire of postmodern fiction's ironic, avant-garde intertextuality, but also as a camp parody, successfully performing a classic work of literature, with few changes, as a horror novel. The most famous of these texts, Seth Grahame-Smith's *Pride and Prejudice and Zombies* (2009), is one I repeatedly return to over the course of this book, and it will form the central example in this chapter. This text takes the story of Jane Austen's 1813 novel *Pride and Prejudice* and reframes it as a zombie apocalypse rather than a comedy of manners.

The irony of *Pride and Prejudice and Zombies*

Pride and Prejudice and Zombies became a publishing success (and a Frankensteinian horror) before anyone had even read a word of the text. A single blogger came across the image for the cover – a mashup in itself, featuring a painting by William Beechey that had been digitally altered by Doogie Horner (see Figure 3.1) – and that image, combined with the book's title, sparked an internet phenomenon. Large parts of the parody enacted by the novel-as-mashup are thus paratextual, inviting readers to develop expectations from a visual preview in the absence of the full text. In similar fashion, when Quirk Books was initially marketing the follow-up *Sense and Sensibility and Sea Monsters*, no part of the remixed novel or its themes was revealed. Instead, the publisher held a contest encouraging people to guess the title of their next mashup. The only details provided were that it would involve another literary classic, and that monsters would once again play a key role in the new plot (Binder 2009, 53). Much of the irony of the novel-as-mashup is situational as well as textual, meaning that whether it is recognized depends greatly on an individual reader's relationship to the appropriated text. Although the novel-as-mashup can usually stand on its own as a narrative, without an understanding of the original text and its history of popular reception, it is difficult to understand the success of mashups like *Pride and Prejudice and Zombies*.

Originally scheduled for July release, the publication date for *Pride and Prejudice and Zombies* was pushed forward by three months to April in order to capitalize on the publicity. Two months before the book was even released, it had been mentioned on more than a thousand different websites (Deahl 2009, para. 7). As of 2013 it had sold over 1.5 million copies in the United States alone, and had been translated into over two dozen languages.[1] Although *Sense and Sensibility and Sea Monsters* (2009) failed to match the sales of *Pride and Prejudice and Zombies*, it too was a popular and financial success.[2] After

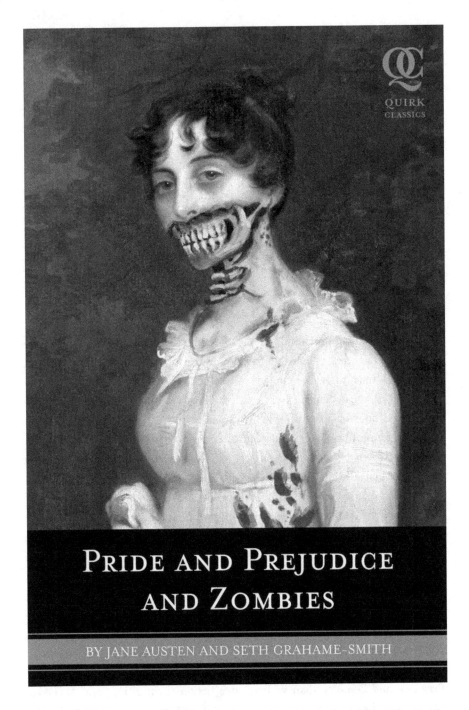

Figure 3.1 Cover of *Pride and Prejudice and Zombies* (2009), © and ™ 2009 by Quirk Productions, Inc. Image courtesy the Bridgman Art Library. Zombification by Doogie Horner. Reprinted with permission from Quirk Books.

the unexpected commercial success of *Pride and Prejudice and Zombies*, a number of other publishers released similar titles. When Lev Grossman of *Time* magazine asked jokingly, 'Has there ever been a work of literature that couldn't be improved by adding zombies?' (2009b, 1), he could not have anticipated how thoroughly his question would be put to the test over the course of the next few years. Following *Pride and Prejudice and Zombies* and *Sense and Sensibility and Sea Monsters* in close succession was Quirk Books's third title in the 'Quirk Classics' series, *Android Karenina* (2010), as well as *Jane Slayre* (2010), *Little Vampire Women* (2010), *Wuthering Bites* (2010), *Alice in Zombieland* (2011), and *Grave Expectations* (2011) from rival publishing houses, to name but a few of the most successful commercial titles. Since 2009, these titles have formed a mini canon within the novel-as-mashup genre.

Although other people have used the novel-as-mashup technique in the past, particularly in the late twentieth century, *Pride and Prejudice and Zombies* was the first written text to employ this technique so commercially and extensively, combining 85 per cent of *Pride and Prejudice* with 15 per cent 'ultraviolent zombie mayhem' (Grahame-Smith and Austen 2009, 3, inside cover). Though successive examples of the novel-as-mashup have tended to supplement their appropriated texts with a much higher percentage of new content, they are still often accused of being Frankensteinian at best, and plagiarist at worst. Some reviewers see the texts as poor or lazy satire, while others read them as successful camp. In terms of genre, the novel-as-mashup often appropriates either realist classics like Jane Austen's *Pride and Prejudice*, or Gothic novels, sometimes resulting in the 'original' and the mashup being shelved together in bookshops (Weston 2009, para. 6; Brownstein 2011, 196). These novel-as-mashup texts are not straightforward Gothic parodies, however, nor are they clear examples of realist historical fiction, a genre they frequently parody. It is also worth noting that the novel-as-mashup is one of the few kinds of Frankenfiction where a reference to the *Frankenstein* mythology is notably absent. From a formal perspective, these texts are very Frankensteinian indeed: literally composed of the pieces of other texts, which they imbue with new and arguably monstrous afterlives. Many reviewers have also noted this connection. Ryan Britt, from fantasy publisher Tor, suggested that 'for the contemporary, uninitiated reader, *Frankenstein* would appear to have more in common with a pop literary mash-up, like *Pride and Prejudice and Zombies*' than with science fiction (Britt 2011, para. 2). David Mattin describes mash-up literature as 'combining two existing works to create a third, *Frankenstein*'s-monster-like new work', and *NME*'s Jordan Basset described the novel-as-mashup genre as 'Frankenstein's monsters of the literary world'

(Mattin 2012, para. 3; Bassett 2015, para. 2). The link to *Frankenstein* is present, but it takes place at a formal level, rather than a narrative one.

As one critic writes of the novel-as-mashup genre, '[i]t's hard to say, in the end, if this is an homage, an exploitation, a deconstruction, or just a 300-page parlor trick' (Anders 2009, para. 5). The novel-as-mashup confuses critics not necessarily because it is difficult to identify it as camp or satire, but because it is parodying multiple related subjects at once, from different ironic perspectives. In addition to parodying the literary classic onto which it is grafted, the novel-as-mashup also parodies the function of the classics, and of historical fiction, at a para- and metatextual level. It also confronts us with the way adaptation studies and historical fiction address questions of historical faithfulness and ethical appropriation, without always considering how literary irony may be misread and misused. As I have established, in the context of most contemporary art, irony is the primary means of revealing that which was hidden or implicit in normative constructions of reality. This irony is certainly not unique to either the twentieth or the twenty-first century. In *Irony's Edge*, Hutcheon points out that 'ours joins just about every other century in wanting to call itself the "age of irony," and the recurrence of that historical claim in itself might well support the contention of contemporary theorists from Jacques Derrida to Kenneth Burke that irony is inherent in signification, in its deferrals and in its negations' (1994, 9). Nearly every age of Western culture has been fascinated with irony – though postmodernism may be the first to so directly acknowledge its own historical contingency.

In the more specific context of postmodern historical fiction, Hutcheon talks about camp irony not only as a literary technique, but as a political tool or force. This places her in contrast with Fredric Jameson, for whom camp (like pastiche) has long lost its political and cultural relevance (Hutcheon 1994, 41, 177). Ironically, to defend their points both Jameson and Hutcheon turn to historical fiction: texts that parody the past. Jameson primarily points to what he terms the 'nostalgia film' (Jameson 1988, 196), and Hutcheon to 'historiographic metafiction', defined as 'those well-known and popular novels which are both intensely self-reflexive and yet paradoxically also lay claim to historical events and personages' (Hutcheon 1988, 5). In their discussions one can already see two conflicting readings of non-oppositional parody emerging. Jameson sees such nostalgic fiction as vacuous and normative, while Hutcheon sees it as self-reflexive and potentially subversive. The reason Hutcheon and Jameson can disagree so fundamentally on this issue is that they each have a very different definition of parody.

Jameson takes a negative approach to camp or sincere historical fiction, as evidenced by his equation of the style with pastiche, or 'blank parody, a statue with blind eyeballs' (1991, 17). For Jameson pastiche is truly empty, devoid of both satirical laughter and the political impulse, essentially representing the antithesis of creativity. He shapes his definition by comparing pastiche to parody:

> Pastiche is, like parody, the imitation of a particular or unique style, the wearing of a stylistic mask, speech in a dead language; but it is a neutral practice of such mimicry, without parody's ulterior motive, without the satirical impulse, without laughter, without that still latent feeling that there exists something normal compared to which what is being imitated is rather comic. (Jameson 1988, 195)

Jameson thus links parody to satire and to laughter, implying that the irony and pleasure in parody is always negative or antagonistic. Pastiche is then framed as 'empty', or bereft of irony, by comparison.

Hutcheon, in contrast, questions the degree to which it is possible to satirize something that is already recognized as inauthentic or ironic. There certainly is an extent to which postmodern fictions have popularized a specific kind of historically minded parody more generally. Both Hutcheon and Colebrook cite postmodern historian Hayden White in their arguments about the serious side of historiographical irony. White asserts that 'every representation of the past has specifiable ideological implications' (1978, 69). Paraphrasing White, Colebrook explicitly highlights the ironic dimension of modern historiography: 'for the historian must *read* the past as if there were some meaning of the past not apparent to the past itself. The past always means more than it explicitly "says"': historical traces and narratives, like fictions, automatically contain an element of irony or distance (2004, 3). As Hutcheon argued in 1988:

> [P]ostmodern fiction has certainly sought to open itself up to history, to what Edward Said (1983) calls the 'world.' But it seems to have found that it can no longer do so in any remotely innocent way, and so those un-innocent paradoxical historiographic metafictions situate themselves within historical discourse, while refusing to surrender their autonomy as fiction. And it is a kind of seriously ironic parody that often enables this contradictory doubleness: the intertexts of history and fiction take on parallel status in the parodic reworking of the textual past of both the 'world' and literature. (Hutcheon 1988, 124)

In other words, satirical representations of ironic states can still be 'seriously ironic' or authentic. Postmodern fiction (and specifically historiographic metafiction) attempts to render the reality of past moments, while always acknowledging the inherent fictionality of this rendering. This again creates a paradoxical irony in which playing with history becomes a serious (i.e. artistically 'authentic') endeavour (Golomb 1995, 20). Frankenfiction is engaged in a comparably ironic relationship with history and the past, though it often uses camp rather than satire to do so.

In much of postmodernism, specifically those texts highlighted by literary scholars, ironic parody tends to be quite politically serious. This is true even though, as Ann Heilmann and Mark Llewellyn argue, 'when fiction looks backward, it does so in a necessarily different and more playful manner than the factual' (2010, 13–14). Consider Sarah Waters's retroactive attempts to mainstream lesbianism by re-imagining the Victorian world in which lesbians were originally 'vilified or eclipsed by the historical record' (Carroll 2010, 195). In so doing, she reveals that historically, lesbians were actually everywhere. Although this restoration is an ironic, fictional one, in that it asks its audience to read something into history that is not explicitly present, as Samantha Carroll points out it is also a very serious act of 'recognitive justice', serving to 'destabilise deep-structure inequalities' (2010, 195). While the object of irony is sometimes made ridiculous in satire, the motivation for the satire is serious, gesturing towards a more 'authentic' reality.

Gothic fiction, likewise, has a clearly delimited and clearly *political* tradition of parodic appropriation. Avril Horner and Sue Zlosnik suggest that Gothic parody can be traced to the very beginning of the genre, and that 'the comic turn in the Gothic is not an aberration or a corruption of a "serious" genre but rather a key aspect of the Gothic's essential hybridity' (2005, 12). That the Gothic does not always take itself seriously is an important factor in its transgressive and political capabilities. Within the context of historical fictions, Gothic parody 'frequently allows a fresh perspective on a changing world, one of accommodation rather than terrified apprehension' (2005, 12). Its sensationalist contexts and narratives offer a non-threatening, self-parodying vocabulary through which to assimilate the frightening and the unknown. This also allows a measure of ironic 'detachment from scenes of pain and suffering that would be disturbing in a different Gothic context', opening new possibilities for engagement (2005, 13). Because of how thoroughly embedded self-parody is within the Gothic, repetitions and clichés that might become tired or signal conservatism in other genres can instead act to revitalize the Gothic's transgressive impulse. For instance, as Kamilla Elliott argues:

> Gothic film parodies go beyond simple mockery to reveal inconsistencies, incongruities, and problems in Gothic criticism: boundaries that it has been unwilling or unable to blur, binary oppositions it has refused to deconstruct,

and points at which a radical, innovative, subversive discourse manifests as its own hegemonic, dogmatic, and clichéd double. (Elliott 2008, 24)

Here familiarity and repetition have a surprisingly critical function, indicating when a particular theme, form, or interpretation has begun to lose its power, or take itself too seriously. Elliott cites the Abbott and Costello mashups of 1948 and 1953, which signal the point at which Universal's monster movies themselves reach peak camp. She also discusses how camp films like *Young Frankenstein* (1974) or *Bram Stoker's Dracula* (1997) parody other key adaptations in the history of *Frankenstein* or *Dracula*, identifying the moments at which certain tropes and representations become fixed. They parody not to comment on sociopolitical reality, but to reveal the structure of the status quo itself. Of course, because of the way they epitomize the objects they parody, these camp Gothic texts often become classics in their own right. The objects of camp are also useful to scholarship because they point to what has become cliché. This process applies to Gothic monsters as well. As Catherine Spooner argues, 'the very familiarity of the twenty-first-century monster opens them up to new comic possibilities' (2017, 122).

As a form of *commentary* on such generic conventions, rather than as a classical adaptation or work of historical fiction, the novel-as-mashup has the potential to be read as a 'serious' or authentic object of criticism – but to what end? Does the novel-as-mashup represent the logical extreme to postmodernism's ironic appropriation of history, as author and critic Charlie Jane Anders (un-ironically) suggested when she wrote: 'Literary Mashups Meet Tentacles. Has All Of Western Literature Been Leading Up To This'? (2009). Or is the novel-as-mashup a camp nod to the realist literary classics of the nineteenth century, riding on the coat-tails of their success, and continually preserving them in cultural memory by bringing them in line with popular culture's current fashions? Camilla Nelson suggests that, at least in the case of the *Pride and Prejudice and Zombies* franchise, the novel-as-mashup has tried to fill each of these parodic positions at different moments in time (2013, 339–40). As I will argue, this is also the case for the novel-as-mashup genre more broadly.

Literature with a twist: parodying the classics

The first and most obvious parody the novel-as-mashup enacts is of classic, canonical literature. Its entire identity is based on the appropriation of certain well-known novels, which many people in the Western world will read during the course of their secondary education, and many others will encounter through a popular film or television adaptation. At the very beginning of the novel-as-mashup trend, *Pride and Prejudice and Zombies* positioned itself as a satirical parody, or 'as a form of populist rebellion against the oppressive cultural authority of Jane Austen's work, particularly as this cultural authority is evinced in the classroom and the lecture hall' (Nelson 2013, 339). In an initial interview with the *Sunday Times*, likewise, Grahame-Smith suggested that he had 'faced the wrath of Austen fans on blogs' for his irreverence towards the classic (Goodwin 2009, 10). Here *Pride and Prejudice and Zombies* unabashedly satirizes contemporary culture's nostalgia for the world and work of Jane Austen, belittling *Pride and Prejudice*'s legacy with the promise to transform 'a masterpiece of world literature into something you'd actually want to read' (Grahame-Smith and Austen 2009, back cover).

Faced with a largely positive reception, however, both the novel's marketing and the text and paratext of subsequent novels-as-mashup quickly shifted their tone. As Nelson notes in a later interview, Quirk Books's head of publishing Jason Rekulak argued:

> Despite the obvious satirical content of the novel, 'Seth is not making fun of *Pride and Prejudice*.' 'He understands that generations of readers love this book.' 'He knew it would be crazy to make fun of it.' He also reaffirmed the cultural status of the Austen brand. 'It's such a landmark and important novel'. (Nelson 2013, 342)

Around the same time, Grahame-Smith also firmly denied that *Pride and Prejudice and Zombies* was a satire, stating 'it wasn't my intention to make fun of the original. *Pride and Prejudice* is a brilliantly written book by a brilliant author, and all I wanted to do was give its themes and characters an absurd canvas to play out upon' (Harvison 2009, para. 12). Grahame-Smith takes the novel's commercial success as a sign that readers understand its 'absurd' humour, and 'see it for what it is – a silly, entertaining way to revisit a timeless classic' (2009, para. 16). This positions the novel-as-mashup as camp, not satire, and subsequent mashup novels followed suit. The back cover of *Jane Slayre* claims, for instance, that it will 'transform Charlotte Brontë's unforgettable masterpiece into an eerie paranormal adventure that will delight and terrify' – elements that are of course already present in *Jane Eyre* (Erwin and Brontë 2010). This again implies that the novel-as-mashup's primary aim is tongue-in-cheek replication, not satirical critique.

Of course, many of the texts appropriated by the novel-as-mashup genre were satirical in their own right, and this humour was often directly aimed at the cultural rites, rituals, and institutions of the age. As Hutcheon notes, '[a]long with Mary Shelley, Emily and Charlotte Brontë, and other women writers, Austen used parody as the disarming but effective literary vehicle for social satire' (1985, 44). Part of the popularity of the novel-as-mashup involves the way it maintains and re-emphasizes what readers already loved about the original text. As one reviewer comments of *Pride and Prejudice and Zombies*, reading it 'means discovering that half of the things you're laughing about were written 200 years ago by Austen herself' (Hesse 2009, para. 23). Some sections and themes are decidedly new, however, and firmly mark the novel-as-mashup as a parodic 'repetition with distance' (Hutcheon 1985, 32). It reproduces classic literature, but in an intentionally crass and campy manner that separates it from a more traditionally 'authentic' (and satirical) parody.

For instance, if we read the novel-as-mashup as a camp parody, its cavalier approach to sex and violence fits Sontag's definition perfectly. Sontag compares the twentieth-century consumer of camp to the nineteenth-century dandy, writing: 'The new-style dandy, the lover of Camp, appreciates vulgarity. Where the dandy would be continually offended or bored, the connoisseur of Camp is continually amused, delighted' (1999, 63). In other words, Sontag argues that where many fashionable, subcultural tastes were once characterized by aesthetically high-minded excess, twentieth-century connoisseurs pursue this same kind of excess through a popular or vulgar aesthetic. Vulgarity, in this case through gratuitous additions of sex or violence to a canonical classic, is a trademark feature of the camp aesthetic. In the case of the novel-as-mashup, these additions do not serve as satirical comments on the original text, but simply as markers of camp excess.

In terms of sexual vulgarity, Quirk Classics titles like *Pride and Prejudice and Zombies* resort to relatively mild innuendo and insinuation. Of Mr Darcy, rather than noting that there is 'something of dignity in his countenance that would not give one an unfavourable idea of his heart' (Austen [1813] 2008, 162), Elizabeth Bennet notes 'something of dignity in the way his trousers cling to those most English parts of him' (Grahame-Smith and Austen 2009, 206).[3] This alteration makes no didactic or critical point about *Pride and Prejudice*; it is simply spectacle. One can also find a myriad of jokes that deliberately misread the nineteenth-century wording of the Austen original, rendered potentially awkward by two hundred years of linguistic evolution. For example, when Elizabeth 'should like balls infinitely better [...] if they were carried on in a different manner' (Austen [1813] 2008, 37), Darcy replies in *Pride and Prejudice and Zombies* with an innuendo: 'You should like balls infinitely better [...] if you knew the first thing about them' (Grahame-Smith and Austen 2009, 45). This elicits a blush from Elizabeth. Such references could also be said to satirize stereotypical Victorian prudery, though of course Austen was not a Victorian author. As I discuss in the next section, the term 'Victorian' has become increasingly synonymous with 'the long nineteenth century'. Characters also remain relatively chaste in *Pride and Prejudice and Zombies*. A text with a more directly satirical stance towards Victorian prudery might have opted for more explicitly sexual content.

The novel-as-mashup's use of violence is often vulgar and campy as well. Blood splatters, limbs fly, and physical violence breaks out at highly inappropriate moments. For the most part, this gore and violence has not been added to produce a genuine sense of horror or revulsion, though the genre does make liberal use of the sensational 'gross-out' moment common in horror film and television (L. Williams 1991, 2; Wu 2003, 87). Although such moments of blatantly gratuitous gore are intended to shock, they do so in a context of fantasy and camp excess that still allows the text to maintain humorous undertones for its target audiences. For instance, when *Pride and Prejudice and Zombies* describes Mrs Long's death in its first horror scene, the mental image of zombies biting 'into her head, cracking her skull like a walnut, and sending a shower of dark blood spouting as high as the chandeliers' is vivid and gruesome (Grahame-Smith and Austen 2009, 14). Because it is juxtaposed with the incongruous location and language of a Regency ball, however, it is read comically.

As mentioned above, initial interest in the novel-as-mashup was precipitated by Doogie Horner's gory re-imagining of William Beechey's portrait of Marcia Fox, on the cover of *Pride and Prejudice and Zombies*. Original illustrations interspersed throughout the pages of the mashups in the Quirk Classics series also play with the juxtaposition of Regency Britain and twenty-first-century horror, though they do not engage directly with any classic artwork the way the cover does. Few of the mashups released by publishers other than Quirk Books contain illustrations inside the text, but most rely on digital manipulation to create a violent or gory (but not horrific) version of an original artwork for the cover. Photoshopped illustrations from Carroll's *Alice's Adventures in Wonderland* are scattered throughout *Alice in Zombieland*, depicting a zombified Mad Hatter, a Black Rat in a waistcoat with pocket watch, or a blood-stained Alice with a disembodied leg in her arms instead of a croquet mallet (see Figure 3.2).

Figure 3.2 Interior illustration from *Alice in Zombieland* (2011), by Sir John Tenniel and Brent Cardillo. Illustration © 2011. Reprinted from the book *Alice in Zombieland* with permission of its publisher, Sourcebooks.

In most cases, the violence in the novel-as-mashup is simply meant to be humorous, seen most clearly when the heroic monster slayer is juxtaposed with the animalized zombie or vampire. For example, a passage near the end of *Pride and Prejudice and Zombies* sees Elizabeth and Darcy stumbling across a group of zombies who have mistaken a patch of cauliflower for pale brains, and are devouring them accordingly. The two consider leaving the zombies to their devices, but then realize that this provides them with their first opportunity to fight side by side, and they happily proceed to put the creatures out of their misery (Grahame-Smith and Austen 2009, 302). This passage is violent but not gruesome, and its description (and depiction, in the accompanying illustration) of the zombie 'unmentionables [...] crawling on their hands and knees, biting into ripe heads of cauliflower' (2009, 302) is deliberately incongruous with Austen's 'high literature' register – particularly as this passage follows Darcy's proposal of marriage, which is left nearly unaltered. In some cases, the cartoon violence of the novel-as-mashup actually lessens the horror of the classic text. Returning to *Alice in Zombieland*, when the Cheshire Cat remarks 'we're all dead here. I'm dead. You're dead' (Cook and Carroll 2011, 83), the March Hare is instead the Dead Hare, and the card soldiers become the 'dead soldiers' in *Alice in Zombieland*, some of the absurdity and darkness of Carroll's original is in fact lost in the conversion, overwritten again and again by the same joke about zombies. The threat of losing one's head in Carroll's text is also lessened, given the fact that most of the characters are already dead, and are already losing body parts at an alarming degree.

In the rare cases where the mashup violence is not overtly campy or cartoonish, it adds drama to scenes that were already dramatic or violent in the original text. When Jane beheads Helen Burns or stakes Mrs Reed in *Jane Slayre*, for instance, her actions are violent, but the tone of the passages themselves are not extremely incongruous with the tone of the 'unaltered' *Jane Eyre*. Both Helen and Mrs Reed die in Brontë's novel (though of course here it is not at Jane's hand), and in both passages the finality and brutality of death are starkly apparent. In the mashup, however, Jane's role is more active. Both events serve as additional steps in Jane's process of self-realization. Jane moves from a passive to an active participant in these deaths: actively able to spare the 'mortal soul' of these women, rather than passively watching them die and be lost (Erwin and Brontë 2010, 505). Within the mashup novel Jane's final, violent actions towards these women are framed melodramatically, but not satirically. Likewise, while the novel-as-mashup's addition of fantastical monsters to classic narratives might be read as satirical, it has the ironic effect of strengthening character motivations, underlining dramatic events and existing character flaws, and thereby bringing the text's 'hidden' meaning or readings to the surface. In *Sense and Sensibility and Sea*

Monsters, for instance, Marianne is initially repulsed by Colonel Brandon not only because of his age and reserved temperament, but also because he is half squid (B.H. Winters and Austen 2009, 37). This alteration emphasizes the reading that these two characters are from metaphorically different worlds, and belong to a different 'species' of people.

Some changes to classic texts made by the novel-as-mashup seem more satirical than others, but with no obvious goal other than to 'fix' or modernize aspects of the original novel's plot and motivations. Instead of spraining her ankle in a rainstorm, Marianne tumbles into a brook in *Sense and Sensibility and Sea Monsters*, where she is attacked by a giant octopus, and is subsequently rescued by a wet-suited and spear-wielding Willoughby (B.H. Winters and Austen 2009, 48). This raises the dramatic stakes of her storyline for modern readers, who may have failed to appreciate the domestic drama and gender representations in the unaltered story. Likewise, *Wuthering Bites*' Catherine Earnshaw is not weakened by a fit of feminine hysteria like her counterpart in Emily Brontë's *Wuthering Heights*, but by a vicious vampire attack (S. Gray and Brontë 2010, 204). This event serves to deepen Heathcliff's guilt not because Catherine must be protected, but because in addition to being a vampire-slaying gypsy he is also a vampire himself. In *Pride and Prejudice and Zombies* it is more than financial need and resignation that causes Charlotte Lucas to marry Mr Collins: Charlotte has been bitten by a zombie, and wants to experience as much as she can of married life, knowing that when the time comes her husband will do her the courtesy of 'a proper Christian beheading and burial' (Grahame-Smith and Austen 2009, 99). This change rationalizes Charlotte's eagerness to marry Mr Collins for the modern reader's benefit, while also re-emphasizing the more mundane tragedy of loveless marriage for the sake of survival presented in the original novel. Zombies also provide an explicit reason for why the militia regiment is stationed at Meryton, something never touched upon in Austen's *Pride and Prejudice*, where the Napoleonic Wars serve only as subtext. In keeping with the camp aesthetic, the novel-as-mashup uses over-the-top performance to render metaphorical readings literal and the literal readings metaphorical. The novel-as-mashup translates the dramatic stakes and motivations for a twenty-first-century pop-cultural context hyperbolically, rather than satirically. It accepts the classic novel's conventions, but also makes them more visible *as* conventions. The very act of having thought so seriously about how to make canonical literature resonate with fantastical monsters also makes the novel-as-mashup a trademark example of camp; it is 'too much' to be truly serious (Sontag 1999, 59).

In addition to parodying the work of classic literature itself, the novel-as-mashup parodies traditional presentations of the literary canon – especially, as Nelson also notes, in scholarly or educational contexts (2013, 339). The cover of *Pride and Prejudice and Zombies*, featuring a portrait image overlaid by a black-and-white title bar, is itself a visual reference to the Penguin Classics series, common to many classrooms, as is the term 'Quirk Classics' (used by Quirk Books to market its novel-as-mashup titles). Many novel-as-mashup texts go even further, fabricating their own 'scholarly' paratexts. Some of these parodies are satirical of their appropriated conventions. Vera Nazarian's *Mansfield Park and Mummies* features a series of satirical appendices: the first opens onto an anatomical cross-section of the human digestive tract, with an arrow pointing to the appendix. In the second 'Appendix', the process is repeated, showing the relevant organ 'After Mummification' in a cross-section of an Egyptian sarcophagus (Nazarian and Austen 2009, 557–63; see Figure 3.3). The book also claims to possess a series of 'Scholarly Footnotes' (2009, front cover), which are in fact little more than comical asides, or scandalized disclaimers from the author regarding the meaning of certain words in Austen's *Mansfield Park*. See the word 'mount', to which Nazarian includes references clarifying that this is 'not in the Biblical sense', or exclaiming: 'Upon my word, not *that* way!' (Nazarian and Austen 2009, 52, 281, original italics). These devices are clearly satirical, mockingly parodying the scholarly editions of classic literature that densely pad the text with complex essays and annotations, transforming it into an object of study or prestige rather than pleasure.

In *Little Vampire Women*, by way of contrast, footnotes are used with camp sincerity. For instance, a footnote on the term 'allium mask' suggests that it was 'Invented by Willis Whipetten (1750–1954) for his son, John, who suffered from dysgeusia garlisima, a chemosensory disorder that makes everything smell like garlic' (Messina and Alcott 2010, 4). While the contents of the footnote are clearly ridiculous, they accurately follow the form and register of a scholarly footnote, and within the context of the narrative they function as such. Likewise, many novel-as-mashup texts include reading group suggestions and discussion guides that contain a strange mixture of satirical irony and camp sincerity. The *Jane Slayre* 'Reading Group Discussion Questions', for instance, contain the following prompt:

> 10. In this novel, killing is a kindness more often than it's a sin. What makes it so in Jane's mind? Do you think she's right in her assessment that she should have killed Bertha Mason and released her from her cursed life? Imagine if Bertha was merely been [sic] mad and not a werewolf – would your opinion be

different? Do you think Rochester would really have minded if Jane *had* killed his wife, or doth he protest too much? (Erwin and Brontë 2010, 395)

Not only is it difficult to find the satire in this discussion topic, but the questions it raises seem genuine, with real-world applications. Asking readers to consider how they would have felt if Bertha 'was merely [...] mad', as of course is the case

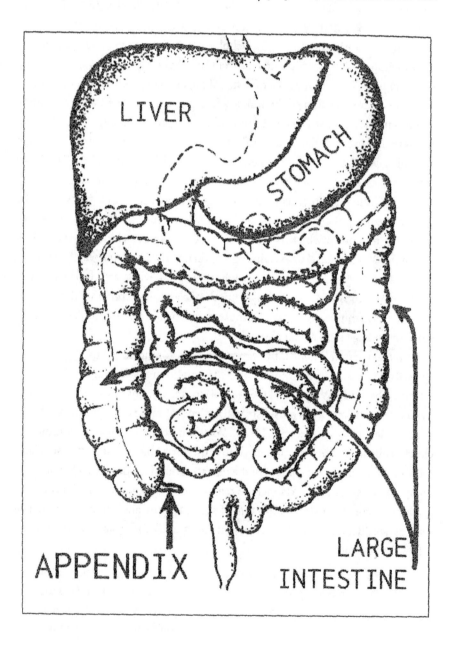

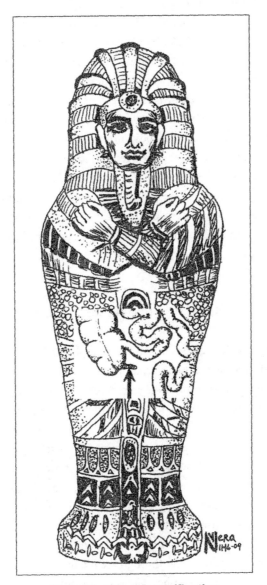

Figure 2: After Mummification

Figure 3.3 'Appendix A' and 'Appendix B' from *Mansfield Park and Mummies* (2009). 'Appendix', courtesy of Pearson Scott Foresman. 'After Mummification', © 2009 by Vera Nazarian. Scans by the author.

in *Jane Eyre*, also draws their attention to earlier feminist readings of Brontë's narrative. Again, this guide implies that the novel-as-mashup text is something to be carefully studied and analysed, despite its status as parody.

Pride and Prejudice and Zombies takes a more satirical approach in its discussion guide. Question eight reads: 'Vomit plays an important role in *Pride and Prejudice and Zombies*. [...] Do the authors mean for this regurgitation to symbolize something greater, or is it a cheap device to get laughs?' (Grahame-Smith and Austen 2009, 319). Although playfully and dismissively framed, this poses a legitimate and self-critical question about the nature of literary irony and interpretation – one that I myself have been seriously and sincerely attempting to answer in this chapter. The *Pride and Prejudice and Zombies* study guide draws attention to our tendency to focus only on the politically or ethically 'authentic' (i.e. culturally oppositional) irony in historical texts and contexts. Through such references, the novel-as-mashup also reveals yet another object of parody: the contemporary historical fiction market.

Parodying neo-Victorianism

In addition to parodying classic novels on multiple levels, the novel-as-mashup is also engaged in a metatextual parody of historical fiction's satirical contexts and conventions. For example, one subset of historical fiction, called 'neo-Victorian' fiction, explicitly returns to the nineteenth-century past in order to revise its construction of social categories like gender, class, sexuality, and race. Neo-Victorian fiction is a type of historiographic metafiction, or postmodern historical fiction that is historically rigorous, self-aware, and self-mocking. Taking *The French Lieutenant's Women* (1969), one of neo-Victorianism's canonical texts, Hutcheon herself explores how 'John Fowles juxtaposes the conventions of the Victorian and the modern novel. The theological and cultural assumptions of both ages – as manifest through their literary forms – are ironically compared by the reader through the medium of formal parody' (1985, 31). Hutcheon specifically describes *The French Lieutenant's Woman* as a satire, which 'parodies the Victorian novel in order to reveal what the Victorian world hid' (1985, 105). The novel-as-mashup has often been brought into discussions of neo-Victorianism precisely because it seems to be commenting on the particular discourse of satirical postmodern irony with which this brand of fiction and criticism is concerned. This discourse is often framed (following Jameson) as a struggle between 'authentic', progressive irony and conservative nostalgia.

For instance, the novel-as-mashup's camp aesthetic potentially defines it as something Christian Gutleben calls 'nostalgic postmodernism'. Gutleben discusses how twentieth and twenty-first-century 'retro-Victorian' (or neo-Victorian) novels portray the nineteenth-century past in which they situate themselves (2001, 5). His analysis of neo-Victorian fiction is split, broadly speaking, into two chronological phases of revisionist texts. The first phase contains those early neo-Victorian texts that resist nostalgia, where 'ironic recycling of the myth-laden Victorian novel was at the avant-garde of postmodernism in Britain' (2001, 120). The second phase, 'thirty years later, after many more rewritings of myths, traditions and genres', finds the neo-Victorian succumbing to nostalgia and realist tendencies, with the consequence that 'the same principle of modernizing tradition appears inevitably less progressive' (2001, 120). From this perspective, the novel-as-mashup could be seen as the culmination of a process of cultural regression. It is highly unlikely that anyone would regard the novel-as-mashup as 'realist' given the fantastical monsters that often populate its pages, but the novel-as-mashup could certainly be accused of having nostalgic tendencies, turning to the past as either an escape from the present or as a calculated marketing strategy. Indeed, although Gutleben's use of the term 'progressive' here is potentially problematic for its emphasis on certain highbrow texts above the middlebrow and lowbrow, his point about the cultural shift away from postmodernism's avant-garde irony (and its emphasis on authenticity) is very germane.

While the novel-as-mashup does not draw on the nineteenth century exclusively, the majority of mashup publications derive their source material from the Regency and Victorian eras of England's literary history. Does the novel-as-mashup fall into this 'neo-Victorian' category? Arguably not if one takes Heilmann and Llewellyn's seminal definition of the neo-Victorian project. They describe neo-Victorianism as inherently metatextual, comprised of texts that 'must in some respect be *self-consciously engaged with the act of (re)interpretation, (re)discovery, and (re)vision concerning the Victorians*' (2010, 4, original emphasis). A certain amount of ironic self-awareness is certainly present in the construction of the novel-as-mashup. Jason Rekulak, who provided the initial idea for *Pride and Prejudice and Zombies*, has cited the internet's myriad publishing options as his inspiration, where artists can allegedly 'get away with' flouting copyright concerns in a way that he, as a traditional book publisher, normally cannot (2009, para. 2). As this sentiment indicates, the relationship between the novel-as-mashup and the texts it appropriates may not be as intimate or traditionally literary as Heilmann and

Llewellyn's definition broadly implies. Again, this suggests that the novel-as-mashup should be read as a camp parody, not a satire.

Although the novel-as-mashup is engaged in metatextual reference, its appropriation of classic literature, verging on plagiarism, is arguably less concerned with the Victorians than it is with their twenty-first-century stereotypes, afterlives, and copyright-free textual legacies. This is also the reason Regency texts like *Pride and Prejudice* can be considered under the neo-Victorian umbrella. Traditional publishing's extensive copyright laws are no doubt partly responsible for the selection of these particular period texts for adaptation, and mashup artists' preference for texts already in the public domain is understandable in this restrictive context.[4] The texts appropriated in the novel-as-mashup also tend to be those kept alive by a seemingly endless series of adaptations, whether for stage, television (especially by the BBC), or cinema. Historiographic metatextuality, then, is not the defining impetus of the novel-as-mashup. Rather than mixing nineteenth-century works with contemporary tastes by metatextual design, the novel-as-mashup seems to be neo-Victorian by superficial coincidence. If this is the case, however, it employs an unusually high proportion of qualities that could be termed 'neo-Victorian' – at least, under many definitions of the term.

Like Heilmann and Llewellyn, Kate Mitchell seeks a more 'authentic', self-aware type of neo-Victorianism in her 2010 study, *History and Cultural Memory in Neo-Victorian Fiction*. She describes the dichotomy in neo-Victorian fiction as follows:

> The issue turns upon the question of whether history is equated, in fiction, with superficial detail; an accumulation of references to clothing, furniture, décor and the like, that produces the past in terms of its objects, as a series of clichés, without engaging its complexities as a unique historical moment that is now produced in a particular relationship to the present. [...] Can these novels recreate the past in a meaningful way or are they playing nineteenth-century dress-ups? (Mitchell 2010, 3)

We can again see an element of humour in this metaphor, in the image of a twenty-first century text gleefully 'trying on' the past in childish play. Mitchell's conception of a 'meaningful' reworking can also be read in the context of artistic irony and authenticity, in which literature should react against cultural and textual conventions. Here the novel-as-mashup clearly falls into Mitchell's second, implicitly meaningless category: it is unabashedly engaged in nineteenth-century dress-ups, delighting in its objects and clichés. In the many illustrations in *Pride and Prejudice and Zombies*, for example, the Bennet sisters are clad in the Regency dresses so often depicted in BBC dramatizations of Austen's novel, but for fighting they wear their 'sparring gowns' (Grahame-Smith and Austen 2009, 130). These gowns remain largely faithful to the BBC aesthetic, but also incorporate steampunk elements like leather corsets and gun belts. The material, historical reality behind certain nineteenth-century garments is glossed over by the popularity of their revised forms in contemporary culture and fashion. In the novel-as-mashup, the corset and the parasol serve a similar function to the zombie as objects and clichés of popular fiction. It is the instant recognizability of these historical items of clothing, made popular in contemporary culture by steampunk and neo-Victorian fiction, that makes them so attractive to novel-as-mashup readers, authors, and publishers. This again highlights the camp function of the novel-as-mashup, engaged in a metatextual parody of neo-Victorianism's superficial conventions and objects, and thereby also demonstrating how those conventions have come to define and dominate the genre.

The novel-as-mashup is designed primarily to parody and entertain, not to satirically 'recreate the past in a meaningful way' in the sense Mitchell describes (2010, 3). The turn of neo-Victorian studies to, as Marie-Luise Kohlke puts it, 'lighter', less satirical forms of writing marks another area of debate in neo-Victorianism, however (2014, 33–4). It is not just a question of whether or not these un-critical texts are funny (a regular bone of contention in the case of the novel-as-mashup), but also whether texts that do not 'promote serious historical insight or revision' can still serve as acceptable depictions of the past, and meaningful additions to the neo-Victorian field (2014, 33–4). Although her analysis of comedic texts maintains a certain level of literariness, Kohlke does conclude that it is not only 'serious' representations of the Victorians that merit academic study (2014, 34). As she demonstrates, metatextuality can extend into the comic mode, expressing a humorous or tongue-in-cheek awareness that still fits into existing neo-Victorian theory on representations of gender, race, and class (2014, 34). It is here that the novel-as-mashup parody of the genre functions – not as an ironic satire of the Victorians, but as a camp performance of neo-Victorianism's allegedly feminist, postcolonial, and egalitarian readings of the nineteenth century. Of course, as Heilmann and Llewellyn suggest, the Victorian influence on the neo-Victorian fiction market generally has less to do with a reading of Victorian realist fiction, and more with 'how contemporary neo-Victorian readers think the Victorian realist mode worked' (2010, 13). The genre is built on a series of preconceptions (and sometimes misconceptions) about the Victorians.

In their introduction to *Neo-Victorianism*, Heilmann and Llewellyn refer to Miriam Burstein's blog post 'Rules for Writing Neo-Victorian Novels' (under the alias 'The Little Professor'). Joining a series of posts by novelists and fellow academics that satirically examine the stereotypes of historical fiction, Burstein's list suggests (among other things) that in neo-Victorian fiction 'All middle- and upper-class Victorian wives are Sexually Frustrated, Emotionally Unfulfilled, and possibly Physically Abused', and that 'All heroes and heroines are True Egalitarians who disregard all differences of Class, Race, and Sex. Heroines, in particular, are given to behaving in Socially Unacceptable Ways, which is always Good' (2006, paras 2, 4). Although the novel-as-mashup does not follow all of Burstein's 'rules', in many respects, it is clearly responding to these stereotypical tropes and traditions of neo-Victorian fiction.[5] It is not the only body of work to do so. In recent years, mainstream neo-Victorian literature has developed its own extensive self-parody. For instance, Caterina Novák describes how the novel '*Dora Damage* [2006] can be read both as a straightforward example of neo-Victorian feminist fiction and as a parody of the genre, in the sense of exaggerating and commenting on many of its key characteristics and offering an important contribution to the debate surrounding its feminist political credentials' (2013, 115). Even if it is not entirely intentional, the novel-as-mashup can still be considered a camp parody – as Sontag suggests, 'pure examples of Camp *are* unintentional' (1999, 58, emphasis mine). In this sense, the novel-as-mashup can be described as neo-Victorian fiction, but also as a work of *neo-neo-Victorianism*, which engages in a camp '*(re)interpretation, (re)discovery, and (re)vision*' of the neo-Victorian genre (Heilmann and Llewellyn 2010, 4, original emphasis).

As in *Dora Damage* and other neo-Victorian novels, one of the most common tropes of neo-Victorian fiction *beyond* the book is what Antonija Primorac describes as a 'loss of Victorian female characters' agency that takes place in the process of "updating" Victorian texts in contemporary screen adaptations through the – now almost routine – "sexing up" of the proverbially prudish Victorians' (2013, 90). Female characters are exoticized and hypersexualized in a way that is presented as feminist, but enacts a '"retro-sexist" [...] conservative treatment of women's agency' (Whelehan 2000, 65; Primorac 2013, 106). In the 2016 film adaptation of *Pride and Prejudice and Zombies*, we can see this same process at work. Lizzie, Catherine de Bourgh, and the other female warriors in the film choose war over domestic work, but they are presented in a way that foregrounds their sexual desirability over their physical ability – played by stunning actresses, dressed in leather corsets and high-heeled boots, and flashing tantalizing glimpses of skin and frilly underclothes to the viewer as they dress themselves for battle. Like many neo-Victorian productions, this film walks 'a treacherous line between sexual and political critique and voyeuristic impulses' (MacDonald and Goggin 2013, 5). This 'sexing up' takes place to a lesser degree in the printed novel-as-mashup, where the male characters are also objects of sexual desire.

Notably, the majority of novels-as-mashup feature female protagonists and narrators. This is partly because of the prevalence of Austen and Brontë mashups, in which women are often the most prominent and well-rounded characters, but the weapon-wielding heroine of the novel-as-mashup is also indebted to third-wave feminism's popularization of female monster slayers. The female action hero has been closely associated with popular feminism since television programmes like *Buffy the Vampire Slayer* aired in the 1990s, and reacts against the idea that stereotypically feminine women are incapable of physical violence or exertion. The female protagonists of novel-as-mashup texts like *Pride and Prejudice and Zombies*, *Jane Slayre*, and *Alice in Zombieland* are transformed into fierce and skilful hunters, alternately vanquishing or redeeming the monsters that cross their path. Slaying allows these women to fill a role often reserved exclusively for men in popular culture, which initially seems like a feminist approach. Rather than being appreciated for her more traditionally feminine qualities of 'wit and vivacity' (Austen [1813] 2008, 71), the Elizabeth Bennet of *Pride and Prejudice and Zombies* possesses great skill in the use of a blade, as well as all the physical and mental stamina that results from hours of meditation in the dojo (Grahame-Smith and Austen 2009, 226). She is a match for Darcy not only in conversation, but also in combat (2009, 151). Although side characters in novel-as-mashup texts often have something to say about these slayer women – in *Pride and Prejudice and Zombies* only unmarried women fight for king and country against the zombie hordes, and in *Wuthering Bites* '[n]o woman of quality concerns herself with fighting bloodsuckers' (S. Gray and Brontë 2010, 411) – the narrative is on the side of those who do take up their weapon of choice against the monsters.

This portrayal of strong women soon reaches its limits, however. Because the stakes of gendered representation are only introduced superficially, the narrative inadvertently naturalizes traditional, binary gender roles. As Tara MacDonald and Joyce Goggin suggest, 'the repeated characterisation of these now-standard figures risks turning them into clichés that reinforce unproductive stereotypes, rather than giving voice to women as distinctive subjects' (2013, 5). The female warriors of the novel-as-mashup are universally white, cis, heterosexual, and sexually desirable 'extraordinary women' (2013, 7), and as a result their 'feminist' struggles lack convincing opposition. In *Pride and Prejudice and Zombies*, Lizzie Bennet is transformed into a postfeminist hero who is capable of doing whatever she puts her mind to, but only because she is not directly faced with oppression. This gender-blind, pseudo-feminist adaptation masks the conventional and conservative gender roles the mashup ultimately promotes. In the end, Lizzie's choice is to give up her sword and her warrior lifestyle in exchange for a wedding ring, and to exchange dominance on the battlefield for a life in the domestic sphere.[6]

Of course, because of the way monsters change the context and stakes of the novel's action, portrayals of villainous or mad women – embodiments of unconventional womanhood and monstrous femininity – also tend to be softened in the novel-as-mashup. Traits that may previously have been associated most strongly (and negatively) with femininity are instead given a fantastical motive. Some women are transformed into fantastical monsters rather than metaphorical ones, as is the case with *Jane Slayre*'s Mrs Reed, Abbott, and Bertha Rochester. Although not absolved of their psychological or emotional faults, they are partially forgiven by the protagonist because it is in 'their very nature' as monsters (and not humans) to behave in such a way (Erwin and Brontë 2010, 76). Any humour drawn from their flaws becomes focused on their fantastical nature, and not their gendered deficits – again distracting the reader from any overtly feminist message in the name of a more 'universal' monstrosity. *Alice in Zombieland*'s Red Queen is demanding and overbearing because she is attempting to hold back a zombie apocalypse, and not because she is a woman in power. Miss Havisham and Estella of *Grave Expectations* are a danger to Pip because they are hunters and he is a werewolf, not because they seek revenge against all men. Ironically, however, turning these characters into fantastical monsters also serves to re-feminize them, more clearly marking them as 'Other' – a category closely associated with feminism and femininity. This re-Othering in the novel-as-mashup takes the focus away from feminism without removing the anti-feminist narrative, in which women who embrace conservative roles are good, and rogue women are 'monsters'. Fantastical monsters thus continue to represent a generalized otherness throughout the novel-as-mashup, though not always as a particular gendered, racialized, or sexualized 'other'. The monsters can be protagonists, antagonists, or supporting characters. More often they simply dismiss the politics of otherness, setting themselves up as post-racial, post-feminist, and post-inequality.

Unlike neo-Victorian fiction, the novel-as-mashup certainly does not make a special effort to include people of colour, or of nationalities not present in the original novels. As I argued in Chapter 2, however, monsters are traditionally associated with otherness in Gothic and horror fiction, and particularly with ethnic minorities. In the novel-as-mashup, this remains the case as well. In *Jane Slayre*, for example, the madness of Bertha Rochester is not only connected to her status as both female and foreign, but also to the fact that she is a werewolf (Erwin and Brontë 2010, 614). Although the werewolf is a fantastical monster, it also has direct cultural connotations of animal emotion and exotic ethnicity, which very effectively link it to Bertha's animalization in *Jane Eyre*.

The novel-as-mashup also maps fantastical monsters directly onto historical categories of otherness for comedic effect, although the ethnic reference or humour used often attempts inclusivity. In *Wuthering Bites*, for example, the outcast gypsies with whom Heathcliff identifies are transformed into a superhuman clan of vampire slayers. As Mr Lockwood notes, 'it is their skill and courage that keep the beasties from devouring all of us and taking over our fair country' (Erwin and Brontë 2010, 15). A notable exception to the novel-as-mashup's 'post-racial' approach to otherness can be found in *Sense and Sensibility and Sea Monsters*, where Sir John Middleton is depicted as a colonial adventurer, who has kidnapped a black woman (his unruly wife Lady Middleton) from Africa. Arguably the target of this satirical reference is imperialism rather than race, but its inclusion in *Sense and Sensibility and Sea Monsters* is unintelligible as a commentary on *Sense and Sensibility*. Neo-Victorian fiction, on the other hand, often features ironic depictions of racial and colonial oppression, potentially aligning the novel-as-mashup with this genre once again. As the film critic Bill Stamets points out, the neo-Victorian film *Black Venus* (2010) depicts the graphic physical and mental exploitation of black freak show performer Sarah Baartman (the 'Hottentot Venus'). In doing so, argues Stamets, the film 'risks committing one kind of obscenity on screen in order to alert early 21st century spectators to its early 19th-century original on stages' (2012, para. 14).

Pride and Prejudice and Zombies offers a different example of a satirical dig at Victorian imperialism, mimicking neo-Victorian fiction with its tongue-in-cheek mention of 'Orientals' – both a reference to the various warrior schools that make an appearance in the book, and to the Victorian terminology that is now politically incorrect. Consider the following passage, which replaces a discussion in *Pride and Prejudice* about inanimate objects (books) with one about people of Asian descent, specifically in the context of martial arts:

Pride and Prejudice	*Pride and Prejudice and Zombies*
'What think you of books?' said he, smiling.	'What think you of Orientals?' said he, smiling.
'Books—oh! no. I am sure we never read the same, or not with the same feelings.'	'Orientals—oh! No. I am sure we never met the same, or had the same feelings toward them.'
'I am sorry you think so; but if that be the case, there can at least be no want of subject. We may compare our different opinions.' (Austen [1813] 2008, 62)	'But if that be the case, we may compare our different opinions. I think them a strange lot—both in appearance and custom, though having studied solely in Japan, I admit that the opinion may be incomplete. I should be most interested to hear of your time in the company of Chinamen.' (Grahame-Smith and Austen 2009, 75)

In this example the satire, though ethnic in nature, is primarily directed at imperialist attitudes towards other nations, and not at the other nations themselves. In a similar vein, this time with a classist component, Lady Catherine de Bourgh constantly insults what she considers to be Elizabeth's inferior training at the hands of 'those appalling Chinese peasants' (Grahame-Smith and Austen 2009, 158), rather than the elite and exclusive Japanese schools favoured by most of the British upper class in this novel. Here, then, ethnicity comes to stand in for class. Reference to 'Orientals' and 'Chinamen' in *Pride and Prejudice and Zombies* is partly in compliance with the novel's addition of martial arts to the classic story, but it also mocks writers of the nineteenth century who used these now-derogatory terms – and parodies the neo-Victorian novelists who use them ironically (see Primorac 2015, 42–3). This is not a satire of Austen; the Orient and Orientalism are largely absent from her novel (though imperialist themes can be found in Austen's work as well; see Said 1993, 80–97). Instead, it is a camp re-enactment of neo-Victorianism's satirical appropriation of the Victorians.

Another example of the novel-as-mashup's camp parody of neo-Victorian fiction (distinct from its use of monsters) can be found in its various portrayals of the class divide. Although the novel-as-mashup generally retains the same class distinctions as depicted in the appropriated texts, certain aspects of the class hierarchy are often re-emphasized or made literal in the twenty-first-century adaptations. In *Jane Slayre*, the Reed family is transformed from figurative blood-suckers into literal ones: they and the families with which they associate are all vampires, the traditional monsters of the upper class. In contrast, the servant Abbot is a zombie, and the typhus epidemic at Lowood becomes an unexpected zombie plague, literalizing the zombie as the working class 'monster of the people' (Grossman 2009b). In light of many Marxist readings of Austen's work, specifically *Pride and Prejudice*, the zombies in *Pride and Prejudice and Zombies* could also be read as an ironic manifestation of the almost-invisible working class in the original novel. After all, the zombie is traditionally read as a manifestation of 'recurrent anxieties about corporeal dismemberment in societies where the commodification of human labour – its purchase and sale on markets – is becoming widespread' (McNally 2012, 4). And as Jo Baker's 2014 novel *Longbourn* suggests, there is an invisible territory to be explored at the edges of *Pride and Prejudice*, in the lives of the Bennet family's numerous but silent domestic staff. Like gender, then, *Pride and Prejudice and Zombies'* satirical reading of monstrous class distinctions does have a theoretical basis in the original text, but like race, in the novel-as-mashup this reading is instead predicated on a parody of neo-Victorian stereotypes, and tendencies towards retellings of classic literature from marginal perspectives.

For example, some mashups choose to make more dramatic comments on the division between the landed gentry and the working classes, though similar sentiments do not appear at all in the original novel. These additions are instead derived from twenty-first-century perceptions of the period. Although *Wuthering Heights* does not really offer any consistent depictions of amicable relationships, an entire passage reflecting an uncaring attitude towards the servants is added to *Wuthering Bites*. Cathy Linton is out visiting her pony in the stables when she stumbles across a vampire attacking one of the household staff. Cathy's first instinct is to shout: 'Get off her this moment. This girl is our maid and she has duties to attend to' (S. Gray and Brontë 2010, 399). When the vampire refuses to retreat, she is forced to kill him before he kills the maid, but only because 'if he killed Sally, I knew it would take days to replace her, as her mother was so difficult to convince sending her after the first four of her daughters were murdered in service here' (2010, 400). Despite her many character flaws, Cathy's life is satirically framed as more worthy of admiration and preservation than that of the servants in *Wuthering Bites*.

To cite another example, *Sense and Sensibility and Sea Monsters* delivers the following excerpt in the middle of the novel. It takes place in Sub-Marine Station Beta, an entirely invented environment that replaces the London of the appropriated text:

> It only contributed to the awkwardness when a loud bang was heard against the glass back wall of the docking; turning their heads, they saw that a servant,

who had been changing the water filtration tank and come detached from the breathing hose of his special Ex-Domic Float-Suit, was clamouring for their attention. The operations of the Station's various life-sustaining apparatuses were meant to be entirely invisible to the inhabitants, and the man's noisy exhibition was a rather embarrassing violation of decorum; Elinor and her guests studiously ignored him, and his increasingly insistent thrashing became the background to the ensuing uncomfortable exchange. (B.H. Winters and Austen 2009, 337)

The choice to invent this scene, and such a callous response from the novel's main characters, represents a political statement by the twenty-first-century author about Victorian class divides, rather than an addition based on explicit evidence in the appropriated novel. Its insertion also undermines Elinor's primary role in the novel as a sensible, sensitive, and sympathetic force, without offering any real substitute or counterbalance. The servants seem to serve little purpose other than to mark the text as set 'in the past', or to admire and assist the novel's main characters.

One notable exception to the novel-as-mashup's parody of neo-Victorian fiction lies with the genre's depiction of heterosexuality. Little effort has yet been made to insert any overtly non-heterosexual relationship into the novel-as-mashup, despite the relatively free reign given to the authors to alter similar aspects of the classical narratives, and despite camp's historical association with drag.[7] Authors and publishers of the novel-as-mashup have avoided making direct engagements with LGBTQ discourse, perhaps assuming that it would alienate portions of their mainstream, Anglo-American audience. Here, again, queer politics are systematically erased from camp to make it more marketable to mainstream audiences, 'safe for public consumption' (Meyer 1994, 7). Occasionally, homosexual subtext present in the source material is even diffused, as in *Jane Slayre*, where Jane is forced to kill her dear friend Helen Burns (now a zombie), with whom she shared an ambiguously intimate relationship. This passage takes place immediately after the one where Helen dies while sleeping in the same bed as Jane, negatively reinforcing homosocial intimacy in a way not present in the source material. Although the girls share a bed in *Jane Eyre*, in Brontë's version Helen is killed only once, by consumption, not a second time by Jane. Most novels-as-mashup are resolutely heteronormative, choosing to update the social roles of the women they feature, but not their pursuit of a monogamous, heterosexual relationship. Of course, even in Frankenfictions that do engage with queer identity, like *Penny Dreadful*, the outcome is not always positive. The most prominent (and long-lived) characters are inevitably those deemed most relatable to mainstream audiences – white, Western, and heterosexual.

Ultimately, none of these mashups satirizes either their contemporary context or the nineteenth-century novels they appropriate. If the novel-as-mashup is a camp performance, there are several moments where the form transgresses camp parody into satire, but in general they reproduce specific neo-Victorian themes and traditions rather than critiquing social or political realities. Just as Gothic parody reveals 'inconsistencies, incongruities, and problems in Gothic criticism', so neo-Victorian parody (including the novel-as-mashup) can highlight boundaries the genre 'has been unwilling or unable to blur, binary oppositions it has refused to deconstruct, and points at which a radical, innovative, subversive discourse manifests as its own hegemonic, dogmatic, and clichéd double' (Elliott 2008, 24). Although it is not satirical of classic literature nor neo-Victorian fiction, then, the novel-as-mashup's camp parody does have the effect of highlighting several of the pitfalls of our ironic relationship, through historical fictions, with the past.

Taking the past seriously; or, the limits of postmodern irony

Sontag separates camp from more didactic forms of irony, suggesting that camp always necessarily 'identifies with what it is enjoying' (1999, 65), albeit at a distance. But even camp parody can become problematic when the object of parody is ironic. As I have argued, postmodern neo-Victorian fiction tends to parody contemporary culture's nostalgia for the past. In a conversation with Mario Valdés, Linda Hutcheon re-visits the subject of postmodern nostalgia, specifically as it relates to irony. For Hutcheon, postmodern irony has an inherently nostalgic aspect, though this aspect is ultimately overwritten. The nostalgic move of postmodern irony is 'both an ironizing of nostalgia itself, of the very urge to look backward for authenticity, and, at the same moment, a sometimes shameless invoking of the visceral power that attends the fulfilment of that urge' (2000, 34). Before being ironically dismissed, the nostalgia inherent in contemporary depictions of the past must first be evoked in all its conservative glory.

Again, this is important because of irony's frequent use as a political tool or weapon. As Simon Critchley argues in his book *On Humour*, irony and humour are actually 'a form of cultural insider-knowledge, and might, indeed, be said to function like a linguistic defence mechanism' (2002, 68). Those who do not speak the language are excluded from the joke, to the point where 'having a common sense of humour is like sharing a secret code' (2002, 68). This system of exclusion is what Hutcheon has referred to as 'irony's edge', which 'manages to provoke emotional responses in those who "get" it and those who don't, as well as in its targets and in what some people call its "victims"' (1994, 2). The victims Hutcheon describes are those people who miss a text's irony entirely, and/or those who are the object of ironic mockery. As both Gutleben and Hutcheon point out, the ethical or politically relevant ironies of one time and place are not those of another. Once-progressive writings can be neutralized or rendered reactionary in later readings. After all, Austen's own ironic writing is now commonly misread as a straightforward, sentimental romance by popular culture. This belies Sontag's suggestion that 'the Camp sensibility is disengaged, depoliticized – or at least apolitical' (1999, 54). The line between inclusive and exclusive forms of irony is often a fine one. This is all the more true when it involves marginalized groups or individuals, or historical trauma.

In its role as parody, the neo-Victorian novel-as-mashup foregrounds the tendency of postmodernist fiction to ironically reproduce problematic ideologies. When attempting to reproduce or adapt the past in fiction, questions of imperialism, racism, and sexism inevitably arise – particularly when we are speaking about the Victorian past. Whether or not a text approaches this past ironically, we can never be sure such irony will be interpreted as intended. Irony (and satirical irony in particular) has an inherently exclusionary function. This means that ironic representation already tends towards exclusivity, whether that exclusiveness is considered to be subversive, oppressive, or simply undirected. Sometimes this function gives power to marginalized groups who are 'in' on the opposition to mainstream culture. Sometimes, however, it can serve to reproduce oppressive power structures. Considering the oppositional or satirical function of irony, Colebrook neatly summarizes this problem as follows:

> On the one hand, irony challenges any ready-made consensus or community, allowing the social whole and everyday language to be questioned. On the other hand, the position of this questioning and ironic viewpoint is necessarily hierarchical, claiming a point of view beyond the social whole and above ordinary speech and assumptions. (Colebrook 2004, 153)

In other words, even when satire questions the common consensus, it necessarily relies on the very framework it criticizes to do so. How can we know something is satirical if we do not also recognize what is expected?

In a continual, familiar struggle, postmodern art has often inadvertently supported or recreated the very systems it attempts to undermine, generally as a result of its ironic structure. As Colebrook points out, postmodern literature 'has been dominated by texts that express a masculinist, imperialist, racist or elitist discourse in order to present the violence of that discourse. [...] And even if one were to decide that such texts were, or ought to be, ironic, this would still allow the violent content to be displayed, enjoyed and popularised' (Colebrook 2004, 157). This issue of ironic reproduction speaks to current concerns within neo-Victorianism as well. Consider Australian Prime Minister John Howard's accusation that postmodern versions of Australian history represent 'little more than a litany of sexism, racism and class warfare' (quoted in Carroll 2010, 191). Analogously, in her 2015 monograph *Neo-Victorian Freakery*, Helen Davies questions whether 'neo-Victorianism distorts freak show performers beyond all recognition, compounding nineteenth-century abuses of vulnerable people' (2015, 3).

Given how the novel-as-mashup parodies not just texts, but genres and textual modes, it might be best to think of the parody found in Frankenfiction as 'meta-ironic'. This (again paradoxical) term is conceived by Hutcheon as follows:

> By analogy, then, we might be able to speak of a 'meta-ironic' function, one that sets up a series of expectations that frame the utterance as potentially ironic. Signals that function meta-ironically, therefore, do not so much constitute irony in themselves as signal the possibility of ironic attribution [...] and operate as triggers to suggest that the interpreter should be open to other possible meanings. (Hutcheon 1994, 154)

Arguably, all irony is meta-ironic, in the sense that no text or statement intended as ironic is also guaranteed to be *interpreted* as ironic either by everyone, or for all time – a problem Hutcheon also acknowledges, but leaves unsolved. For Colebrook this problem is inherently humanist, and 'may well be tied up with the long history of Western subjectivism: the idea that behind language, actions, difference and communication there is a ground or subject to be expressed' (2004, 20). By assuming that one meaning must be 'true', we inadvertently privilege one meaning, usually offered by those in places of power, over another.

Colebrook, drawing on Jacque Derrida's post-structuralist theory, argues that 'all speech is potentially ironic, both because a concept has a sense we neither author nor control *and* because there are *non*sensical forces at work in the articulation of concepts' (2004, 169, original italics). Colebrook sees these nonsensical forces as the ways in which unintended meaning can be written or read into all communication. In cultural criticism today, the difficulties inherent in this assumption are under continual scrutiny. Colebrook's tentative solution to such difficulties is this:

We would need to acknowledge the problem of sense or meaning beyond manifest intent, as in classical irony, but we would also need to read for the inhuman, machinic or errant forces that preclude such a sense from governing the text. (Colebrook 2004, 169)

In other words, we must continue to search for ironic or alternate readings of texts, while also remaining open to the possibility of a third, as-yet-unknown way, where meaning runs rampant.

Although it frequently abuses canonical, 'establishment' texts, the novel-as-mashup's neo-Victorian parody is also guilty of the exoticized depiction (and exploitation) of potentially vulnerable people. For example, in *Sense and Sensibility and Sea Monsters*, Lady Middleton's attempts to escape back to Africa are a running joke. Although they are intended for comedic effect, they reference a very real power dynamic, both between husband and wife and between master and slave. Likewise, despite the Barthesian 'death of the author' and the New Critical step away from authorial intent, readings of *Sense and Sensibility and Sea Monsters* are complicated by the fact that the author, Ben Winters, is himself a middle-class man of European descent, profiting from a story in which a white, middle-class European man exploits a black African woman. Rather than challenging the exploitation of various groups and individuals, many works of Frankenfiction – including the novel-as-mashup – risk perpetuating unwanted sentiments, stereotypes, and ideologies, particularly if read un-ironically. Through its use of 'meta-ironic' markers like fantastical monsters, steampunk gadgets, plagiarism, and genre bending, however, the novel-as-mashup makes un-ironic readings more difficult (though not impossible).

Ultimately, rather than attempting to parody a literary classic 'in ways that enrich the narrative without derailing it', as Samantha Carroll advocates in her analysis of neo-Victorian fiction, the novel-as-mashup confronts us with the possibility that enrichment and derailment may not be the only two options available (2010, 183). Moreover, it suggests that these two options need not be mutually exclusive. Rather than critiquing directly, as satirical parody does, the novel-as-mashup mobilizes both the nostalgia contemporary culture evinces for the textual past *and* the satirical responses to such nostalgia through camp. As a result of this broad focus, the critique enacted by the novel-as-mashup is generally not very deep or particularly political – at least, not in the way Hutcheon (or many a neo-Victorianist) describes it. It does point to the ethical and political limitations in the way these historical fictions ironically represent the past, however.

Beyond postmodern irony

In the introduction to their 2014 collection *Neo-Victorian Literature and Culture: Immersions and Revisitations*, Nadine Boehm-Schnitker and Susanne Gruss argue for an extension of the definition of neo-Victorianism that moves beyond postmodern irony:

> Even though postmodernity remains a helpful reference point for academia, writers and artists, neo-Victorianism has moved beyond postmodern concerns such as intertextuality, self-reflexivity or metafiction. Despite postmodernity's ongoing relevance, neo-Victorianism calls for newly calibrated tools of analysis which enable us to approach it as a symptom of a contemporary literature and culture which more strongly integrates questions of ethics, reconsiders the author, allows the referent to become visible again behind the veil of material signifiers, and plays at and with practices of immersion. (Boehm-Schnitker and Gruss 2014, 2)

The novel-as-mashup certainly presents us with some of these tools. Its recycling of neo-historical texts in a (post-)postmodern context makes us aware of the genre's 'inconsistencies, incongruities, and problems' (Elliott 2008, 24), and offers us an opportunity to revive and re-evaluate these ironic discourses. For all its conservative motives and methods, the novel-as-mashup's camp parody of neo-Victorianism can be a valuable tool, highlighting the fault lines in historical fiction's use of postmodern irony.

For Hutcheon, it is precisely such deferral, present to a certain degree in all historiographic metafiction, that finally creates space for 'a consideration of the different and the heterogeneous, the hybrid and the provisional. This is not a rejection of the former values in favor of the latter; it is a rethinking of each in the light of the others' (1988, 42). As Spooner too suggests, Gothic revivals, comic vampires, and other parodic texts and figures 'are not a dead end, the sign of a tired and played-out tradition: rather comedy has, from the beginning, offered a way of continually interrogating that tradition, and in doing so, renewing and refreshing it' (2017, 143). Frankenfiction's parody of historical fiction's tropes and conventions should ultimately allow for the formation of new and unexpected connections, and the divestment of old stereotypes. This, I would argue, is something the novel-as-mashup certainly offers – even if its greatest capacity for considering difference exists outside the mashup narrative itself.

While in this chapter I discussed the novel-as-mashup's parody of realist and historical fiction, in the next chapter I will explore how Frankenfiction's relationship to historiography and historical fiction functions in the visual arts, where the object of parody or remix is not a literary text, but a visual historical trace. Because these appropriations often infringe on a boundary between history and fiction that is seen as absolute, their insertion of monsters into historical scenarios has a more direct impact than a fantastical narrative might. While some Frankenfictions attempt to make monsters a 'natural' part of history, the artists Travis Louie, Dan Hillier, Colin Batty, and Kevin J. Weir make the idea of a natural history monstrous.

Notes

1   For an excellent overview of *Pride and Prejudice and Zombies*'s publication history and marketing strategies, see Binder (2009) and Nelson (2013). It is increasingly rare in the publishing world to sell 1.5 million copies of a single novel. To put this in perspective, sales for all of Sarah Waters's books combined just hit the one million mark in 2014 (O'Keeffe 2014). Although it was a box office failure, even the 2016 film adaptation of *Pride and Prejudice and Zombies* met this number. Domestic ticket sales for the film are estimated at 11 million (1.3 million viewers, at an average ticket price of $8.50) ('Pride and Prejudice and Zombies' 2016).

2   This may also be due to the relative popularity of *Pride and Prejudice* above Austen's other novels. Sales data for *Sense and Sensibility and Sea Monsters* is scarce. For an estimate that places it at the fourth most successful mashup novel in terms of sales (after *Pride and Prejudice and Zombies* and Adams Media's 'Wild and Wanton' editions of *Pride and Prejudice* and *Persuasion*), see Riter (2017, 72).

3   Naturally, this is not the first time characters from Jane Austen novels have been sexualized. One of the most famous examples is a scene from the 1995 BBC adaptation of *Pride and Prejudice*, in which Mr Darcy emerges from the water in a transparent shirt. This scene has become so well known it was satirized in the ITV miniseries *Lost in Austen* (2008), and commemorated with a 2013 re-enactment in Hyde Park (Lyall 2013). Nelson suggests that *Pride and Prejudice and Zombies* is more indebted to such adaptations than it is to Austen's novel (2013, 342). Similarly, the mashup *Alice in Zombieland* takes its name from the 1951 Disney film adaptation *Alice in Wonderland* rather than Carroll's *Alice's Adventures in Wonderland*.

4   To date, the only novel-as-mashup to be published through official channels in conflict with US copyright law is *The Late Gatsby* (Klipspringer and Fitzgerald 2012). This book is only for sale outside the United States, where different copyright laws and lengths apply, and it is currently only available as an eBook.

5   Burstein writes that 'Any novel based on an actual Victorian literary work must include considerable quantities of Sex' (2006, para. 9). This tends to be true only of the novel-as-mashup texts that juxtapose classic literature with erotic fiction (Sinclair and Brontë 2012; I.J. Miller and Brontë 2013; Spector and Wilde 2013), rather than with horror fiction.

6   As Nelson notes, of course, the sequel to *Pride and Prejudice and Zombies – Dreadfully Ever After* (2011) – 'opens with Elizabeth bitterly regretting the diminution of her freedom' (Nelson 2013, 347).

7   An exception can be found in the *Pride and Prejudice and Zombies* discussion guide, though its engagement with LGBTQ discourse is painfully conservative. Namely, in a reference to stereotypes of the 'butch' or unfeminine gay woman, the narrator asks whether Elizabeth Bennett's 'fierce independence, devotion to exercise, and penchant for boots' might mark her as 'the first literary lesbian' (Grahame-Smith and Austen 2009, 319).

4

Remixing Historical Fiction

Did I request thee, Maker, from my clay
To mould me Man, did I solicit thee
From darkness to promote me?

(Milton [1819] 2003, 256; Shelley [1831] 2015, 1)

This passage from *Paradise Lost* takes on an ominous echo as the epigraph to *Frankenstein*. It speaks less of creation, and more of reanimation or revival, teasing out the reader's dark associations with the origins of Frankenstein's creature. Of course, in Frankenstein's case the metaphor is even more ominous: in contrast with the biblical creation of Man, his creature is not formed of inert and shapeless clay, but from the dismembered pieces of humans and other animals (Shelley [1831] 2015, 46). These objects have shifted from living to dead, and were meant to remain at rest. What gives Victor Frankenstein the authority, this passage seems to ask, to reassemble the pre-existing (if disused) pieces of other bodies into such a monstrous new whole? And is the creature or the creator responsible for the results of this resurrection? The creature certainly did not ask to be given such monstrous life, and in the course of Shelley's novel, it becomes clear that he would rather not be assembled at all.

In the context of this book, we might ask whether the act of Frankenfiction is comparable to the monstrous birth and abandonment of Frankenstein's creature, for in addition to the many other parallels it invites, the *Frankenstein* myth can serve as a metaphor for historical revival gone wrong. What gives Frankenfiction the right to dredge up past texts and artefacts for popular entertainment, and why, in addition to recycling historical modes and aesthetics, does it intentionally revive them in a monstrous fashion? What are the implications of a Frankensteinian resurrection of past texts and traces? In Chapter 2, I discussed how Frankenfiction conceptualizes monsters at a narrative level in various media (novels, comics, and television), and in the previous chapter I took a step back to examine the genre's parody of other forms and narratives. In this chapter, I will focus once again on meaning generation at the level of narrative, considering what it means that Frankenfictions are *historical* monster mashups. What is 'history', and how might our relationship to it be rewritten through Gothic remix? As *Frankenstein* also suggests, the answer to these questions depends partly on the material being recycled. In Chapter 2 I looked at several adaptations of literary monsters, set in a fantastical past. These fictions were constructed from the parts of other, literary texts, in a way that was both legally and ethically defensible. Legally because the texts they appropriated are long out of copyright, and ethically because these appropriated texts were predominantly fictions. *The League of Extraordinary Gentlemen* could be labelled a wilful misrepresentation of literary fiction, but it would be more complicated to accuse it of misrepresenting cultural history.

Of course fictions, unlike other historical artefacts, *do* ask readers to 'promote' them from darkness. Art is generally open to being resurrected and given new life, though like Frankenstein's creature, an artist may not always be appreciative of monstrous, distorted, or fragmented resurrections. This might be the case, for instance, in situations where an adaptation takes an opposite political stance to that found in its alleged source text. In a culture where creator-figures remain highly authoritative, adaptations are often expected to conform to the intentions of an original author (as I will discuss in Chapter 5). In the previous chapter, I considered the implications of 'monstrous' adaptation in textual mashup. In this chapter, I will once again take a multimedia approach, examining the way four visual artists construct their Frankenfictions. This approach also allows us to move away from the usual assumptions associated with text-to-screen adaptations. The images in this chapter draw inspiration from textual fictions, but also from the parts of other images, and other visual and aesthetic traditions. What ethics and aesthetics are involved in appropriating historical objects, which are *not* accompanied by the kind of implied consent that literary fiction offers adaptors? What happens when the adaptor or remixer appropriates an object that is meant to represent an objective or historical reality, rendering it fictional? As I will demonstrate, depending on the source this appropriation can raise a very different set of questions, and can generate diverse types of narratives.

I have chosen to use visual Frankenfictions to illustrate this discussion because, though they are the least 'readable' in the sense of printed words on a page, they are still thoroughly 'narrative'. Anne Quéma, for instance, argues that 'pictures can adopt a narrative form and also rely on the kinesis of the eye for their meaning to emerge' (2007, 97). And Gillian Rose suggests that 'modern societies make meaning through visual imagery now more than ever before' (2005, 67). The histories images can construct are also uniquely persuasive, and often received with greater authority than written histories. Photography in particular 'is regarded as showing the truth of things, how things really looked when the shutter snapped' (G. Rose 2005, 67). In reality, however, an image (whether illustration, photography, or other medium) is never a straightforward truth. As Rose argues, 'different identities, different subject positions are reiterated in highly complex ways by visual images' (2005, 69). The visual medium opens a window into a moment in time and space in a way that creates dramatic tension, and requires interpretation. Kate Mitchell takes this metaphor a step further, giving it a historical dimension, when she writes about photography in neo-Victorian fiction. Here, the image acts as a medium in the spiritualist sense of the word, 'channelling the past and forming a geometry of connections with the present' (Mitchell 2008, 81).

In addition to the meaning made through visual imagery, the way texts and images interact can also spawn a new set of narratives and paratexts. This is made explicit in Travis Louie's captioned portraits, one of the examples in this chapter. I specifically discuss examples of visual art here, rather than book illustration or marketing art, in order to isolate the way Frankenfiction 'adapts' and addresses the past through its material traces. But my analysis of Frankenfiction's visual narrative strategies could apply to any of the texts in this book. Indeed, many of these same tactics can be found in the way *Penny Dreadful* – a show that relies as heavily on literary language as it does on the visual – draws on the Gothic aesthetics of decadence and excess to create a sense of drama. Likewise, *Anno Dracula*'s re-designed 2011 cover aligns it with twenty-first-century neo-Victorian fiction, rather than the twentieth-century vampire fictions of Anne Rice indicated by the 1992 editions.[1] Of course, the adaptive process occurs in slightly different ways across different media. In contrast with these more hybrid, literary dramas and 'image-texts', the majority of the artists I discuss in this chapter – Dan Hillier, Travis Louie, Colin Batty, and Kevin J. Weir – prioritize visual language, rather than spoken or written language, to create their fictional, Gothic histories.

In the Gothic, and in Gothic historical fiction, a distinct aesthetic has emerged. Allan Lloyd-Smith, for instance, describes the postmodernization of the Gothic in the twentieth century, in which the 'Gothic heritage becomes *Heritage Gothic*, a use of now conventional tropes that is legitimized simply through previous practice' (2004, 126; cited in Spooner 2006, 34). As the Gothic turns to the past for its clichés rather than its symbols, does it lose its transgressive ability to re-imagine history, as Christian Gutleben suggested of neo-Victorian fiction? Moreover, why do we feel compelled to consume stories set in the past, instead of addressing those same issues in a present-day context? For many Gothic scholars, the answer to this question has to do with the twenty-first-century's own deep entanglement with the past, and insecurity about the future. Looking at the ways 'the past' manifests in the narratives of our Gothic present may not tell us why contemporary culture remains obsessed with falsifying the past, but it does show us that the meaning we draw from these texts is always multiple, with implications that extend beyond the Gothic past's flashy surface and into its frightful depths. In the Gothic, then, we find a useful vocabulary for theorizing Frankenfiction's particular engagement with pastness.

The Gothic and historical fiction

Many critics point to the continuing importance of historicity and the past in Gothic fiction. Markman Ellis argues that the Gothic 'is itself a theory of history: a mode for the apprehension and consumption of history' (2000, 11). Sean Silver, likewise, describes how important 'the Gothic way of telling history' has actually been to 'the development of the modern British nation-state' (2014, 6). The genre's anachronistic way of imagining grand and ancient pasts consistently impacts on how we view our national history in the present, he argues, and perfectly describes 'the experience of modernity as continually routed through and ruptured by the past' (2014, 9, 12). For Chris Baldick, the Gothic's 'historical fears derive from our inability to convince ourselves that we have really escaped from the tyrannies of the past. The price of liberty, as the old saying tells us, is eternal vigilance' (1992, xxii). As a genre, then, the Gothic is 'profoundly concerned with the past, conveyed through both historical settings and narrative interruptions of the past into the present' (Spooner 2006, 9). This is also true of Frankenfiction, and the genre's engagement with the past is particularly direct in the visual arts, as I will examine shortly.

Of course, these points about the importance of history in the Gothic are all complicated by the genre's love of fakery and embellishment. As Catherine Spooner notes, '[t]he construction of fake histories is integral to Gothic texts' (2006, 38). Hogle, likewise, writes that the Gothic is 'grounded in fakery' from its earliest origins (2012, 497). This is especially acute in Frankenfiction, with its tendency to parody and camp. And it is partly for this reason that we must describe Gothic revivals as Frankensteinian stitch-work – they are never seamless. Gothic narratives are not meant to be read as authentic or to be taken seriously, and yet they often express and embody very real and serious anxieties. This intentional fakery, combined with the Gothic's narrative and political relationship with the past, makes it especially interesting to compare the genre to that of historical fiction. As Diana Wallace has powerfully argued, 'the early roots of historical fiction are deeply entangled in the Gothic tradition, so deeply that it is often difficult to separate the two genres' (2012, 136).

Wallace suggests that the most useful way to separate these two genres might lie in their attitudes toward the past. She writes: 'historical fiction [unlike the Gothic] proper is defined partly by its eschewing of the fantastic, the supernatural, and (ironically) the "fictional" in the sense of the invented or imaginary' – rather than the inherent fictionality of objective reality described by postmodern philosophers (2013, 3). Fantastical Gothic fictions do not necessarily pretend to be objectively realistic, or to convey historically plausible events. Instead, they suggest how history itself is both uncomfortably real and increasingly distant or surreal. In the words of Daniel Baker, writing about Susanna Clarke's fantastical alternate history *Jonathan Strange and Mr Norrell* (2004), rather than prioritizing an accurate representation of history, such fantasy 'works to make the familiar unfamiliar. The historian's job is often to explain the transition between these states. The historical novelist similarly explores the dissonance and displacement between then and now, making the past recognizable but simultaneously authentically unfamiliar' (2011, 4).

In the case of Frankenfictions and other Gothic texts, this effect is achieved through a process of alienation. Bertolt Brecht describes how alienation takes place in theatre, where a scene is played 'in such a way that the audience was hindered from simply identifying itself with the characters in the play' (1964, 91). Within the visual arts, Brecht describes an image 'painted in such a way as to create the impression of an abnormal event' (1964, 91). Essentially, the effect of alienation is to draw the spectator's attention to the unnatural nature of the artwork itself, ultimately transforming the text into a kind of Gothic metafiction. It is a 'special technique' which allows the artist or performer to 'underline the historical aspect of a specific social condition' (1964, 98). In other words, sometimes to capture the authentic nature of a specific historical event or condition, one must first de-naturalize it, transforming it from a timeless or 'universal' occurrence into a dramatic and alienating one (1964, 96).

This tactic is taken up by each of the four artists I will discuss. Although Hillier, Louie, Batty and Weir are not theatre performers, their work might fall under Thomas Leitch's seventh definition of adaptation as a kind of performance. In

'Adaptation and Intertextuality', he writes that '[e]ven adaptations in the same medium as their alleged originals, like translations into a new language, pose as bringing these original works to new life' (2012, 99). From this perspective, visual Frankenfictions very explicitly perform and revive historical objects and moments for our entertainment. These visual histories are pleasurable in a distinctly Gothic and distinctly campy way. As Susan Sontag writes, 'Camp sees everything in quotation marks. It's not a lamp, but a "lamp"; not a woman, but a "woman." To perceive Camp in objects and persons is to understand Being-as-Playing-a-Role. It is the farthest extension, in sensibility, of the metaphor of life as theater' (Sontag 1999, 56). By self-consciously posing as historical artefacts, these Frankenfictions draw attention to the clichés and elisions in our present-day constructions of 'the past'.

The 'look' of the past: Visual Gothic histories

Many scholars of the Gothic seem primarily interested in film, television, and the novel, but Gothic historical fiction (in the broadest sense) manifests itself in many other media as well. I have already characterized the Gothic as 'a complex mesh of intense trans-medial energies' that extended beyond written narrative into the visual from its earliest days (D.J. Jones 2011, 11). Citing various critics, Gilda Williams catalogues several aesthetic qualities that are particularly prominent in the visual Gothic, including 'fragmentation, subverted notions of beauty, dramatic lighting' as well as its recurring 'visual triggers', like 'the emphasis on surface and texture', 'the literalization of idea into form', 'claustrophobic space and disintegration, signalling a history of unhappy relations with the past', and 'the voyeuristic and theatrical framing of a scene often belonging to a specifically female position as an outsider' (2014, 420). Continuing the obsession with the body in the Gothic visual aesthetic is the deliberate insistence on 'viewing the physical "body-in-pain"', 'the subtle but constant uses of skin to signal monstrosity', and 'the blurring of forms to suggest undecided material and ontological states' (2014, 420). For Williams, the Gothic forms a 'flexible cluster of visual traits, combined with a narrative-based and often dramatic context recounting a set of oppressive conditions usually inherited from the past' (2014, 420–1). Together, these characteristics help distinguish the things we call Gothic from related categories in the visual arts. They will also prove useful in the following discussion of the way the visual arts can serve as a kind of Gothic historical fiction.

Spooner likewise suggests a number of features that can be identified as part of the 'Gothic style', breaking them down into two broad categories. In popular culture, this includes 'intensive chiaroscuro, crowded space, intricate detailing, distorted proportions, a saturated colour palette, ornate fonts and deliberately retro or aged styling'. Gothic in the fine arts, in direct contrast, is often 'governed by the adoption of narrative themes and tropes of the Gothic rather than a consistent "look"' (Spooner 2014, 184–5). On the one hand, then, we see a move towards the Gothic in popular culture that deliberately distorts the past, and appropriates its objects at the expense of their contexts. This is the aesthetic most readily associated with Frankenfiction. On the other hand, the fine arts have adapted the Gothic's themes and tropes to create a new kind of historiography, or history writing. Sometimes, this is at the expense of the Gothic's overt fakeness, and potentially at the expense of its ability to transgressively transform our perceptions of the past.

The work of visual artists like Travis Louie, Dan Hillier, Colin Batty, or Kevin J. Weir demonstrates the potential for a third aesthetic path, between the fine arts and popular art. Each artist produces Gothic remediations, in one sense or another, of historical 'texts' and material traces. Each image layers new meanings and visual histories onto old ones, while demonstrating how the 'story' of the past repeatedly erupts into the present. In this they evoke the Gothic 'multiple-image' apparitions and juxtapositions of the magic lantern (D.J. Jones 2011, 37), though each artist uses different technologies to create their modern phantasmagoria. Louie uses acrylic paint layered over graphite sketches to mimic the soft-edged photographic style of the late nineteenth century, while Hillier digitally alters existing Victorian engravings and images. Weir makes animated GIFs (a moving, digital image particularly popular on social media sites) using old wartime photographs from the Library of Congress's copyright-free image archive. Batty takes an even more direct approach to appropriation and intermediality, hand-painting each cabinet card in his collection to include Gothic monsters, aliens, and various other figures from popular culture.

Each artist's work is grounded in stories and narrative. For Batty, the cabinet cards he alters already depict scenes that are humorous or monstrous, and readily lend themselves to caricature. Weir takes a similar approach, engaging with the darkness and emotion in the historical images he appropriates. Hillier's work primarily attempts to produce a dramatic sense of atmosphere in the viewer, transporting them to 'somewhere a little bit mysterious' ('Dan Hillier's Illustrations [sic] Detailed Images Resemble a Balance of Both Modern and Victorian' 2014, para. 8). Louie, the most traditionally narrative artist of the four, maintains several notebooks in which he writes about the worlds the subjects of his paintings inhabit. These stories are fully formed before he paints a single stroke on the canvas, and Louie in particular sees his work as a kind of historical writing, or even a kind of neo-historical revision (J.A. Winters 2015, para. 3).

Significantly, all four artists are also engaged in the visual remediations and narratives of people. Historical portraiture has its own set of significations and ethics. The story these artists express, even when it is presented through a light or pleasant aesthetic, is ultimately not a comfortable one. It belongs to the domain of the Gothic, and to the dark past (and present) it evokes. In the case of Frankenfiction more broadly, monstrous historical portraiture also raises important questions about the ethics of 'disfiguring' individual historical portraits and images. As I argued in the previous chapter, traditionally postmodernism is more concerned with the stimulation of action or affect than it is with the ethics of appropriation or the misinterpretation of its representations. Postmodern art is speaking to an audience that is 'in' on its ironic statements. By this logic, appropriation is always acceptable as long as it is able to 'invent allusions to the conceivable which cannot be presented' – that is, as long as it is authentic (Lyotard 1984, 81). Frankenfictions are explicitly inauthentic, and in this chapter we will continue to explore what happens when this kind of appropriative art commits 'to surface and to the superficial in all the senses of the word' (Jameson 1984, xviii). In *The Postmodern Condition*, Jean-François Lyotard suggests that 'the postmodern artist or writer is in the position of a philosopher; the text he writes, the work he produces are not in principle governed by preestablished rules, and they cannot be judged according to a determining judgment, by applying familiar categories to the text or to the work' (1984, 81). As I argue throughout this book, Frankenfictions *are* clearly 'governed by preestablished rules'. They openly advertise their indebtedness to – and manipulation of – earlier texts and tastes. They also *can* be 'judged according to a determining judgment', though not in a general sense. Each of the artworks in this chapter engages with preestablished rules and texts in unique ways, and the ethics and aesthetics of that engagement differs accordingly.

Sublime metamorphosis: Dan Hillier's Victorian illustrations

Dan Hillier's artwork sets out to make the past strange and sublime, and to create a peculiar, Gothic pleasure in Victorian otherness as it does so. Of the four artists in this chapter, Hillier's work is perhaps most deserving of the term 'mashup', taking prints and pages from old issues of the *Illustrated London News*, magazines, and anatomical textbooks, and combining them in works of collage that create a distinctly different story than that of the originals (Ramsey 2014, para. 2). Going back to Sonvilla-Weiss's definition of mashup, in Hillier's work 'the original format remains the same', though of course it is scanned through a computer in between printings, and it 'can be retraced as the original form and content' (2010, 9). Of course, this definition again proves questionable for several reasons. Namely, how far can an image be altered before it is no longer recognized as the 'original', and how does a digital copy of a printed or engraved illustration still count as an 'original' format? Both a digital and a paper 'print' are mass reproductions, but each is mediated in a different context. Additionally, certain aspects of images are arguably more iconic (and thus more readily retraceable) than others, particularly in portrait or subject-oriented art. We could likely identify Sandro Botticelli's Venus (from the *Birth of Venus*, 1486) in a collage, but would we recognize the flowers drifting in the background? Although much of Hillier's collage is performed in the computer programme Adobe Photoshop, he also does extensive pen-and-ink work, again altering the form of the original. Sometimes this is on top of scanned collages, sometimes on its own, but Hillier's additions are always at a level of detail that leaves the viewer unsure of what is new and what is appropriated from other images. Because Hillier's style of inking matches the images he appropriates so precisely, there is always some doubt as to which additions are his, and which belong to the nineteenth-century engravings.

Hillier is part of a much larger body of artists that draw directly on the legacy of Victorian illustration. For instance, Claudia Drake, George K. (alias olex oleole), and Ian Goulden (alias seriykotik1970) all create digital collages of Victorian illustrations and woodcuts. Other artists like Kelly Louise Judd and Mad Meg work in watercolour and pencil rather than Photoshop, but still often imitate the visual technique of collage, using a similar range of styles and source materials. Most of these artists work primarily in black and white, mimicking the monochromatic palette of Victorian lithographs, though Judd's work is highly evocative of some of William Morris' Victorian textile prints. Of these artists, however, Hillier is one of the few to consistently bring fantastical creatures or classical 'monsters' into his work; most rely only occasionally on juxtapositions between the human and the animal or inanimate to create their surrealist scenes. In addition, none are as commercially successful as Hillier, who sells art prints of his work on his website, but also tote bags and t-shirts.

He also works as a professional illustrator on various books and projects (see, for instance, Hillier's work in Lovecraft 2017).

Although Victorian illustration is the dominant aesthetic in most of his images, Hillier also cites 'ancient art – cave paintings, medieval bestiaries, Egyptian art, Buddhist and Christian iconography' as sources of visual and thematic inspiration (n.d., para. 9). In terms of linking Hillier's work to an older artistic tradition, surrealism and the absurdist collages of Max Ernst serve as a useful starting point. In his *Une semaine de bonté* (1934, trans. *A Week of Kindness*), Ernst also uses Victorian illustrations to create monstrous human hybrids in collage, themed around a series of classical, animal, and nature motifs. The exact sources for Ernst's *Une semaine de bonté* are uncertain, though he is thought to have used illustrations from Jules Mary's *Les damnées de Paris* (1883), as well as numerous works by the nineteenth-century illustrator Gustave Doré (Appelbaum 1976, v), who is also a clear reference point for some of Hillier's pieces. Hillier himself cites *Une semaine de bonté* as a particular inspiration in his own style of collage, though there are a number of important distinctions between Hillier's work and the absurdist aesthetic ('Dan Hillier: Artist Interview' 2015, para. 8). Where Ernst's juxtapositions point to the absurdist futility and destruction of human endeavour and achievement, Hillier's intentionally reference spiritualism and the rejuvenating power of the unknown, a distinction I will return to shortly. Hillier's engagement in illustration work is also comparable to Ernst's, who illustrated numerous books, including several editions of Lewis Carroll's writings. Hillier's work has adorned album covers (*Falls* by Royal Blood, 2014), advertising campaigns (notably the 'Wonder Season' at Shakespeare's Globe, 2016), and illustrated editions of classic texts (like *The Call of Cthulhu & Other Weird Stories*, The Folio Society, 2017). Hillier's own participation in these markets gives his appropriation of Victorian illustrations, an explicitly commercial art form, additional significance.

It is difficult to pinpoint one specific type of Victorian illustration that Hillier's work appropriates, primarily because as his career has progressed he has turned to various different – and in many ways more visually complex – styles. Additionally, Hillier frequently deletes the background from his images, reducing the illustrations to a figure (or figures) suspended in white space. This distinguishes them from many Victorian book illustrations, which often feature detailed backgrounds and elaborate settings, and gives Hillier's work a stronger visual parallel with the illustrations in, for instance, nineteenth-century fashion magazines. Unlike these object-oriented fashion illustrations, however, Hillier's artwork incorporates grotesque or monstrous elements like tentacles and bones. These figures are not monstrous in the socio-political (and socially central) sense suggested by twenty-first-century monster theory, but in the classical sense of 'hybrid creatures' who disrupt 'the notions of separation and distinction' that underlie normative constructions of 'individual autonomous selfhood': the minotaur, the conjoined twin, the giant (Shildrick 2002, 2). They are inhumanly – or superhumanly – embodied, both inspiring wonder and suggesting disintegration. In classical and medieval imagery, for instance, Margrit Shildrick suggests that the 'hybrid signalled not just absolute otherness, but the corruption of human form and being' (2002, 16). While she is talking specifically about human/animal hybrids in this example, human hybridity with animals, plants, or technologies all serves a similar function in Hillier's art.

Additionally, rather than serving to showcase an outfit or accessory, as a fashion illustration might, the isolation of Hillier's characters on a white background produces the 'sense of enclosure in space' Chris Baldick associates with the Gothic mode, alongside temporal inheritance and disintegration, though in this case the space tends more to agoraphobia than claustrophobia (1992, xix). In an image called 'Aperture', for instance, two ornate, winged figures appear to be flying endlessly through the vastness of space and time, carrying an array of ancient and Gothic structures on their backs (Hillier 2015a). Hillier's practice, in his later work, of constructing a dark and intricate domestic or nature scene inside of a human silhouette creates a similar effect (see Figure 4.5, for example). Hillier's use and juxtaposition of textures also echoes the 'subverted notions of beauty' and the obsession with skin and the body Williams identifies as markers of the Gothic visual aesthetic (2014, 420). In Hillier's case, the beauty his work subverts is that of the visually unified, clean, and realist illustration, which exists only in service to the objects it sells. A good example of this is 'Snake' (Figure 4.1). This image of a snake-woman or mermaid, though not uncommon in late Victorian art, is marked here as monstrous by a long, coiling tail. The snake woman is attired in a manner appropriate to a costume drama, and though it is unclear whether she is dancing or about to deliver a chiding blow to an unseen figure, she is armed with nothing more than a hand fan, rendering any potential violence charming or comical, rather than terrifying. The image is balanced and built of bold, curving lines, and indeed captures the stylized black-and-white aesthetic of a Victorian fashion magazine even as it evokes the Gothic theme of balance between stricture and excess. Hillier himself hints that Gothic alienation may be closer to the surface of such illustrations than one might assume, citing 'the melodrama and the pathos that so many of those old images encapsulate' as one of the inspirations for his work ('Dan Hillier: Isn't Life Surreal?' 2012, para. 1).

Figure 4.1 'Snake' (2006) © Dan Hillier.

'Snake' could easily be gruesome or terrifying in the hands of another, less stylized artist, but aside from the woman's tail and the dark shading of her skirt and shawl, the image is neither particularly Gothic (in the visual sense) or frightening. Although the snake tail is highly detailed, and the overall image is clearly that of a classical, hybrid monster (images of Lamia, or of sea serpents and sirens spring to mind), there is no glistening hide, and no hint of sharp edges, fangs, or gore. The snake-woman's shawl and skirt serve to safely bind and restrain her, and her prim white jacket, fan, face, and flower provide visual and textural contrast with the dark, coiling tail. These accessories are illustrated in enough detail that we might assume they, too, were designed to sell fashion objects, but the image's fantastical additions, derived from a different illustration and context, resist this reading. The coexistence of these two conflicting aesthetics creates narrative drama. Where the appropriated images may have invited consumers to imagine wearing a certain product, or to picture the events described in a written adventure, the combined image creates a story of its own, independent from (and primary to) any written text. Hillier takes these Victorian illustrations and offers them as images with their own inner life, capable of transgressing the bounds placed upon them by the page, and by their status as commercial or supplementary art. Of course, this move reacts more against the *disappearance* of illustration as an art in its own right during the twentieth century than it does the practice of illustration in the nineteenth. Although illustrations and wood prints were extremely popular in Victorian books and magazines – hence the term 'illustration' in reference to 'a pictorial representation of a text' (J.Thomas 2016, 617) – they were quickly usurped by the photograph by the end of the century, especially following the commercialization of lithograph printing (Wakeman 1973, 37). Julie Codell also describes how central and 'crucial illustration was in the competition among periodicals' (2016, 387). The full wealth of this visual material has only recently begun to be rediscovered by academics, but as it passes out of copyright, visual artists have taken renewed notice of it as well. For the Victorians themselves, as Julia Thomas argues, book illustrations were 'not to be overlooked or taken for granted but closely studied'; Edward Burne-Jones suggested that viewers should 'learn to read a picture as one would a poem', examining them 'carefully and critically' (Burne-Jones 1856, 59; cited in Julia Thomas 2016, 620).

In Hillier's work, adapted illustrations become their own interpretations, and some take on a life of their own. In 'Snake', the woman's coiling tail and raised arm also combine to create a striking sense of movement, as though she could come to life – or sprout other, more monstrous features – at any moment. This is a dynamic found in much of Hillier's earlier work. 'Snake' is an image that is visually related to Hillier's series of neo-Victorian tentacle collages.[2] In these pieces (2006–7), he takes Victorian engravings of otherwise 'normal' individuals, often depicted in private or family situations, and uses contemporary titles to frame them in close, familial relationships (e.g. a father, a mother, an uncle). In a nod to H.P. Lovecraft's horror fiction, Hillier replaces various appendages with tentacles (see Figure 4.2). In visually referencing Lovecraft, Hillier also evokes images of enormous, slumbering monsters of the deep, which are familiar in twenty-first-century popular culture through gaming and memes. These stand in sharp contrast to the formal, familial figures from whom the tentacles sprout. One effect of this repeated juxtaposition is that, despite the absurdity of the images themselves, their stylistic presentation as illustration has a naturalizing

Figure 4.2 'Mother' (2006) © Dan Hillier.

effect, rather than a surrealizing one. This effect works both ways. After immersing oneself in Hillier's illustrations, one begins to see the same Gothic possibilities in the lines of other, more realist illustrations as well. Hillier's work thus appears to invoke the supernatural in the mundane, and his addition in later work of intricate landscapes and religious iconography are all the more striking for their juxtaposition with these same Victorian fashion magazine cuttings and, subsequently, book illustrations.

Hillier's tentacle figures, which are presented in a series of dramatic poses, often appear to be reacting to their own monstrosity with either dismay or wonder. In 'Father', the man pictured has raised his left hand to his face in despair, turning away from his right hand, which is transformed into a branch of tentacles. In 'Mother' (Figure 4.2), a woman with clasped hands gazes wistfully into the middle distance, as though concerned that passers-by might take offence at her octopus skirt and legs. This too is a tactic Brecht attributes to theatrical alienation, describing how a performer in Chinese theatre 'expresses his awareness of being watched', and will 'openly choose those positions which will best show them off to the audience' (1964, 92). The sense of drama created by the subjects' poses and expressions in Hillier's tentacle portraits is what narrativizes and historicizes the work, making the viewer think not just about the image, but about the metatextual nature of its presentation and appropriation.

In addition to fashion illustration, Hillier also engages with nineteenth-century art illustration like that of *fin-de-siècle* illustrator Aubrey Beardsley, best known for his work on *The Yellow Book* (1894–7), an illustrated quarterly. Writing about Beardsley, whose bold, stark black-and-white imagery could be compared to 'Snake' and related works, Brigid Brophy notes:

> His portraits, including those of himself, are less portraits than icons. He is drawing not persons but personages; he is dramatizing not the relationships between personalities but the pure, geometric essence of relationship. He is out to capture sheer tension: tension contained within, and summed up by, his always ambivalent images. (1968, 14)

Sontag goes even further, placing Beardsley's art in the 'canon of Camp', because of its extreme stylization (1967, 19, 278). While it may be too bold to compare these two artists in terms of historical prestige and influence, in Hiller's early collage we find a visual tension and geometric symbolism evocative of what Brophy sees in Beardsley's illustrations. Looking at 'Snake' alongside 'The Black Cape', for instance, although Hillier's style is much more rounded and realistic than Beardsley's, there is something similar at play in the way each image balances between realism and stylization, suggesting a movement from the one to the other (Figure 4.3). Both images clearly represent human figures, but the slight asymmetry of the pose, the use of black and white to draw the eye to shapes rather than details, and the sense of imminent movement in each figure's posture all suggest that the figure is about to transform into something else – something more abstract and inhuman.

In Hillier's later work, which focuses more on detailed, single-subject portraiture than dynamic multi-character scenes, this stylized, dramatic tension is less apparent, replaced by an existential tension rather than a relational one. Conversely, while the sense of repressed wonder and the sublime in Hillier's Gothic histories is hinted at in these earlier works, his more recent pieces carry this imagery – and its Gothic historical narrative – much further. For example, a later series from 2011 involves portraits of what appear to be wild animals and plants (birds, deer, flowers, etc.) wearing human faces as masks.

Figure 4.3 'The Black Cape' (1894) by Aubrey Beardsley. Given by Michael Harari, in memory of his father, Ralph A. Harari. Hi-res scan courtesy of the V&A.

In most, the eyes of the human face or mask are vacant, allowing a glimpse of roots, coils, feathers or flowers through empty sockets. These images are again printed on a white background, but in contrast with Hillier's tentacle portraits, the subject's silhouette is teeming with intricate detailing of flowers, horns, plants, and feathers. These darkly shaded areas of detailing form a marked contrast to the white human masks that overlay them. This, again, is a Gothic feature. As Spooner writes, the 'erasure or effacement of the body beneath the mask is a recurrent feature of Gothic fictions' (2004, 6). These figures are again monstrous in the classical sense, bringing two disparate, binary elements together in one body. In 'The Way' (Figure 4.4), for instance, a figure wearing

Figure 4.4 'The Way' (2011) © Dan Hillier.

a suit and a feather headdress looks sidelong at the viewer through owl eyes. Hillier destabilizes the categories of human/inhuman in this image, but also of male/female, as the figure wears a gentleman's suit but has a very feminine jawline and mouth, and the ornamentation of the head and position of the feathers suggests a woman's hair or hat. The figure is also neither old nor young, displaying a smooth face, but a sombre expression and eyeless, ageless stare that suggests something much older.

Unlike Hillier's earlier tentacle portraits, these masked subjects are illustrated in a style more akin to (and more likely appropriated from) what Paul Goldman terms 'High Victorian' illustrators: a group of academic and 'literary artists' who imbued their works with clear visual and narrative references, often to classical literature and mythology illustrators' (2004, 1, 209). Hillier appropriates their style, and occasionally their subject matter, but not necessarily their message. Instead, his later work still fits best with the 'art for art's sake' stylization of Beardsley and the Aesthetic Movement, despite a scant visual relationship to Beardsley's own bold, abstracted designs. With their iconographic shapes and compact lines, Hillier's recent artworks are also more recognizably related to twentieth-century surrealists or pulp fantasy illustrators like Max Ernst or H.R. Giger.

Again in contrast to Hillier's earlier pieces, in portraits like 'The Way' the movement is not in the subject's body, but in the plants, animals, and landscapes that threaten to spill out of it. In some of these portraits the performative mask of humanity is already slipping, and the human face is uncannily doubled – a Freudian device common in Gothic fiction, which points to a psychoanalytical or surrealist reading of Hillier's work. The subject appears to be looking in multiple directions at the same time, both forwards and back, in transition from something old to something new. In these images, a Gothic sense of spatial and temporal disintegration is strongly visible. Not only are the appropriated illustrations undercut by monstrous or sublime new shapes, the subjectivity of the figure depicted is at risk of exploding into wild and multiple fragments. Here, rather than explicitly revelling in historical barbarism as one might expect from a Gothic narrative, Hillier's mask portraits illustrate a playful approach to the idea of 'natural' history, both in the sense of the environment and of historiography or heritage. Mediated through historical illustrations, they merge the human and the botanical into one highly organic, but decidedly stylized image. Notably, unlike Hillier's tentacled characters, these faces wear expressions of serenity, contentment, and quiet wisdom. Far from revitalizing the Victorian illustrations they appropriate, then, Hillier depicts these subjects as serene and silent monoliths, at once in the past and beyond it, forever fused into a hybrid, otherworldly creature. The titles of many of the images ('Lark', 'Trickster', etc.) contribute to this effect, framing the figures they depict as archetypes of nature, pagan gods, or tarot figures. They also underline the subconscious presence of a sublime otherness beneath the human mask of subjectivity. In a staging that seems highly metaphorical, these figures literally wear the skin of their predecessors, using their illustrated likenesses to further unfathomable agendas. In many ways, these images might also be read as depicting unconscious or repressed memories, surfacing in the form of dreams or hallucinations.

More recently Hillier's work has shifted again, from binary hybrids, recognizably inspired by individual illustrations, to more complex and 'elemental' bodies, landscapes, and bodyscapes (B. Harvey 2016, para. 5). His work still maintains the overall aesthetic of a surrealist, nineteenth-century illustration, however. These later scenes draw on wildly different themes and imagery, but in each case, like Hillier's mask portraits, they gesture towards the unconscious aspects of the subject – and the appropriated Victorian illustrations – that they depict. In 'Lunar Seas' (Figure 4.5) or 'Cellar Door' (Hillier 2015b), human outlines cut away to landscapes that seem to hint at the inner workings of their minds and imaginations. In 'Throne' (Hillier 2014a), a human figure with a lion's head presides over a scene painted into its body, of a pack of wolves running on a mountaintop. 'Untitled' (Hillier 2014b) depicts a woman in a religious pose, whose head has been expanded into a geometric pattern of nerves and blood vessels, suggesting through visceral imagery the new 'life' imagined in faith or religious experience. Here the scenes and dark detailing inside of the human silhouettes has almost completely consumed the subject, and in some cases spills out into the white space around the subject to form a background. Where Hillier's earliest images conveyed mystery and interiority through action, these images directly reveal the subject's unconscious, interior life, offering a wealth of imagery and a 'web of intertextuality' up for interpretation (G. Rose 2005, 72, 82).

Hillier illustrates his fantastical reading of historical, material reality like a picture book, unpacking and warping the various links, impacts, and repercussions of this historical visual style. Taken in chronological progression, Hillier's work seems to show the slow disembodiment of the Victorian subject, which is transformed from a physical being into something mutable, sublime, and deeply spiritual. Where absurdist artists like Ernst illustrate the collapse of human subjectivity and meaning with their juxtaposition between various images and styles, however, Hillier explores the new kinds of meaning and subjectivity that might rise up precisely in this space of juxtaposition. These meanings

Figure 4.5 'Lunar Seas' (2013) © Dan Hillier.

are monstrous in the sense that they are sublime: resisting categorization and understanding, and pointing to the boundaries of rational knowledge, language, and discourse. Hillier's combination of stylized illustration and sublime figures, projected onto a white background, transforms the commercial function or absurdist nihilism of these appropriated objects into a Gothic self-awareness that is weighty with historical imagery, but also filled with a sense of wonder. Hiller's most recent images more subtly emphasize the reading his tentacle and portrait collages suggest overtly, revealing the hidden beauty, drama, and mystery within historical material, which ultimately comes at the cost of that material's transformation into something new.

Hillier's Frankenfiction relays a Gothic history of repressed wonder and difference, in which visual representations of the Victorians sprout strange appendages, and slowly grow more overgrown, wild, and sublime. In doing so, these images reflect on their own appropriative action. They also offer one example of how a Gothic revival or exhumation of past texts can be visual, but still explicitly 'textual' or narrativizing. In this case, the politics and ethics of appropriation are still relatively straightforward, and the juxtaposition of different visual styles is rendered less jarring by the same aesthetic of Victorian illustration that naturalizes their more monstrous elements. An illustration, like a novel, is not a direct representation of a real or historical moment, and so its manipulation – a fiction building on a fiction – is arguably unlikely to shock or alienate viewers today. Each of the following works responds to the ethics and politics of appropriation, which relate steadily more closely to the aesthetics and traces of documentary photography in various ways.

Foreign animals: The immigrant portraiture of Travis Louie

Dan Hillier's visual Frankenfiction tells a sublime, Gothic story using a highly stylized and surrealist form. The resulting work makes the viewer reflect on broad themes and psychological, unconscious questions, but has little to say about the ethics or politics of specific images or epochs. The work of Travis Louie, on the other hand, directly addresses a historical gap in representation by appropriating a realist, photographic aesthetic. His work has less to do with illustration, save for the fact that it is done with a similar set of tools. Louie paints in graphite and acrylics, but approximates the science of photography. Like Hillier, Louie sells prints of his work on his website, though of the two he is more firmly situated as an independent fine artist. In the most literal sense, Louie's work is not Frankenfiction at all, if Frankenfiction must always include mashup's direct appropriation of other texts in their 'original form'. The elements Louie brings together are painted wholly by him, though models are used for certain images. He does, however, see his work as yet another iteration of the persistent need to represent the familiar and the popular in new ways. In his paintings image and text work as independent but interconnected objects, both staged as historical artefacts and played against each other to create surprising and sometimes uncanny effects. This, combined with the monstrous neo-historical world his characters occupy, brings his work back under the purview of Frankenfiction.

From the moment Louis Daguerre announced his perfection of an early photographic technique, later known as the daguerreotype, in 1839, photography and the natural sciences 'formed an immutable bond' (Nathan 2011, 379). The 'camera-as-eye analogy', highlighted by several scholars and scientists at the time, emphasizes 'the perceived veracity of photographic images', despite continued professional and technological challenges to this perception (2011, 380). Indeed, as I will discuss in the following section, from its earliest days photography was used to create fictions as well as document realities. As John Harvey writes, photography is 'at one and the same time an instrument for scientific inquiry into the visible world, and, conversely, an uncanny, almost magical process able to conjure up the semblance of shadows and, with it, supernatural associations' (2007, 7). Louie plays with the visual aesthetic of this technology in order to make precisely this argument.

Although there are many contemporary artists painting in a photorealistic style (examples include Gerhard Richter, Richard Estes and, more recently, Nicholas Middleton), and even some working in the style of Victorian photography, few apply this photorealistic technique to fantastical creatures, and none quite as successfully as Louie. Louie has been 'photographing' monsters since the early 2000s. These paintings begin with a story, written by Louie and based on his observations of strangers – for instance the 'unusual people' living in his grandmother's building in New York ('Conceptual Realism – Travis Louie' 2013, para. 1). This story can be anywhere from a few words to a few paragraphs long, after which Louie sketches his characters in graphite. Next, he applies layer after translucent layer of acrylic paint in a variety of monochromatic shades. This creates a gently glowing, almost translucent effect that mimics the way old photographic plates react to light. The finished painting (which often, like many old photographs, tends to be quite small) is then mounted in a vintage frame and displayed next to the story or phrase that inspired it. The end result is uncannily photorealistic, and were it not for the fact that the characters Louie paints are almost always fantastical, one might be inclined to assume that many of his images were in fact Victorian and Edwardian photographs (Voynovskaya 2015, para. 1). In particular, the blurred or translucent edges are reminiscent of a mid-nineteenth-century daguerreotype.

This faithful adaptation of the photograph into the painting is very intentional in Louie's case, and is something he is vocal about in many interviews. In his own words:

> There's a quality of 19th century photography that represents a simpler time. When these pictures were taken, there was still this innocence that allowed people to be fooled by simple photo retouching and double exposure techniques in 'spirit' photography or those wonderful photographs of 'fairies' staged and taken by Elsie Wright in 1917. Before photography we only had eyewitness accounts and physical evidence. When I paint my characters with a resemblance to tin types and cabinet cards, it allows them be more plausible in the mind's eye. (Leavitt 2013, para. 6)

It is this technological 'innocence' that Louie aims to recapture in his art. By setting his narratives and characters in the past, Louie authenticates them, much as a traditional costume drama or other work of historical fiction might – though of course this sense of realism is immediately broken by the fantastical subjects in the images. Still, everything Louie does in the visual part of his art contributes to this performative sense of faux-historical authenticity and earnestness. As Nastia Voynovskaya writes on the art website *Hi-Fructose*: 'Though filled with fantastical characters, [Louie's] works have an effect of verisimilitude much like historical documents from the Victorian and Edwardian periods' (2015, para. 1). Although he is a painter rather than a photographer or digital artist, by choosing portrait photography as his representational aesthetic, he also draws attention to the power of the photographic medium to establish historical authority.

Where the images themselves are whimsical, the uncanny and unfinished stories he writes about each character's past are thoroughly Gothic: repressed histories that, although they preceded the images, are presented as secondary. On some websites (including, occasionally, Louie's own) they do not appear alongside the image at all. Many are quite difficult to locate online, with a few only available through Louie's social media accounts. These 'hidden' histories often tell a very different story from the images they accompany. Where the work's visual aspect contributes to an aesthetic of historical 'verisimilitude', the fantastical subjects and attached text deliberately alienate the viewer, transforming the whole into an explicitly Gothic fiction. 'Pals' is one example of this dynamic (see Figure 4.6). Two semi-human figures stand side by side, facing the viewer head-on and clad in simple dresses with their full bodies visible. They stand against a plain background, painted at the bottom with a faint flower pattern that appears to be some kind of curtain or screen. The fact that they are holding hands and smiling leads us to assume that they are the

Figure 4.6 'Pals' (2006) © Travis Louie 'One cold December day, Herbert and Lawrence lost a bet.'

'pals' indicated by the title of the work. The caption, however, reads: 'One cold December day, Herbert and Lawrence lost a bet' (Louie 2006b). This supplies us with more information about these two characters, while itself raising additional questions. Are Herbert and Lawrence women, for instance, or was the price of the bet they lost having their portrait taken in drag? The figures' garb, as well as the shapes under the dresses, indicates a female or feminine body. The facial hair of the left figure, however, is ambiguous. Does this image represent two summer (or springtime) friends who lost a bet in December, and are thus no longer on speaking terms? The aesthetic of photographic authority and 'innocence' that Louie cultivates is deployed in a way that places it in contrast with Louie's own framing of the works in his descriptions and interviews. While the image directs viewers to 'read' the narrative one way, the caption intentionally alienates them from the image, presenting it as staged and incomplete, and pointing to a more ambiguous reading. This relationship between image and caption is consistent throughout Louie's work. The revelation of an ambiguous or dramatic past is another trope of Gothic fiction, though in the case of 'Pals' what Louie's narrative caption reveals appears relatively innocuous.

Louie describes his portraits as filling in history's visual blanks by supplementing images of white, middle-class Victorians with literal alien immigrants. Through his art he comments on our attitudes towards the foreign, and on the experience of immigration more generally. In this sense, Louie's monsters operate very much as Cohen describes, and as the monsters in mashups like *The League of Extraordinary Gentlemen* or *Penny Dreadful* also function. Here, fantastical monstrosity becomes a symbol for racial or ethnic otherness, though Louie also appeals to the 'friendly monster' trope so prevalent in twenty-first-century pop culture. Louie has explicitly tied his decision to reproduce the Victorian photographic motif to 'the immigrant experience in North America from the late 18th century through the early 20th century', which he sees as 'a convincing record of such things' (J.A. Winters 2015, para. 12). Some of his captions also place the subjects in the UK, suggesting his works actually encapsulate the Anglo-American immigrant experience, rather than just those immigrants who passed through Ellis Island. Himself a descendent of Chinese immigrants, Louie recalls seeing old, black-and-white photographs hanging in the homes of childhood friends, and wondering why his family had none. Quite simply, he discovered, his ancestors were too poor to afford this kind of historical capital, and so their image has since faded from memory (Wolfson 2011, para. 1; Meyers and Beard 2013). For Louie, this lack of retrospective representation is yet another contributor to present-day racism and discrimination (Erlanson 2009; Leavitt 2013). This perspective transforms his paintings from whimsical historical fictions into Gothic tales of historical absence.

Fittingly, around the same time that Louie began painting neo-historical monsters, a new book collecting the work of Augustus F. Sherman was published to much media interest and online scrutiny (Sherman and Mesenhöller 2005). Sherman was an amateur photographer working as Chief Registry Clerk at New York's Ellis Island from 1892 until 1925, and he photographed some of the 12 million immigrants to pass into the United States before the station closed in 1954. Many are pictured in their native dress (see 'Dutch woman', Figure 4.7). These portraits are accompanied by the subject's country of origin, and occasionally a date or additional descriptor, but no names are given. In addition to being portraits of people, then, the individuals represented by Sherman in these photographs become symbolic of a particular race, ethnicity, or nationality. Like Louie's, Sherman's images are clearly staged or posed,

Figure 4.7 'Dutch Woman' (1905) by Augustus F. Sherman, from The New York Public Library. 'Sad Miss Bunny' (2011) © Travis Louie. 'While posing for a formal portrait, young Miss Bunny had a sad feeling when her hands touched some rabbit fur. She had always wondered what had happened to her family. She never found out that they were devoured by wild dogs. At a young age, she was discovered wandering the woods outside Hastings, was adopted by a wealthy London family, and lived what many would consider a charmed life.'

ceremonial rather than candid – unlike Lewis W. Hine's factory photography, for example, which attempts to capture the working conditions of child labourers (see Hine 1908, 1911). Nevertheless, there is a certain sense of directness or frankness to Sherman's photographs that has led many commentators to regard them as documentary, with all the connotations of honesty and authenticity that this label implies. There are several important distinctions between these actual immigrant portraits and Louie's Gothic historical fictions, however.

By manipulating a realist, photographic aesthetic with paint rather than chemicals or electrical charge, Louie is engaged in an act of Gothic fakery, doubling the thing that is already an uncanny double. The uncanny, generally manifested in the form of 'a doubling, dividing and interchanging of the self [...] the repetition of the same features or character-traits or vicissitudes, of the same crimes, or even the same names through several consecutive generations' (S. Freud [1819] 2001, 233), finds a natural home in the photograph and other modern technologies of reproduction. Although Sigmund Freud himself never links photography and the uncanny, Margaret Iverson draws on Roland Barthes's *Camera Lucida* in a 1994 article to note that the 'nature of the medium as an indexical imprint of the object means that any photographed object or person has a ghostly presence, an uncanniness that might be likened to the return of the dead' (Iversen 1994, 450). Given enough time or distance, all photographs become uncanny objects of potentially Gothic significance. Here we are talking about that aspect of the uncanny (or 'un-homely') which, in Freud's words, is 'in reality nothing new or alien, but something which is familiar and old-established in the mind and which has become alienated from it only through the process of repression' ([1819] 2001, 240). Once again we find the concept of alienation on display, in a sense very similar to Brecht. By drawing attention to the photograph's status as an uncanny replication of events distanced from us by time and context, an artist or performer might comment more effectively or emotionally on the unique historical moment that created it.

Louie's use of alienation to construct a repressed and politicized historical fiction can be found at both the visual level of the portraits and the textual level of the captions. It seems quite possible that Louie is referring to Sherman's photographs when he speaks of the 'convincing record' of the North American immigrant experience. In any case, comparing his work to Sherman's produces some interesting contradictions. See Figure 4.7, in which Sherman's photograph 'Dutch Woman' is juxtaposed with Louie's painting 'Sad Miss Bunny' (elsewhere titled 'Young Miss Bunny' or simply 'Miss Bunny'). Although the subject of each of these photographs is quite different, they resonate in similar ways in terms of the response they are designed to elicit from contemporary viewers. Both are posed, in partial profile, in what appear to be clothes chosen specifically for the occasion. Both gaze hopefully into the distance, as though they are gazing towards the future (or into the past). In each image, similar lighting and costuming techniques are used to simultaneously draw attention to the subject's eyes and to a particular aspect of their otherness, encouraging both empathy and curiosity. In the case of 'Miss Bunny', it is animal ears rather than a national headdress that marks her as other. Her clothes belong to the 'neutral' realm of costume drama, which transforms middle- and upper-class fashion from across the nineteenth century into uninflected 'historical' garb.

Of course, this choice is anything but neutral. As Spooner argues in *Fashioning Gothic Bodies*, 'the body in Western culture is inarticulate except through clothes', which are 'above all a means of inserting the self into social discourse, literary or otherwise' (2004, 3). Where the Dutch woman's national clothing marks her as poor, exotic, and other, Miss Bunny's 'neutral' dress signals her successful assimilation into Western society. Her identity as a rabbit has been overwritten by her new, human identity. In a way, Louie's portraits are thus as much an image of cultural erasure as they are of historical revision. Spooner's analysis of the symbolic function of clothing in Gothic fiction also supports this reading. Citing Alexandra Warwick and Dani Cavallaro, she notes that: 'The wearing of clothes is the emblem of the obedient and improved (absented) body' (1998, 84; quoted in 2004, 12). By wearing clothes at all Miss Bunny marks herself as more than an animal or inhuman monster, and by wearing the 'right' clothes she becomes socially and culturally invisible.

The seeming neutrality of her fashion choices is deceptive, however, for Miss Bunny's body (and her past identity) is not so easily absented. As Spooner notes, '[t]he monster stands for body as garment' (2004, 11). Miss Bunny's inhuman fur serves as a symbolic national or ethnic dress in this narrative, just as the Dutch woman's literal garments, and sets her apart as other. From the caption to the image, we learn that Miss Bunny's status as a subject, rather than a commercial object, is less assured than she may know. This description relays how she was lovingly adopted into wealth by humans after her parents met a gruesome end, eaten by wild dogs. We also learn that, in a ghoulish twist, the material under her hands in the portrait is rabbit fur, which gives her 'a sad feeling' when she touches it. This Gothic revelation suggests that although she is safe for the moment, at the whims of her adoptive family she might end up in the same position as the rabbit whose fur decorates their house. The caption also relays the loss of her past and her heritage in exchange for the chance at a new life. Rather than presenting an unquestioning and utopian illustration of multiculturalism and hope, then, Louie's immigrant portraits represent a dark and troubled past, concealed through successful but still tenuous integration into a new environment, and a drastic change (and repression) of one's personal identity. In telling Miss Bunny's tragic story, rather than leaving her to the audience's visual assumptions, language also serves to humanize her – just as it does for Frankenstein's creature in Shelley's novel.

Sherman's hopeful portraits arguably also conceal a dark and oppressive past that is only briefly addressed in their 2005 reprinting. In addition to giving Americans a vivid look at the individuals who helped make up the 'great melting pot', Ellis Island station (and its portraits) also serves as a grimly reflective record of shifting attitudes towards immigrants (see Bayor 2014; Fleegler 2013; Desforges and Maddern 2004). Around 250,000 of the 12 million who attempted to enter the United States during the station's existence (1892–1954) were turned away on the grounds of disease, insanity, or criminal record. Notably, in the 1920s, the stream of immigrants was sharply restricted on the basis of national or ethnic origin, as immigrants from Southern and Eastern Europe were considered inferior to the earlier immigrants from Northern and Western Europe (see Roediger 2005). Before the station closed in the 1950s, Italian, German, and Japanese resident aliens were detained there during the Second World War. The portraiture of the 'native' and the foreign national has a complex, often tragic history in the United States.

Not all of Louie's 'monsters' are harmless, but all seem friendly, which is another key part of Louie's Gothic historical narrative. Old photographic styles have been used to create horror in many online projects,[3] but Louie's work falls well outside of this genre. In his image 'Mr. Sam' (2014b), the monster's large, pointed teeth are offset by his kind expression and the flower perched on his head. Louie is adamant that his monsters not be read as frightening (Meyers and Beard 2013; Maxwell 2015), and the same tools that he uses to create the impression of authenticity are also employed to render his monsters disarming. The soft glow produced by his acrylic layering technique and the monochromatic tones are more evocative of the tamer, more visually 'innocent' era of silent film than they are of either horror or thriller aesthetics.[4] A sense of historical time is much easier to pin down in his artwork than a geographical space, though neither is entirely straightforward from an aesthetic standpoint. This is because Louie's work frequently draws on a 1950s aesthetic as well as a Victorian one – again, a controversial period in the United States from the perspective of race relations. Here Louie is specifically interested in the future-focused imagery of the Atomic Age, and though his work has moved increasingly towards this time period, the aesthetic is often visible in his Victorian pieces as well. In 'Sea Monkey Princess' (2008), the figure's dress is Victorian, but her fins and bulbous antennae, bright lighting, and far-gazing expression echo early science fiction pulp art. In this aspect Louie's work strays from the Gothic aesthetic, though as Spooner points out in her most recent monograph, optimism and hope are becoming increasingly central to post-millennial Gothic (2017, 3). Its 'histories' are also becoming increasingly futuristic. As Dale Townshend argues, the contemporary 'notion of a "Gothic World" is [...] the disturbing vision of the monstrous future', rather than 'a vision of a glorious past world' (2014, xxxvi). The borders of this new, twenty-first-century Gothic aesthetic are still taking shape.

This same strange aesthetic, at once monstrous and hopeful, historical and futuristic, is also at work in portraits like 'The Ghost of Abigail' (2009), or 'Emily' (2006a), in which the horns, hair, and staging of the figures pictured again evokes the retro space imagery of 1960s science fiction. When combined, these two aesthetics – Atomic and Victorian – work together to create a strange and timeless nostalgia for a more hopeful moment. Aesthetically, these images do not only look backward. They are situated specifically in a past that looks forward (a *retrofuturistic* one). Louie confirms this aesthetic, writing: 'I almost get that sense that people were more hopeful about the future in North America than they are now and that played into a sense of wonder that is very important to me' (J.A. Winters 2015, para. 12). It is their hope that makes his paintings futuristic more generally, even as they draw on problematic pasts. In the caption for 'Sea Monkey Princess' (2008), for instance, we are told that Lady Abigail (no relation to the Abigail Fitzsimmons in 'The Ghost of Abigail') is the last of the royal line, hinting that some disaster befell her family or her people. Her short life is spent managing and avoiding 'royal intrigue', in which she is disinterested. Her image – bright, soft, and warm – shows no trace of this tragedy. Lady Abigail's eyes look away from the camera, the corner of her mouth ever-so-slightly upturned in a smile. The viewer can only imagine she is thinking about spending 'her days with her briny relatives, blowing bubbles and exploring': an imagined future she will never experience, but enjoys forever in this frozen moment.

Louie's retro portraiture can be split into two broad categories: monster portraits and companion species portraits. As we have seen, the first category places monsters and otherworldly creatures (singular or plural) at the fore. Louie's second type of painting, the companion species portrait, also draws on a Gothic aesthetic. These portraits feature a human figure and an animalistic or alien one together, in a configuration that indicates curiosity, friendship, or symbiosis. In paintings like 'The Thompson' (2013b), 'Dorothy and her Damsel Fly' (2011a), 'Miss Lucy and Her Hat Monkey' (2013a), or 'The Family Yeti' (2011c), darkly-attired Victorians pose with their companion animals. Unlike Louie's monster portraits, these images depict a relationship between humans and their monsters that examines Victorian attitudes of exploration and curiosity. While the images themselves often suggest that it is the humans who rule over the monsters, the accompanying captions add an additional layer of ambiguity. In the caption for 'The Thompson', a monster is discovered in Harry Thompson's backyard and named after him in traditional nineteenth-century fashion. From Louie's painting, however, it is unclear who is the monster and who is Harry Thompson. The giant creature depicted lays a hand on the human figure in a possessive gesture, hinting that it may be the man (not the monster) who was 'unearthed by workers who were installing a slate patio' (Louie 2013b).

Like Miss Bunny, the animals and monsters in these companion species portraits are painted both literally and figuratively as immigrants, exiles, objects of colonial conquest. In each caption, however, the question of who is the conqueror and who the prize is made uncertain. For instance, several paintings in this series follow the tale of Oscar Pennington, 'the foremost cryptozoologist in the 19th century' (Louie 2014c). Oscar's life and explorations are full of monsters. The first painting, 'Oscar and the Truth Toad' (2011b), tells us that in 1895 'a large toad broke into Oscar's house'. Oscar could not rid himself of this toad, but upon discovering that it compelled people nearby to tell the truth, he took to wearing it on his head. Oscar's further adventures include his photography of the giant 'Bat of Exmoor' (2015a), the eventual acquisition of another monster in Malaysia (a giant tarsier that 'attached itself to Oscar and for the next 27 years, it did not leave his side'; see Figure 4.8), and an encounter with the 'Miss Emily Fowler & Her Spider' sideshow (2014a), among many others (Louie 2015b). In 'Oscar and the Giant Tarsier' (Figure 4.8), Oscar poses with his furry Malaysian companion in a manner evocative of Victorian hunting photographs, but the tarsier looks much more triumphant about Oscar's discovery than Oscar does. All the paintings in this series tell a story of Oscar's imperial conquests that echoes many familiar nineteenth-century narratives, but each ultimately demonstrates how he is mastered by the creatures he discovers, rather than the other way around. In these and other companion portraits, then, Victorian capitalist and colonialist stereotypes are often reversed, lending the images a post-colonial air as well as a fantastical one.

Louie's Gothic historical fictions depict the past as a place that is sometimes dark and dangerous, but paradoxically it is also one of inherent optimism, where we can live in harmony with strange creatures. In these companion animal paintings, as in Louie's monster portraits, the aesthetics of realist historical documentation are appropriated first to draw in, then to alienate the viewer, in

Figure 4.8 'Oscar and the Giant Tarsier' (2014) © Travis Louie. 'Oscar Pennington was a naturalist and was known as the foremost cryptozoologist in the nineteenth century. Early on in his career, many of his colleagues disagreed with his theories and practices. They characterized his field of study as "searching for faerie tales". After the incident with the "truth toad", he managed to alienate himself from the London zoological society. Undaunted, he set out in the Spring of 1847 to follow reports of a giant mammal that was thought to be extinct. Upon his arrival in a small village in the kingdom of Sarawak in Borneo, he met up with English adventurer, James Brooke. Together, they were able to track down the legendary creature known as Tarsius Praegrandis or simply the giant Tarsier. They were able to find a colony of them in the Northern region in what is now known as Malaysia. A rather larger specimen attached itself to Oscar and for the next twenty-seven years, it did not leave his side.'

order to comment upon the gaps in other visual histories. Colin Batty, the next artist I will discuss, takes a very different approach to both the photographic aesthetic and the ethics of visual historiography.

Meet the family: Colin Batty's Victorian cabinet cards

Colin Batty is a British sculptor and painter primarily known for his work on Hollywood films. The website that hosts his work claims that he 'sculpted the original Halcyon model kits of the Alien, the Predator, and the Queen Alien', linking him to H.R. Giger, whom I mentioned in my discussion of Dan Hillier's work (Wellins n.d., para. 1). Batty's previous work includes Paul Berry's short film adaptation *The Sandman* (1991), reworking a classic Gothic tale that Freud also discusses extensively in his essay on the uncanny. Batty has also worked on a number of Tim Burton's projects, specifically *Mars Attacks!* (1996) and *The Corpse Bride* (2005), meaning he has been a part of creating the camp-but-creepy 'Burton' aesthetic that Spooner describes as increasingly influential on contemporary Gothic (Spooner 2017, 66). This affiliation occasionally shows in his work as well. The figure in Batty's piece 'Brainiac and Son' (Batty 2014c), for example, bears a strong resemblance to the aliens from *Mars Attacks!*, for which Batty sculpted the original model of the head.

At the beginning of this chapter, I referred to Mitchell's metaphor of the photograph as a spiritualist medium. At photography's birth in the early nineteenth century, she writes, 'it was greeted as a ghostly medium that could supplement memory, function as time's receptacle, and pledge to remember in the face of loss' (Mitchell 2008, 82). In the case of Victorian practices like spirit photography, this idea becomes more literal. My introduction to Louie's art suggested that photography was an emblem of an authentic and scientific reality, but as John Harvey argues, both '[s]piritualists and scientists claimed to be able to see and visualize otherwise invisible and intangible realms' (2007, 72). Likewise, there are many examples of Victorian photography that are expressly fictional and fantastical – the Pre-Raphaelite photographer Julia Margaret Cameron, who staged scenes from contemporary poetry and classical mythology, and whose images accompanied Alfred Tennyson's *Idylls of the King and Other Poems* (1875) as illustrations, is just one example.

In addition to revealing the unseen and unexplored for science, photography also attempted to penetrate the veil between the physical and the metaphysical. Victorian customers paid death-bed photographers for portraits of their recently deceased children and family members, and spirit photographers for a glimpse at the ghosts and other spiritual beings that they believed shared their material plane. Pre-photographic depictions of spirits and the dead may have commonly 'served as didactic images, designed to stir, sober and encourage onlookers to prepare for death, flee from sin and fear judgement' (J. Harvey 2007, 21-2). Death-bed, and especially spirit photographs, in contrast, may have 'helped turn grief into belief, and enabled the bereaved not only to come to terms with their loss but also to know with certainty that the great divide that separated them from the departed could be bridged' (J. Harvey 2007, 58). Photography as a medium was still associated with authority and reality, then, but in this case what it claimed to reveal went beyond physical reality.

At first glance, some of Batty's more recent work is strikingly reminiscent of spirit photography. His project 'Meet the Family' uses over a hundred cabinet cards: postcard-style portraits popular from the late nineteenth century (circa 1870) to the end of the First World War. Cabinet cards served a number of functions, but often acted as a kind of calling card or memento, kept as souvenirs, given or posted to friends, or left behind to indicate the person depicted on the card had visited. These vintage cards depict real people, now long dead, in highly staged poses. Batty was able to purchase a number of these cabinet cards in bulk from a thrift store (Hardison 2014, 1). He paints ghosts, monsters, pop culture icons, and various absurd objects directly onto the cabinet cards, matching the style of the existing black-and-white image. These revised cards depict nineteenth-century figures, sometimes in the presence of a ghostly or demonic figure; at other times part of their head or body is obscured by a supernatural object, or a relic of another time and place. As in spirit photographs we often find 'manifestations of partial ghosts – incomplete by virtue of appearing either headless or as a head only [...] or else to a certain extent hidden, truncated or obscured' (J. Harvey 2007, 16). Both the physical cards and their digital reproductions are currently displayed in and sold through the Peculiarium Gallery, a kitsch curiosities museum in Oregon which also markets Batty's work online. This exhibition venue has the added effect of paratextually framing the cards as a conspiracy magazine discovery, or a freak show exhibition.

Batty's cabinet cards are intended to be overtly fake, or even patently ridiculous. Consider 'Blobby McGee' (Figure 4.9). Because of the way sections of the woman's body have been painted out, and other sections have been added, in her new form she resembles a human lava lamp – an invention that would not exist for more than a century. This absurdist aesthetic echoes Batty's other independent work, which often involves garishly coloured caricatures of well-known people and characters. Like Louie and Hillier, Batty's work engages with the fantastical and the supernatural, but his cartoonish exaggeration of real people's existing features distinguishes him from these artists. Their subjects may be monstrous, but are highly stylized in terms of composition in a way that situates them more firmly in the traditional world of illustration or fine art. Likewise, though his work is strongly alienating, Batty often employs the comic mode rather than the uncanny to achieve this effect. Batty's cabinet cards ultimately make monstrous caricatures of the people depicted. Each image exaggerates features already implicitly present. On one markedly unaltered card, Batty transforms an unusually photogenic and wholesome-looking man into Superman (Batty 2014m). In some images, Batty's caricatures are overtly satirical, toeing the line between comedy and offence. One card takes a married couple who originally looked 'very much alike, and rather formal', and turns one – the wife – into a hand puppet (Bromwich 2015, margin notes). Batty comments that '[w]hich one is operating which is open to debate, I think' (Bromwich 2015, margin notes). This statement is clearly intended to satirize a stereotypical (and rather misogynistic) view of marriage. In Batty's own words, the cabinet cards 'suggest their own stories', but what we see in his revisions are clearly his own 'readings' of the images (Bromwich 2015, para. 1). As with Louie's paintings, this adds a narrative element to the artwork, though where Louie's monsters are inviting, in Batty's case it is the cabinet cards that represent the uncanny 'ghostly presence […] the return of the dead' (Iversen 1994, 450), while his monstrous alterations provide the parodic, often satirical narrative.

Despite this element of visual comedy and frequent absence of horror, Batty's work is still resolutely Gothic. In the previous chapter I discussed the way the Gothic employs the comic mode to mock and revise its own tradition. As part of that discussion, I referenced Avril Horner and Sue Zlosnik, who write:

> [P]arody can offer Gothic a comic turn. This turn frequently allows a fresh perspective on a changing world, one of accommodation rather than terrified apprehension [… by] offering a measure of detachment from scenes of pain and suffering that would be disturbing in a different Gothic context. (Horner and Zlosnik 2005, 12–13)

By this analysis, Gothic comedy would serve the opposite function to Brecht's alienation effect, drawing the viewer's attention away from historical drama and emotion rather than towards it. Of course, in Batty's cabinet cards, the subjects are generally white, well-to-do, and seemingly free of pain or suffering. Instead, it is Batty who inserts the element of disturbing otherness, monstrosity, or

Figure 4.9 'Blobby McGee' (2014) © Colin Batty. Courtesy of Peculiarium.

suffering into the images. Batty's is predominantly a popular, visual comedy that borrows the superficial stock imagery of the Gothic, not a literary, textual one that draws unironically on Gothic modes and themes. This is reflected in the images he creates.

In each cabinet card, Batty caricatures Gothic themes and subjects, including monsters, history, traditional gender roles, and the secret family past. Some cards transform their subjects into classic horror monsters that the Victorians themselves created, like the werewolf in 'Wolfman Jacket', and Frankenstein's creature in 'Frankenvintage Seated' (Figure 4.10; Batty 2014q, 2014h). However, the representations of these characters are drawn from their twentieth-century iterations, and not from the Victorian tales and illustrations that introduced them. This causes the viewer to reflect on the irony that the monsters for which the Victorians are best known are not *visibly* Victorian, and were in fact only secured as popular icons by later, cinematic revivals. These images are now the ones we, and the Victorian figures in these two cabinet cards, must respond to. Kamilla Elliott describes this as a 'Gothic triptych' (i.e. a folding artwork consisting of three parts, hinged together), through which a foundational adaptation can 'look back to earlier Gothic films and forward to later ones' (Elliott 2008, 30, 26). So 'Frankenvintage Seated' (for instance) is really an adaptation of James Whale's 1931 *Frankenstein*, which itself looks back to Shelley's text.

Some of Batty's images make a more direct visual link to a Victorian past, and at these moments, when the images verge into the spiritual and the mystical rather than the comic, they are less abrasively satirical. Cards like 'Chimp Siblings' or 'Elephant Dude', invite comparisons to well-known Victorian freaks like Stephan Bibrowski (a.k.a. 'Lionel the Lion-faced Boy'), or Joseph Merrick the 'Elephant Man' (Batty 2014e, f).[5] Still others, as indicated above, draw inspiration from Victorian spirit photography, or from 1950s images of alien sightings (Batty 2014a, i, o). One image, 'Two Ladies and a Thing', bears an especially strong and disconcerting resemblance to a post-mortem photograph (Figure 4.11). When Batty's images most closely – and thus nostalgically – mimic Victorian spirit photography, avoiding anachronistic caricature, the alienation is just enough to produce an awareness of the image's context and mediated nature, but not enough to provoke distancing laughter or scorn.

Several images satirically reference conservative ideas about femininity and domesticity, depicting Victorian women as robots or puppets to convey a lack of mobility, autonomy, or personhood (see Batty 2014g, k). At the same time, however, they draw the viewer's attention to the fact that these historical issues remain relevant. In 'Fembot', for instance, the female subject's head has become detached, suspended from a series of metallic tubes and revealing robotic cables inside. The caricature is inspired by the insinuation that the Victorian

Figure 4.10 'Frankenvintage Seated' (2014) © Colin Batty. Courtesy of Peculiarium.

woman is a metaphorical 'robot', empty of human feeling and a slave to social programming. This image also evokes continuing depictions of the female body as robotic servant in film and television, however, from Fritz Lang's *Metropolis* (1927) to the retro-futuristic Hanna-Barbara cartoon *The Jetsons* (1962–87), to

Figure 4.11 'Two Ladies and a Thing' (2014) © Colin Batty. Courtesy of Peculiarium.

Alex Garner's 2014 thriller *Ex Machina*. That such images remain relevant is indicative of the state of Western gender roles more broadly.

In fact, most of Batty's gendered satires address present-day society, rather than teasing out historical issues. In another set of cabinet cards, 'Melissa Muscles' and 'Captain Clevage [*sic*]', the subject's head has been transposed onto the body of an apparently different gender (Batty 2014d, 1). The first image bears a similarity to vintage images of circus strongmen, and the second is visually resonant of mid-twentieth-century pinups, rendered incongruous by the subject's luxurious moustache. Both images also echo Marcel Duchamp's gender-bending 'readymades' – for example *L.H.O.O.Q., or La Joconde* (1964), in which Duchamp has drawn a goatee onto Leonardo Da Vinci's *Mona Lisa* (1503–6). Not only are the bodies in Batty's cards incongruous with the subject's visibly masculine or feminine facial features, these revealing images and twentieth-century references are incongruous with the stereotypical Victorian prudery imagined by twenty-first-century audiences. Batty's titles for the cabinet cards, which alliterate like a cartoon character's, also contribute to the ridiculous tone his work creates. Of course, the 'joke' of these images only works because gendered body norms persist in the twenty-first century. By constructing these images as ridiculous, then, Batty draws attention to the problematic depictions of gender that populate the contemporary media landscape. This is an absurdist move rather than a didactic one, but Batty's cabinet cards still hint at a regressive link between the past and the present. If one looks hard enough, his caricatures suggest, we will see ourselves, our strange cultures, and our own flaws reflected in the images of our past. We are our own freak show.

Batty reinforces this idea by framing his cards as a family photo album. The photobook collection of his cabinet cards, edited by Mike Wellins and Lisa Freeman, contains little background or introduction to the work contained within its pages. It does, however, include an epigraph and postscript which help to give the collection some context. The epigraph, attributed to American novelist Mark Twain, reads 'A man with a hump-backed uncle mustn't make fun of another's cross-eyed aunt' (Wellins and Freeman 2014, epigraph). This is part of a longer excerpt from an interview, published in the *New York World* on 11 May 1879, in which Twain explains why he never wrote a book about England:

> I have spent a good deal of time in England [...] and I made a world of notes, but it was of no use. [...] No, there wasn't anything to satirize – what I mean is, you couldn't satirize any given thing in England in any but a half-hearted way, because your conscience told you to look nearer home and you would find that very thing at your own door. A man with a hump-backed uncle mustn't make fun of another's cross-eyed aunt. (Twain 1997, 111)

Although it is possible that the use of this epigraph refers to the British origin of the cabinet cards, it more likely suggests a motivation for Batty's alienating imagery. Rather than acting from some urge to preserve history or write immigrant identities back into public memory, as Travis Louie does, Batty's caricatures suggest that 'we' – the white, Western public – were as barbaric and ridiculous then as we are now, and we may as well laugh at this fact.

The photobook's postscript presents a similar reading of Batty's images. Attributed to another British novelist, Dodie Smith, it states: 'The family – that dear octopus from whose tentacles we never quite escape, nor, in our inmost hearts, ever quite wish to' (Wellins and Freeman 2014, postscript). This sentence forms part of a toast in Smith's play *Dear Octopus* (1938), which depicts the relationships between three generations of a large family, going back well into the nineteenth century. In the context of Batty's work, this citation seems to suggest that instead of trying to escape history, we might approach it in a spirit of generosity, enabled not by temporal distance from our strange ancestors, but by our awkward identification with them, through laughter at them.

A handful of Batty's images abandon both caricature and Victorian imitation to create a surreal character more comparable with Louie's work (Batty 2014b, n), or with Hillier's (Batty 2014j, p). 'Snake Boy', in particular, echoes the stylization and motion of Hillier's 'Snake', or Beardsley's 'The Black Cape' (Batty 2014p). Although both Batty and Louie paint photographic approximations of historical moments, however, a dramatic difference between the two is that, unlike Louie, Batty's work has no clear ethical goal, positioning itself on the side of nihilistic absurdism. At first glance, Batty's images seem to possess the 'posture of critique, even assault' that Sanders attributes to appropriative works (2006, 4). While Batty's cabinet cards often satirize their subjects at a narrative level, in terms of style and form most are pure camp, suggesting 'that however reflexive we are we will only know reflexivity' (Travers 1993, 128). It is difficult to find the moral commentary in an image like 'Blobby McGee', which, to appropriate Jerome de Groot's description of historical exploitation, seems to be 'wrong just to be wrong' (de Groot 2016, 176). Rather than appealing to the realism of the photographic aesthetic, Batty turns to its spectrality and sensationalism. Despite this turn his work demonstrates none of the deeper aesthetic significance Hiller's does, however. His cabinet cards represent an act of pure, transgressive pleasure.

Batty's caricature of past artefacts clearly places his cabinet cards within de Groot's definition of historical exploitation, though they are still relatively inoffensive when compared to a sexually explicit or violently graphic television programme like *Spartacus: Blood and Sand* (which de Groot cites as an example of the genre). Just as Batty's impressions of these photographic subjects inspired his manipulations of their cabinet cards, however, so his alienating caricatures inevitably lead the viewer to speculate about the lives, personalities, and stories of the individuals depicted. Of course, Batty's acts of historical appropriation are much more Frankensteinian in this respect than those of the other artists I have discussed. Those depicted on the cabinet cards certainly do not 'ask' to be remade in monstrous fashion. Although cabinet cards were not expressly intended to serve as private images, they were *personal* ones. Since the nineteenth century photography has developed as 'a medium through which individuals confirm and explore their identity, that sense of selfhood which is an indispensable feature of a modern sensibility' (Holland 2004, 119). Although these cabinet cards no longer 'belong' to anyone, in the sense that they were discarded or sold, and the subjects anonymous and forgotten, they still display the likeness of real people, to the extent that appropriating them feels almost like appropriating that person's identity. This also raises the question of what should be done with historical traces and remains after those they represent are gone. In this case, we have little access to the original context or creative decisions behind the images, as they were never archived or entered into historical record, passing from a thrift store bargain bin straight into Batty's creative control.

In many cases, these photographs are the last remaining historical trace of that individual's life. Where Dan Hillier's art erodes and defaces Victorian illustrations through digital reproduction, those images still exist elsewhere in their unaltered forms. Colin Batty paints directly onto the cabinet cards, destroying the artefact as he reinterprets it and effectively painting that individual out of history even as he paints them into art. He creates historical absence, rather than filling in historical blanks as Louie does. Charlotte Cory, another cabinet card artist who creates her mashups digitally rather than physically, refers to the frequent 'claims of the photographer printed proudly on the back – often in French to enhance the aura of artistry: "Les clichés sont conserves"; "Negatives are always kept"; "Copies may always be had"' (Cory 2007, 2). Of course, in most cases this is no longer true, as the photographer's shop has long since gone out of business, and the cards themselves are 'preserved for a posterity that is no longer interested' (2007, 2). In the case of Batty's cards even the 'original' copy is no more. And yet, while we might argue that Victorian illustration and the photographic aesthetic have become part of 'Heritage Gothic' (Spooner 2006, 34), losing their signifying potential and becoming the 'clay' of *Paradise Lost* rather than the recognizable limbs and organs of *Frankenstein*, the same cannot quite be said of the actual, historical object of the photograph. We still feel a twinge at the thought of these likenesses being defaced or lost. In Batty's case, the 'freak show' parody his cabinet cards enact is ultimately acceptable because his subjects are white, Western, and middle class, but also safely anonymous. This sets it apart from the work of the fourth and final artist in this chapter, Kevin J. Weir.

Flux machine: Kevin J. Weir's animated horrors

Based on the various definitions I have offered for Gothic historical fiction, the work of the fourth and final artist in this chapter, Kevin J. Weir, is simultaneously the least and the most Gothic. It is the least Gothic because, as per Diana Wallace's distinction between the Gothic and other historical fiction, visually it is the one least grounded in 'the fantastic, the supernatural, and (ironically) the "fictional" in the sense of the invented or imaginary' (2013, 3). Although Weir's work tells a fantastical story, the images he utilizes are all from the genre of documentary history, taken from the Library of Congress' public domain archives. Overriding this historical realism, however, is how Weir's GIF art brings these images together into a story, literalizing Baldick's claim that the Gothic's 'historical fears derive from our inability to convince ourselves that we have really escaped from the tyrannies of the past' (1992, xxii). It is also the least transformative of the four bodies of work, because Weir simply combines existing images and animates them. In some cases he simply animates the background of a single image (Cocozza 2014, para. 1). The end result of Weir's appropriation is ultimately all the more ghoulish and surreal precisely because it is grounded in the real, and the photographic. Rather than 'writing' new histories, Weir simply animates existing ones.

There are few comparable bodies of work to be found in contemporary visual art. Short for 'graphics interchange format', the GIF medium generally uses the comic mode, rather than the Gothic one (Uhlin 2014, 522). GIFs are also slowly becoming a favoured medium among fine artists (2014, 518), who depict more dramatic or abstract scenes, but nothing quite as historically appropriative as Weir's work. Rob Walker, the creator of the Victorian Cut-Out Theatre, appropriates Victorian illustrations to make short, narrative comedies, but these are again very different in tone and aesthetic to Weir's photographically based GIFs. The closest one comes to approximating these GIFs is in the very earliest short films, like those of George Albert Smith (1864–1959), which seldom ran longer than a minute and contained no sound. Although GIFs represent a relatively recent addition to the world of art, in many respects they *are* essentially short, silent films on a continuous loop. In Weir's words, they are the 'shortest of stories' (Cocozza 2014, para. 2), though as I will demonstrate, they differ from short films in at least one important way.

Weir's project, *The Flux Machine*, began not as an expressly artistic endeavour, but as an attempt to improve his Photoshop skills (O'Reilly and Heilpern 2016). He works as a full-time designer in advertising, and though his *Flux Machine* GIFs began as a hobby, they have since led to new commercial opportunities as well. For his animations, which each take around a week to build, Weir draws 80–100 frames in Photoshop, 'cutting things out into layers, moving them a little bit, making a new layer, moving that a little bit' until the moving image can be compiled (Cocozza 2014, para. 1). The end result is an endlessly looped video that is between ten and twenty seconds long, shared freely on Weir's website. Because the images he uses are all from iconic historical archives, Weir is able to use the uncanny, repetitive qualities of the GIF medium to show viewers an endlessly repeated historical moment, disrupted by the tools, tropes, and figures of Gothic alienation to produce the appropriate sensations of surprise and horror in response.

Weir's work often lacks the degree of warmth, whimsy, or comedy found in the other artists' projects. His monsters are not friendly like Louie's, nor are they stylized and sublime like Hillier's. He also does not attempt to critique our nostalgia for a better past through absurdist caricature, as does Batty. Weir's aesthetics have been unfavourably compared to the Monty Python cartoons of Terry Gilliam, particularly in several images that involve anthropomorphized buildings (Weir 2012g; see the comments section in Cocozza 2014), but these comparisons, though understandable, are ultimately unjustified. In addition to being black and white – unlike much of Gilliam's work, which is in vivid technicolour – Weir's images are far grimmer in tone than Gilliam's, lacking the satirical elements that they maintain. Although Weir's GIFs do not generally appropriate personal photographs, the publicity that war photographs receive as objects of shared cultural memory renders them problematic on a different, often more powerful level. It is precisely this devotion to emotional authenticity and photographic realism that makes Weir's work such a disturbingly effective illustration of the Gothic's troubled relationship with the past. These images do not represent a new kind of monstrosity or aesthetic. They are simply another iteration – another performance – of old ones.

The sense of alienation and uncanniness in Weir's work has three primary sources. Firstly, his images are familiar: the 'homely' to the uncanny's 'un-homely' (*unheimlich*). Unlike the other three artists in this chapter, Weir uses

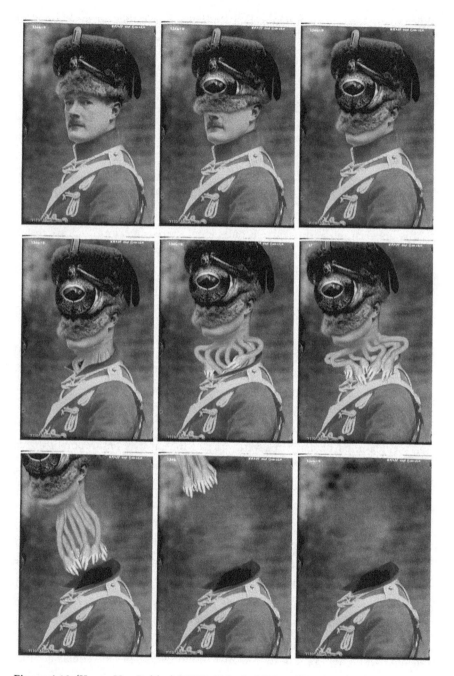

Figure 4.12 'Krupp Von Bohlen' (2012) © Kevin J. Weir. GIF expanded for still reproduction.

images of well-known people and events, which are easily traceable in the Library of Congress archives. Each GIF starts as a single, still image, and many of the characters depicted are named, historical figures (Weir 2011, 2012a, d). Their names and faces are may well be known to contemporary viewers, though their images represent a kind of familiarity that belongs to the realm of public memory and history, rather than personal recollection. When the images move, usually only after several seconds, this initial sense of familiarity is disrupted. In 'Krupp Von Bohlen' (Figure 4.12), for instance, a giant eye opens in the subject's face, which then proceeds to sprout a dozen legs and leap away from the neck, out of frame. This renders the image uncanny both through movement, an attribute not normal to the photographic medium, and through the monsters and fantastical images it reveals. Still images and objects are also less threatening than moving ones – as Victor Frankenstein recounts, what was beautiful before he imbued his creature with the spark of life became monstrous once it begins to stir (Shelley [1831] 2015, 48). This uncanny movement is also a key narrative element. In a piece called 'Doberitz', for example, if the GIF is broken down into still images it becomes virtually impossible to even see the monster's hand emerging from the laundry chute (Weir 2012e). Movement literally makes the horror happen. In the case of these old documentary photographs, animation has much the same effect as colouration might, making the images feel less temporally distant and thus (when they contain graphic or disturbing images) more shocking. Although films certainly existed in the time these photographs were taken, we are not used to seeing moving images from this period, whereas still photographs commonly feature in news reports, on memorials, and in other regular, commemorative media. When the images are made to move, then, the moment becomes startlingly 'real' to the viewer, closer to our own contemporary forms of mediation.

Secondly, in addition to using images of familiar people, Weir strays from the nineteenth century into the twentieth, and into the iconic genre of wartime photography. These images are already ominous, not only because they are historic and uncannily familiar, but because of the horrific events the photographed scenes represent. Those pictured in images like 'Peekskill', 'Doberitz', or 'Decoy Howitzer' (Weir 2012c, e, f) have since died, for instance, perhaps even on the battlefield. With the animation and combination of these images with fantastical elements, viewers experience these past horrors through the lens of historical fiction, but without the use of a single 'original' image. Like the wartime scenes, the monsters, ghosts, and other figures that populate Weir's GIFs are taken from the Library of Congress' stock image library (Cocozza 2014, para. 4).[6] This arguably makes Weir's historical fictions the most unsettling, and certainly the most Gothic, of the four artists. As Weir describes, the images have also 'gotten a little dark' as he has increasingly researched the 'actual history' of the appropriated photographs (de Bruin-Molé 2016, para. 10). In other words, the more Weir learns of the historical context of the images, the more effectively he can adapt his animations to reflect that context, and to convey the Gothic horror they capture. Ironically, his initial selection of the images for his project was more random – they were easily available, copyright-free, and offered a dramatic, visual tension that invited interpretation. This again speaks to the ethics and responsibility of archived material. Is it the photographer who should be concerned with the legacy of their images, or the person who appropriates them? Richard Huyda has suggested that more could be done by the archivist to protect photographs from 'misrepresentation and distortion by the user in whatever ways possible', including more contextual and technical detail in standard cataloguing procedures to help ensure that images are not taken out of context (Huyda 1977, 12). In practice, we not all creators, recorders, and users are equally dependable in this regard. Ultimately, the burden of responsibility lies with us all. Weir's is a borderline case – his appropriations of these historical images are not openly disrespectful or satirical of those pictured, as are Batty's. The potential is there for the material to be misappropriated and abused, however.

Finally, each of Weir's GIFs also gestures towards a sense of historical repetition more generally. In each image, the ghostly traces of those soldiers and events depicted are never at rest. Instead, they are caught in an uncanny, Gothic repetition. In 'Decoy Howitzer', for instance, the moment of a soldier's death is replayed over and over again (Figure 4.13). A dark mist spills out of the nearby cannon before resolving itself into a dark double of the soldier, stealing his own 'ghost' or life force, and dragging him out of frame. The historical soldier depicted in the image may well have survived the battle, but here he becomes emblematic of the millions who died in the trenches of the First World War, some by this very cannon. This creates a sense of fascination and horror, as the viewer is forced to consider the historical impact of this moment *ad infinitum*. It also represents an engagement with the abject, through the visual encounter with the corpse – in this case literal rather than implied. Evoking Brecht, Julia Kristeva compares such encounters with a theatre performance, where 'as in true theater, without makeup or masks, refuse and corpses *show me* what I permanently thrust aside in order to live' (1982, 3, original emphasis).

Figure 4.13 'Decoy Howitzer' (2012) © Kevin J. Weir. GIF expanded for still reproduction.

Going back to Baldick's comments on the effects of Gothic history, Weir's images literalize the fearful idea that the 'price of liberty [...] is eternal vigilance' (1992, xxii). To avoid repeating the past we are forced, horrifically, to return to it, and to re-live it continually. And re-live it we do: Weir's *Flux Machine* has received hundreds of thousands of visitors, and currently has more than 2,500 backlinks from other websites. As I mentioned above, the *Flux Machine* project has led to similar, commercial work for Weir as well, including a series of mock-historical GIFs for the film *Miss Peregrine's Home for Peculiar Children* (2016) – another Tim Burton project (Weir 2016). In a sense, then, these images are also part of the broader spectacle of war created through popular history and fiction. This spectacle glorifies barbarism even as it depicts it, turning it into a product of Gothic consumerism that provokes 'a gleeful shudder even as we congratulate ourselves on the collective progress of humanity' (Spooner 2006, 20).

Not only does Weir effectively convey historical horror through Gothic reproduction, he also does so in a way that is resolutely digital. This has a number of narrative and aesthetic repercussions. For instance, what Weir particularly likes about the GIF format is how 'it allows you both to use suspense and to freeze one moment' (Cocozza 2014, para. 8). The idea of suspense may initially seem to run counter to the looped nature of the GIF, which repeats the same series of images over and over again. By manipulating the length of time at the end of each loop, however, Weir creates a moment of calm in the image, in which everything returns to normal. This pause between loops sometimes extends to as much as eight seconds. Before every loop of the gif exists a moment where the viewer wonders whether things might turn out differently. As interviewer Paula Cocozza notes, however, 'it is just a moment of illogical hope' (2014, para. 8). The cycle cannot be changed.

As Quéma writes of H.R. Giger's Gothic images, the 'viewer is trapped in that fantastic moment of hesitation […] Although the means of representation are mimetic, the framed misshapen reflection undermines the principle of mimetic reproduction' (2007, 99). Despite the realist quality of the still images Weir appropriates, in a Todorovian moment of fantastical hesitation between the uncanny and the marvellous, the viewer is repeatedly thrown into uncertainty. In 'Peekskill' (Figure 4.14), for instance, it takes a full seven seconds for the image to move. On the first viewing, during this period the viewer's gaze is focused on the foreground, and the four soldiers dug in to the side of the hill. By the time the movement in the background begins to draw the viewer's eye, two of the soldiers have already been reduced to skeletons. The GIF quickly completes its animation loop, in which the passing monster consumes the souls of the other two soldiers, transforming them into skeletons as well (which takes around two seconds), followed by a three-second pause and a fade to black. Then the sequence repeats again. On the second viewing, the seven-second wait feels much longer, because now the viewer is focussed on the background, caught in motionless hesitation while they await confirmation that what they think they have seen is 'true'. Weir's GIFs trap the viewer in a single past moment, which is repeated over and over again. His images are thus fantastical and Gothic in a way only the GIF can achieve, because through alienation they approximate moments and objects that are mimetically un-representable. Graig Uhlin, for instance, argues that the GIF's 'repetition indicates that a viewer is not guided along by a narrative structuring of time. The viewer is rather caught up in the GIF's temporal suspension: to view it is to be captivated' (2014, 520).

Like Louie, Weir does not automatically turn to the familiar archetypes or popular monsters that Hillier or Batty might use. 'Bangor Fire' and 'Peekskill' feature shadowy monsters that are more productively compared to internet horror figures like the Slender Man than to classical or Victorian monsters (Weir 2012b, c). Weir does explicitly rely on familiar images and emotions, however.

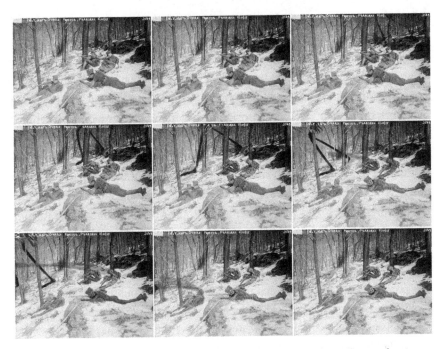

Figure 4.14 'Peekskill' (2012) © Kevin J. Weir. GIF expanded for still reproduction.

This is another function of the GIF. Uhlin cites the way short GIF loops often serve to summarize the emotional content of entire film and television scenes, within the animistic context of early cinema criticism:

> Just as the totemic object serves as a visual, material emblem of that which cannot be held, or grasped in its totality – that is, the spirit of the forest – the GIF animation stands in for what is unable to be circulated. They are tokens of spectatorship; they retain the memory of the spectatorial experience beyond its initial encounter.
>
> [...]
>
> Its meaning is generally not ambiguous. Rather, geared for maximum impact and immediacy of effect, GIFs do not depend on contextual cues to be understood. (Uhlin 2014, 520, 523)

To illustrate what is meant by this statement, I will again turn to 'Decoy Howitzer' (Figure 4.13) as an example. In the first frame, before the GIF begins to move, the original image already has an emotional resonance that is associated with its status as a wartime photograph. Weir takes this emotion and animates it, forcing the viewer to watch the soldier's essence repeatedly being stolen by a monstrous force. This transforms it into a totemic representation of the event it depicts. Now, regardless of whether or not this soldier died on the battlefield, his image has become emblematic of the fallen soldier, the horrific loss of life brought about by the First World War, and of war more broadly. It no longer depends on historical context to convey this particular historical emotion. This transformation, combined with the original image's age (i.e. outside living memory), gives Weir's GIFs a sense of horror without also provoking an ethical objection, like images of London's burning Grenfell Tower or the 9/11 'Falling Man' might.[7]

Ripping such emblematic images out of their original historical context, only to translate them into a medium usually reserved for comic gestures and facial expressions, could well be seen as ethically objectionable. But in turning such a moment into a performance of perpetual alienation, a GIF also allows the spectator to notice the moment's unique emotional resonance, and to appropriate this for their own ends. Drawing on Laura Mulvey's definition of the 'possessive spectator', a cinephile who appropriates publicity stills in 'an act of violence against the cohesion of a story, the aesthetic integrity that holds it together, and the vision of its creator' (2006, 171), Uhlin explains why GIFs do not fall into this same category. Specifically, GIFs appropriate the images of familiar people and situations, but these are *meant* to be shared out of context. Unlike publicity stills, GIF creation instead 'entails liberating the image from its source, not to possess it, as Mulvey indicates, but to give it away, to pass it over to a community of users who then determine its meaning' (2014, 524). Weir, likewise, takes a source image not to possess or erase it, but to freely share an intense, emotional emblem of that image with a new audience, where it no longer requires a historical context to convey the appropriate Gothic historical narrative. The use to which this emblematic history is put is ultimately up to those who share it. They decide where, when, and in which contexts Weir's images will be spread.

Unnatural history

If the visual adaptation and appropriation enacted by these four visual artists can be read as a performance, as I argued using Leitch's definition in Chapter 1, then the Gothic and the uncanny are part of the visual performer's alienating toolkit, allowing them to reproduce (through fiction) the drama of a historical moment in relation to present-day concerns. Frankenfictions go beyond the 'textual' in the literal sense. As I have demonstrated in this chapter, however, they are still readable as narratives, and even as adaptations, whether through their own narrative arrangement or through the juxtaposition and re-contextualization of the texts they appropriate.

Each collection of images utilized by Hillier, Louie, Batty, and Weir comes with its own set of aesthetic and ethical implications. The Victorian advertising and popular illustration used by Hillier has a strong, symbolic language, but with relatively few ethical responsibilities. Louie constructs his own ethical obligations, borrowing the aesthetics of personal and portrait photography to imbue his fantastical, painted subjects with a sense of identity and history. Batty's cabinet cards invert this logic, and these ethics, taking the personal portraits of real people and making them public, transforming them into freak show performers for their twenty-first-century descendants. Weir's wartime GIFs, in contrast, are both ethically and aesthetically volatile, taking iconic images that are traumatically engrained in public memory and using fantastical imagery to re-emphasize their horror to the contemporary viewer. All four artists estrange viewers from their 'historical' images by filling them with physically fantastical – if symbolically resonant – creatures from popular culture.

Quéma argues that Gothic representations 'do not cancel out ideological dogmas, but by estranging the subject from dominant discourses and by violating ideological norms of reality and knowledge, they lay bare the coercive aspects of social and cultural laws' (2007, 114). Although she uses the term estrangement rather than alienation, the process Quéma describes can be related to Brecht's alienation effect. As Gothic fictions, Frankenfictions alienate their audiences from historical realities, not necessarily to critique them, but to reveal their contingencies and re-examine their status as universalizing emblems. Frankenfictions demonstrate that the ethics and aesthetics of past images *do* matter, but not always in the ways that we might expect. In the words of Fredric Jameson, twenty-first-century Frankenfictions represent a return to 'all of the affect (depth, anxiety, terror, the emotions of the monumental) that marked high modernism', but combines them with the 'aesthetic play' and 'fancy' of postmodernism. As Jameson points out in his critique of Lyotard's definition of postmodernism, this is precisely 'the moment in which aesthetics gives way to ethics' (1984, xviii). In the case of Frankenfiction, however, this is a moment of ethical deferral. Rather than drawing attention to the shocking nature of historical imagery, or even to the shock of its appropriation, Frankenfictions shift this moment of revelation onto the perpetual normalization of the past and its images. History has not ended – historical discourse has simply shifted modes from modernist realism to postmodernist authenticity. In rendering the historical traces it appropriates strange and alienating, Frankenfiction's popular engagement with the past brings the ethics and aesthetics of historiography after the 'end of history' into question once more (Lyotard 1984, 73). Crucially, it does so not to dismiss the importance of history and historical discourse, but to demonstrate its continued relevance in new forms and registers.

Let us return, then, to David Gunkel's assertion in Chapter 1 that mashups must 'give up the ghost', or move away from the traditional models of authorship and originality defended by adaptation studies (2012, 82). Each of the artists in this chapter relates to history through the Gothic, using fantastical monsters and images. While none of these artists attempts to be historically accurate in the academic sense, each appropriates historical traces in order to communicate a particular sense of the past and its monstrosity. For Hillier, monsters are history's sublime gift, revealing the hidden strangeness and wonder in even the most 'natural' images of the past. In Louie's work, monsters are our absent ancestors and companions, and he provides a kind of alternative, photographic personal 'history'. Batty's familial caricatures remind us that the Victorian past is as strange as our own present, and Weir's animated monstrosities enthral us with history's lived horrors. All focus on making the past exotic again, alienating and denaturalizing it in order to communicate its uniqueness as a series of historical moments, images, and traces. They also demonstrate how reliant our own media, aesthetics, and historiography are on specific readings and images of the past. From these visual Frankenfictions, we can once again see that the ghost of history always remains with us.

In this chapter, then, as in Chapter 3, I looked at texts that appropriate the material traces of the past – in this case visually and through narrative, affiliating themselves with a clearly defined and long-established aesthetic, and transforming these historical documents of the past into 'original', fantastical, and commercial products. In the fifth and final chapter of this book, I will explore how Frankenfiction appropriates the discourse of authenticity and originality itself.

Notes

1   *Anno Dracula*'s original cover is image-centric, using a pair of white gloves, muted colours, and metallic lettering to mimic other late-twentieth-century horror and historical romance novels. In the 2011 re-release, the cover's bold colours and text-focused design of a 'faux Victorian music-hall poster' are more closely aligned with

trends in twenty-first-century literary fiction, specifically in the fantastical neo-Victorian subgenre (de Bruin-Molé and Stiff 2015, para. 7).

2   Hillier's work is no stranger to neo-Victorian scholarship. It was part of Sonia Solicari's 'Victoriana: The Art of Revival' (2013b) exhibition. It has also been featured in the academic journal *Neo-Victorian Studies* (Solicari 2013a), and on the cover of the academic monograph *Deviance in Neo-Victorian Culture: Canon, Transgression, Innovation* (Tomaiuolo 2018).

3   Many of the works on the urban legends website 'Creepypasta' fall into the category of photographic horror, most famously the uncanny series of 'Slender Man' images, all of which depict a tall, thin, faceless man in a suit. He appears in photographs from many different locations, and across many time periods ('The Slender Man' 2015).

4   Louie also cites early and silent film directors as influences, including F.W. Murnau, Fritz Lang, Orson Welles, Robert Siodmak, Robert Aldrich, Jacque Tourneur, and cinematographer Greg Toland ('Travis Louie Profile' 2010; Wolfson 2011).

5   These particular cabinet cards strongly resemble the work of Charlotte Cory, a mashup artist who combines scanned *cartes de visite* with her own photography and taxidermy to create animalistic 'Vistorians' (Cory 2018). In reference to the publication of Charles Darwin's *On the Origin of Species* in 1859, she comments: 'It is a strange fact of history that [... t]he first generation of people to be photographed were also the first generation of people to realize that they were closely related to the animals' (Cory 2007, 4). Her art is an extended meditation on this idea.

6   In one image, 'Princess Juliana', Weir actually printed the digital archive image, singed the corners, and re-scanned it in order to create the final 'burning paper' effect in the GIF (Cocozza 2014, para. 4).

7   It should be noted that both 9/11 and the Grenfell Tower fire have an extensive afterlife in GIF form, both in the context of respectful commemoration, and in conspiracy forums or joke sites (andycimex 2010; Thompson 2016; Joseph 2017).

5

Appropriating the Author

It is true that I am very averse to bringing myself forward in print; but as my
account will only appear as an appendage to a former production, and as it
will be confined to such topics as have connection with my authorship alone, I
can scarcely accuse myself of a personal intrusion.

(Shelley [1831] 2015, vii)

Mary Shelley's preface to the revised 1831 edition of *Frankenstein* is full of
fascinating statements (and contradictions) about the nature of authorship. In
many ways, her description of her role in the novel's creation prefigures discussions
that are still ongoing in twenty-first-century remix culture. Throughout this
book, I have discussed what separates adaptation from remix and appropriation,
using Frankenfiction to demonstrate how the boundaries between them are not
always clearly defined. In Chapter 2, I looked at Frankenfiction's appropriation of
historical monsters. Chapter 3 discussed Frankenfiction's parodic stance towards
the texts and traditions it appropriates, and Chapter 4 explored Frankenfiction's
use of the visual as well as the verbal to construct its Gothic historical fictions.
I have also touched on several of the ethical and sociopolitical implications of
Frankenfiction's appropriation of different sources and subjects. In this final
chapter of my discussion, I will examine how Frankenfictions frame the figure
of the 'original' author. Our conception of authorship has changed dramatically
over the past three hundred years. What kinds of dynamics are at work when an
author from a twenty-first-century context adapts or appropriates the work of an
author from an eighteenth- or nineteenth-century one?

This question also has implications for the distinction between adaptation
and remix or mashup. Whether a story is original or derivative depends largely
on how we define an 'author', and on the relationship between author figures.
Adaptations are 'authorized' to a certain degree – that is, they are produced by
one author figure, and pay a certain level of homage to another, 'original' author
figure. In the introduction to this book, I cited Linda Hutcheon's definition

of adaptations as works that are conceptualized, created, and recognized '*as adaptations*' (2013, 6, original emphasis). Hutcheon's definition claims to sidestep the common 'fidelity' discourse, but she explicitly excludes things like 'music samplings', '[p]lagiarisms', and 'fan fiction', either because they engage too briefly with their appropriated texts, are not acknowledged as adaptations, or are not 'authoritative' (2013, 9). The problem with this last distinction is that authority, by definition, only focuses on one relationship: that between an 'original' author and a 'derivative' adaptor or plagiarizer. As Marilyn Randall writes, plagiarism 'implies mechanical reproduction, and therefore the absence of talent and work', but mechanical reproduction plays a role in most modern art (2001, 30).

Walter Benjamin hinted at the rise of reproductive art in in 1935, when he wrote that '[a]round 1900 technical reproduction had reached a standard that not only permitted it to reproduce all transmitted works of art and thus to cause the most profound change in their impact upon the public; it also had captured a place of its own among the artistic processes' (2004, 1235). Plagiarists are engaged in the practice of mechanical reproduction, certainly, but so are critics, art dealers, and artists themselves. As Pablo Picasso and other twentieth-century appropriative artists have famously (and pointedly) suggested, 'bad artists copy. Good artists steal' (Quentel 1996, 39).[1] In copyright law and in adaptation discourse, the division between 'original' and 'derivative' constructs the original author's work in a way that masks its similarities to the copyist or plagiarist. All artists are dependent to some degree on the works that came before. In the case of twentieth-century collage artists, this reliance is especially marked, but even a literary novelist must draw on the conventions and characterizations pioneered by others in order to make their own work relatable. Not even authors who are considered the greatest or most original are entirely independent of their environments. Often, the reverse is true. As Anthony Mandal argues in *Jane Austen and the Popular Novel* (2007), for instance, Austen was certainly a talented and persistent writer, but 'the immediate print culture she encountered and engaged with' was also 'fundamental to Austen's literary career' (2007, 3). Mandal traces Austen's themes, characters, and genres across fictions of the late eighteenth century, establishing that she 'was as much an accomplished reader as she was a determined author' (2007, 216). This is a key component of the strength and continued endurance of her work.

The distinction between the 'author' and the 'plagiarist', as I will argue, is much finer than we are often given to believe, and is determined largely by an economics and politics of whose art is most culturally 'legitimate'. The modern preconception of the author as wholly original, which has its roots in the

Romantic period, is greatly indebted to both the image of the Romantic genius and the rise of copyright law. While the desire to protect the rights of the working author seems innocuous, the Romantic authorship model has been contested for numerous reasons since its consolidation at the end of the eighteenth century, and its exclusionary socioeconomics continue to have a profound impact on the politics of authorship, even – or perhaps especially – in Frankenfiction. Such remixes often claim egalitarian or anti-establishment stances while in practice doing little to change the status quo. In the first part of the chapter I will consider how the authors of Frankenfiction frame their relationship to the authors of their appropriated material (where such details are available), referring to the related histories of Romantic authorship, postmodern authorship, and media fandom. Often Frankenfiction's appropriation of classic literature has the effect of highlighting the 'greatness' or 'genius' of the appropriated authors, but it also confers a certain authority on the remixer or adapter, who claims an intimate relationship with them. In the second part of the chapter I will analyse one of the contradictory ways this authorial confluence is framed: through depictions of classic authors. To illustrate this, I will focus on what we might call the most literal of Frankenfictions: stories which, through fictionalized versions of *Frankenstein*'s author Mary Shelley, interweave the fantastical world of Frankenstein's creature with the historical context of the novel's origins.

Frankenfiction and Romantic authorship

The myth of the original author has its roots in the deeply gendered systems and terminologies of Romanticism, a movement at its height when Shelley published *Frankenstein*. Romanticism is still deeply embedded in twentieth and twenty-first-century cultures of creativity. After all, to mother a text still implies something quite different than to father one. The very use of this reproductive metaphor often directly hinders the establishment and acknowledgement of women in artistic fields, rather than making them more visible in a powerful and positive way. In Western cultures, motherhood continues to suggest nurturing, collaboration and self-sacrifice, and is inevitably positioned as somehow lesser than the foundational, authoritative model of fatherhood. This is reflected in artistic creation as well, in which the Romantic naturalization of authorship as an inborn gift serves to create a sociopolitical distinction 'between creative ("productive") and pseudo-creative ("reproductive") imagination' (Battersby 1989, 100). For the Romantics:

[A] great man struggled to produce, driven even harder by unconscious forces within him. Creation involved suffering, pain and tears. Work (even sweat) was involved; but the outcome was not a soulless 'mechanical' product. It was 'natural' and 'organic', and was likened to the (previously despised) processes of being impregnated and giving birth. (Battersby 1989, 73)

Despite this liberal use of pregnancy and birth imagery, Romantic writers conceptualizing their 'natural' greatness often deliberately excluded female artists, whose work was considered lacking in the masculine effort and skill required for genius. Although they could be biologically productive, women's art was considered inherently reproductive, and where 'great' female authors did appear, they were regarded as exceptional and unnatural (Battersby 1989, 42). While parenthood may have become more privileged as an artistic metaphor, only men could produce great art.

Romantic genius and originality are inextricably linked to value – both moral and financial. Frankenfiction stands as a testament to this fact, demonstrating how thoroughly (and profitably) works can remain linked to their authors even through the most dramatic of transformations, and even after that author's copyright has expired. It was only from 1710 that public legislation protecting the work of individual authors existed, however, and only in 1911 (1978 in the United States) that the present formula – the life of the author plus twenty-five to a hundred years (depending on location) – would be legally established. And it was largely Romantic arguments that became the foundation of this new legal terminology. As Olufunmilayo Arewa notes, contemporary copyright law is still 'deeply influenced by Romantic authorship and other conceptions of creativity that [...] emphasize the unique and genius-like contributions of individual creators' (2013, 69).

The Romantic poet William Wordsworth was himself a famous proponent of copyright law, even arguing for 'perpetual copyright' (Woodmansee and Jaszi 1994, 4). He countered publisher objections that a more stringent copyright 'would tend to check the circulation of literature, and by doing so would prove injurious to the public' by citing literature's greater value – both moral and financial ([1815] 1974, 310). The production of great literature, he argued, was contingent on the ability to neglect present concerns in favour of visionary works 'which look beyond the passing day, and are desirous of pleasing and instructing future generations' – in other words, work which self-consciously constructs its own originality and genius ([1815] 1974, 310; see also Woodmansee and Jaszi 1994, 5). Kristina Busse describes his definition of valuable art as 'a thinking and writing that is radically new and different, that is original rather than transformative of older ideas' (2013, 51). Such a definition was also clearly needed 'in order to establish authors as owners of ideas – ideas as commodities that can be owned and sold' (2013, 51).

Of course, the value judgement of what is 'pleasing', valuable, or forward-looking is not only based on a work's objective qualities. In Wordsworth's case, this was to establish the value of so-called good books against the work of 'useful drudges', who are 'upon a level with the taste and knowledge of the age' (Wordsworth [1815] 1911, 104). Practically speaking, the 'useful drudges' Wordsworth notes here would have been novels and popular fictions, quite possibly written by women (Mellor 1993, 1, 7; Mandal 2007, 13–14), whose works were not perceived as being of lasting value to 'future generations' (unlike Wordsworth's own poetry and literature). Wordsworth is certainly not the only Romantic author to make a political distinction between 'literature' and 'injurious' writing. As Battersby points out, the 'distinction between "imagination" (a good thing, and characteristic of the genius-mind) and "fancy" (an inferior thing, and characteristic of those who merely fake genius) lies at the heart of Coleridge's literary theory' as well (1989, 100). When 'legitimate' authors set out to protect the integrity or originality of their authorship, they are always protecting it *from* someone else.

As Kate Flint points out, writing about the heyday of Gothic and sensation fiction in the mid-nineteenth century, many well-established arguments linked women to bad fiction and moral depravity. Some feared that 'certain texts might corrupt her innocent mind, hence diminishing her value as a woman'; others argued 'that she, as a woman, was particularly susceptible to emotionally provocative material' (1992, 22). The novel, as a female-associated form of popular fiction, was the target of much social and moral anxiety in the nineteenth century. Too much trivial fiction might induce weaker-willed readers (particularly women and the working classes) to be led into depravity (Mitchell 2012, 124). As Battersby argues, such concerns are simply extensions of the Romantic logic of genius in which art is '*dis*placed male sexuality ... but *mis*placed female sexuality' (1989, 42, original italics).

Moral dangers aside, women continued to be avid readers and writers of the Gothic and other popular fiction throughout the nineteenth century (Halsband 1976, 55; Battersby 1989, 5). The idea that popular literature was somehow degrading, or something to be protected against, also persisted in various forms well into the twentieth century, when postmodernism began to collapse such distinctions between the popular and the literary. As Frankenfiction can attest, however, the Romantic idea of the 'original' author still persists.

Frankenfictions all possess easily identifiable authors – that is, the most prominent remixer involved in a particular work of Frankenfiction. In most cases, however, they also have a clearly identified 'original' author: the renowned figure who created the appropriated text. Most of these people did not write in the Romantic period themselves, but the image of these authors and their work conveyed in Frankenfiction is heavily reliant on the Romantic authorship model. Classically 'Romantic' author figures like William Shakespeare, Jane Austen, Mary Shelley, Charles Dickens, and Charlotte Brontë have each been the object of Frankenfiction's appropriations, and few Frankenfictions borrow extensively from lesser-known authors. Famous authors and their 'value' and 'authenticity' are crucial to Frankenfiction's recognizability as remix, and to its commercial success.

Despite the fact that most twenty-first-century texts are clearly the work of multiple individuals (e.g. writers, editors, illustrators, publishers), many creators of Frankenfiction advertise their appropriation as a direct partnership between a past author and a present one. For instance, most novel-as-mashup texts cite the original author and remixer as co-authors on the front cover. Team mashups like *Anno Dracula, Penny Dreadful, The League of Extraordinary Gentlemen*, and *The Extraordinary Adventures of the Athena Club* take an approach that more closely resembles traditional adaptation, in which the new work takes shape in the constant company of dog-eared copies of the original author's work. Kim Newman, John Logan, Alan Moore, and Theodora Goss each fall back on the Romantic model in their texts and interviews, extrapolating an original author persona and perspective from a particular body of classic work. When discussing an aspect of *Anno Dracula*'s socioeconomic subtext, Newman suggests that this is something he 'got from Stoker' (Donoghue 2012, para. 6). Here he is not referencing the actual text of *Dracula*, but his own informed speculation about Stoker's intentions for the novel. Writing about how 'powerful' and 'moving' he found Mary Shelley's *Frankenstein*, Logan likewise cites 'the themes that Mary Shelley plays with' – specifically the binary nature of monstrosity (Thielman 2014, para. 4). This again is a reference to interpretations of the text rather than the text itself, framed through authorial intention. The authority of these remixers is primarily as devoted readers, who can claim to mediate between the audience and a particular author's work through superior knowledge.

For visual storytellers like Kevin J. Weir the situation is somewhat different, as the images he appropriates are not directly associated with famous artists. When asked for influences, however, even visual artists tend to cite the authors or production companies behind their favourite films, books, and comics.

Weir offers a list of names, rather than works, when asked about 'specific kinds of monsters and horror' that inspire his own art: 'Lovecraft, Tolkien, Terry Gilliam, Cyriak (incredible animator) and Miyazaki' (De Bruin-Molé 2016, para. 9). Dan Hillier cites his indebtedness to Max Ernst ('Dan Hillier: Artist Interview' 2015, para. 8), and Travis Louie is described as having made 'thousands of sketches of genre characters like Godzilla, King Kong, and a host of creatures from Ray Harryhausen movies', or drawing on the visual style of 'directors like F.W. Murnau, Fritz Lang, Orson Welles, Robert Siodmak, Robert Aldrich, Jacque Tourneur [*sic*], and cinematographer, Greg Toland' ('Travis Louie Profile' 2010, paras 1, 3).

The Romantic idea of the sole, original author is clearly still alive and well. The twentieth century and the postmodern turn have altered our perceptions of this figure in several important ways, however. Like the Romantic author, the postmodern author figure is fundamentally reliant on notions of originality and value. Postmodernism has also continued to privilege the genius of certain kinds of artists and authority over others – though for markedly different reasons, and through different naturalizations. As I will demonstrate in the following section, Frankenfiction is also thoroughly indebted to this later discourse on authorship.

Frankenfiction and the (un)death of the author

The Romantic model of authorship, based on the value and authority of an original genius, persisted virtually unquestioned until the mid-twentieth century. At this point, the Western authorial model shifted once again, this time following academic scholarship and criticism. One of the earliest scholarly attacks on the Romantic author model can be found in W.K. Wimsatt and Monroe Beardsley's 1954 discussion of the 'intentional fallacy'. This essay was a reaction to established scholarly practice, echoing the Romantic model, of linking a work to a god-like author figure as an original piece of intellectual property. Wimsatt and Beardsley explain how 'the design or intention of the author is neither available nor desirable as a standard for judging the success of a work of literary art' (1954, 3). This counters the insinuation of Wordsworth and other Romantics that certain texts were rendered visionary by their great authors, who were inherently able to 'look beyond the passing day' ([1815] 1974, 310; see also Woodmansee and Jaszi 1994, 5).

Of course, when we speak of the famed 'Death of the Author' in postmodernism, we are referring not to Wimsett and Beardsley, but to Roland Barthes's essay of

1967. Barthes also writes of the uselessness of assuming an author's intention or vision, with reference to the model of the original author/genius:

> We know now that a text is not a line of words releasing a single 'theological' meaning (the 'message' of the Author-God) but a multi-dimensional space in which a variety of writings, none of them original, blend and clash. The text is a tissue of quotations drawn from the innumerable centres of culture [...] the writer can only imitate a gesture that is always anterior, never original. (Barthes 1978, 146)

For Barthes, then, the author in postmodern criticism is effectively dead, replaced by a more reader-focused form of textual interpretation. This postmodern perspective was itself enabled by the Modernist movement, with its associated practices of collage, absurdism, and abstract art – all widely considered precursors to twenty-first-century remix culture. Ironically, of course, many Modernist authors (and postmodern ones) still enjoy a level of authority similar to that of the Romantics.

Michel Foucault catalogues a similarly conflicted state of affairs in 1969, critiquing the Romantic model of authorship while noting its continued prevalence. For Foucault, this model was inherently flawed because texts are merely 'objects of appropriation' (1980, 124). It is the author, not the text, that solidifies the distinction between valuable 'literary' production and worthless 'popular' production – but the author is merely a kind of collector, utterly defined by his or her sociopolitical context. As Foucault writes, however, even the postmodern scholars of his time still spoke of literary 'initiators' in terms of originary genius: individuals (Foucault cites Ann Radcliffe and Sigmund Freud) who 'cleared a space for the introduction of elements other than their own, which, nevertheless, remain within the field of discourse they initiated' (1980, 132). Even as he acknowledges the author's continued power, Foucault nevertheless extolls the virtues of 'a culture where discourse would circulate without any need for an author', where questions like 'Who is the real author?', 'Have we proof of his authenticity and originality?', and 'What has he revealed of his most profound self in his language?' would become obsolete (1980, 138). Note the gendered language and pronouns employed in Foucault's discussion of authorship.

While Frankenfiction owes a great debt to the Romantic authorship model, it is unlikely this form would have achieved such prominence without the changing notions of authorship prompted by these works of twentieth-century literary criticism, as well as the advent of postmodernist and poststructuralist thought across the humanities more broadly. Frankenfictions uphold the Romantic authorship model insofar as they operate like adaptations: when they pay homage to the great authors whose work they borrow. Following the pattern of postmodern literary criticism, however, the way creators of Frankenfiction establish themselves as authors, alongside the classic authors they appropriate, is through the postmodern construction of the reader as 'author', or primary meaning-giver. Like adaptors, mashup artists are often framed as *superior* readers, who see the potential inherent in a text, and the unique ways it can fit with other texts.

Accordingly, creators of Frankenfiction often describe a coincidence or 'eureka' moment in which these gaps in the text become clear to them. Quirk Books's head editor Jason Rekulak's story about the inspiration for *Pride and Prejudice and Zombies* reads like a Dadaist cut-up experiment. Rekulak allegedly sat down with a pair of lists, one of literary classics and one of pop culture icons (pirates, zombies, werewolves), and began drawing lines between the two until one combination struck him (Wagstaff 2009, para. 3). Seth Grahame-Smith describes another coincidence in the inspiration for his follow-up to *Pride and Prejudice and Zombies*: a book which draws excerpts from former US president Abraham Lincoln's personal correspondence. 'I kept noticing that every bookstore I walked into had a big Lincoln table, full of books about him. Now, it so happened that this was also the point where the *Twilight* phenomenon was reaching critical mass. So next to every Lincoln table there would be a vampire table' (Sharkey 2010, para. 30). This meeting of *Twilight* and Abraham Lincoln's bicentenary commemorations allegedly produced *Abraham Lincoln, Vampire Hunter* (2010).

For Kim Newman, a longstanding fan of vampires and horror, the 'flashpoint' for *Anno Dracula* came more eruditely (Barr 2015, para. 10). While he was researching interpretations of 'Victorian and Edwardian apocalyptic fiction' for a university essay, he realized that his interests and studies were not so far removed from each other, offering potential threads for connection to the careful reader (Barr 2015, para. 10). Other authors of Frankenfiction cite similar moments, in which a text metaphorically speaks to them. Seth Grahame-Smith describes how in re-writing *Pride and Prejudice and Zombies* as a mashup, he felt almost as though 'Jane Austen was subconsciously setting this up for us' (Grossman 2009a, para. 5). Similarly, of his cabinet cards Colin Batty describes how they 'suggest their own stories. Some are just crying out for me to stick something in there' (Bromwich 2015, para. 1). In this case, gendered imagery is evoked once again, in the form of the pen, paintbrush, or other phallic symbol that penetrates the text with its incisive, masculine authority (S.M. Gilbert and Gubar 2000, 3–7). These accounts of inspiration still refer to the author or 'intention' of the text, but in a way that highlights the mashup artist as reader or observer. Of course, it takes much more than observation to do the actual work of authoring and publishing a text, but this is not the image Frankenfiction generally seeks to promote.

Frankenfiction does not 'kill' the author in the sense of granting anonymity or irrelevance, then. Even when Frankenfictions deconstruct the classic author through parody, travesty, or irony, they are only able to do so by building on an established and persistent understanding of that author's intention for the work, of the appropriated text as original, and of their own work as derivative. Busse attributes this authorial un-death to the strength of the Romantic authorship model. Building 'on a popularized version of Wordsworth and the Romantics,' she writes, 'most aesthetic theories of modernity have been vested in the myth of originality, and it is from this mindset that we have inherited the popular belief that continues to value originality even as we have long entered an age of mechanical reproduction where creativity often takes quite different guises' (2013, 50). Frankenfiction thus draws attention to one of the major problems with the postmodern authorship model. In some situations, it has become acceptable to disregard or obscure the author, but in the realms of copyright law, mainstream publishing, and popular culture, the author is still very much alive. Despite her appropriation by Quirk Books, Jane Austen remains as popular as ever following the release of *Pride and Prejudice and Zombies*, and her 'co-author' Seth Grahame-Smith, though not elevated to the same level, has received wide recognition for this and subsequent mashup works. Inevitably, it is the same authors who were canonized in the eighteenth and nineteenth centuries whose legacy persists today. By attaching one's work to theirs, twentieth- and twenty-first-century remixers can still attain a kind of fame and genius by proxy.

Some mashup critics have prematurely hailed remix culture as the ultimate realization of the postmodern author model, and the final death of the author. David Gunkel, for instance, has written on the implications of Barthes' theories of authorship for remix culture. Quoting Barthes, he states:

'Once the Author is removed, to claim to decipher a text becomes quite futile' (Barthes 1978, 147). Accordingly the objective of the reader, listener, or viewer is not to unearth and decode some secret meaning situated outside of and just below the surface of the text, but to engage with the material of the text itself, to disentangle and trace out its various threads, and to evaluate the resulting combinations, contradictions, and resonances. (Gunkel 2012, 91)

In order to decipher a text, the reader must become a kind of author, actively engaging with and reassembling the material of the text. This, Gunkel argues in the rest of the article, is what mashup does when it re-imagines other texts: it creates meaning by pulling the material of the text apart and re-weaving it. In his reasoning, as in much of postmodern criticism, the idea of the original author or context should be even less relevant in a monster mashup like *Pride and Prejudice and Zombies* than it is in other fictions (2012, 91). As I have argued throughout this book, quite the opposite is true in Frankenfictions.

This post-authorial argument also ignores important sociopolitical aspects of mashup technique more broadly. As Mickey Vallee argues, Gunkel and other critics have 'taken the mashup as a virtual utopia, devoid of traditional authorship, an ironic pastiche that deflates narrative in favour of ironic distanciation' (2013, 77). Although it blends multiple discourses and registers, the effectiveness and popularity of the mashup form relies heavily on the appropriation of highly recognizable figures, and binarily opposed cultural categories. Repetition and reinforcement of such opposing categories can also occur despite intentions to the contrary. As Camilla Nelson points out, though it was originally publicized as the work of an 'anti-fan', the publishers of *Pride and Prejudice and Zombies* quickly realized what a 'saleable commodity' Austenmania actually was, eventually offering a side-by-side reading of the two texts with a trailer advising readers that 'it is in fact far preferable to "Read 'Pride and Prejudice and Zombies' alongside Jane Austen's original text"' (2013, 341).

In addition, when it makes use of self-reference, the text and paratext of the mashup tend to refer to their appropriated texts from the perspective of their juxtaposition, rather than their selection. This focus, while demonstrating mashup's transgressive *potential*, can also mask the processes and systems of power behind its creation and popularity. In other words, mashup is often (but crucially, not always) successful because of the texts and figures it appropriates, rather than the form into which it appropriates them or the uses to which it puts them. This link is especially clear in adaptations and Frankenfictions. For example, *Pride and Prejudice and Zombies* offered a surprisingly nuanced exploration of the border between monster and monster hunter, hinted at the continuities between Jane Austen's culture and our own, and successfully combined a literary classic with lowbrow pulp horror. Its financial success resulted more from the clever, if contentious, juxtaposition of Austenmania with zombiemania than from this skilful combination of monsters and literary classics, however, as the diminished success of subsequent mashup titles would demonstrate. Rather than challenging either the conventions of the publishing industry or the prominence of Jane Austen's work and themes, *Pride and Prejudice and Zombies* ultimately reinforced both. *Pride and Prejudice and Zombies* was popular because *Pride and Prejudice* is popular, a status which the appropriation only emphasized.

Of course, not all works of Frankenfiction are binary remixes, or remixes that appropriate primarily from two clear sources, as described by Vallee. The issues of popular appropriation he raises extend to other kinds of remix as well, however, and are ultimately symptomatic of a wider problem with popular perceptions of authority and textuality. In referencing the popular, Vallee highlights the tendency of popular culture towards conservative ideologies, avoiding radical or progressive politics that might jeopardize its marketability, and its continued status as 'popular' (2013, 82–3). Interestingly, for Vallee this problem is deeply grounded in identity politics. Behind cosmopolitan claims of revolution, hybridity, and empowerment, he argues, lurks a tendency to naturalize ideologies by labelling them as 'post-ideological' (2013, 88). Where the Romantic author model naturalized the individual author/genius, then, the postmodern author model performs a similar feat by rendering the author invisible. The author is still present in a legal and popular sense, but is rendered immune to criticism and critique by the unfashionability of author-centred discourses. In this case, as Margie Borschke argues, remix 'is less a description or explanation of a practice than it is a defense of one' (2017, 35), a blanket valorization of certain systems of appropriative acts.

As Vallee highlights in his analysis of the aural mashup and remix culture, the key issue with much recent scholarship on mashup and remix is that it is too optimistic about the form, and not cynical enough about its applications (2013, 77). For Vallee, scholarship often overlooks the way the representation of identity in the mashup replicates existing cultural binaries, instead focusing on how mashups seem to embody 'the promise of unity and coherence that is lacking within the symbolic order' (2013, 85). He questions why, if the musical mashup seems designed to free us from the 'historical weight' or burden associated with adaptive texts, 'so little has been done to perturb the well established fantasy of crossing boundaries that has characterized the virtual cosmopolitanism of the popular music industry for over a century' (2013, 96).

Instead of a disruption or transgression of traditional authorship, then, we are left with a paradoxical situation. As Vallee persuasively argues, the mashup deconstructs various binary oppositions (normal versus other, past versus present, high culture versus low culture), but is 'silent regarding the inner mechanisms of the system it deconstructs, for even though users actively create multiple lines of flight, they are unidirectional: towards the social imaginary of pop cosmopolitanism' (2013, 96). In the case of the literary mashup *Pride and Prejudice and Zombies*, for example, despite the much-lauded transformative *potential* of such a text on the form and composition of the publishing industry, no such transformation has yet taken place. The literary mashups that go on to achieve financial or cultural success are still generally those produced by major companies and publishing houses, and by a largely white, middle class, and male body of authors and publishers.

In the mass media system, likewise, little has been changed by the popularity of the literary mashup, and the controversy or monstrosity of the text itself in fact distracts from this conversation. In general, the appearance of mashup in certain high art products is not indicative of a collapse between high and low culture in which artists can be, as it were, socially mobile. Instead, both groups are now simply dominated by the same, largely homogenous collectives of people. The danger here is that, although many critics advertise the progressive potential of the mashup, the empowerment against classism, racism, and capitalism they note is simply masking and reinforcing a conservative, cosmopolitan ideology of uniformity. In attempting to appeal to everyone, such texts suppress potentially revolutionary perspectives, in practice ensuring that only 'safe', mainstream perspectives are put forward. In this way, they preserve the status quo rather than disrupting it, meaning that the mashup often reinforces the same binaries it claims to deconstruct.

In a superficial sense, then, a mashup returns to pre-Romantic ideas about creativity, where a good copy is as valuable as a good 'original'. If this were the case overall, however, then in mashup the figure of the author should play a very small role. This, as we can see from the examples of Frankenfiction I have given in this book, is not the case. Sometimes the mashup author is dismissed, but the appropriated author is very often key – especially in the literary mashup. This may be because the Romantic aesthetic is still valid in postmodern popular culture, or it may be that it holds particularly strong sway over the literary arts. Either way, Frankenfictions use the figure of the author in a way that demonstrates several of the problems inherent in implementing the 'death' of the author in popular culture. Popular strategies of author promotion or erasure often serve to reinforce the same pre-existing prejudices, even when they seem to reject them. To illustrate this point, we must turn to the emergent authorship model of twenty-first-century mass culture. As Robin Walz writes, traditionally 'mass culture is produced by an entrepreneurial elite and marketed to the general population, while popular culture is generated by the people (*populo, menu, peuple,* the folk) themselves' (2000, 7). In this definition, popular culture is seen as 'low' or unsophisticated, while official culture (mass culture or media culture) is dominated by an educated elite. Over the past fifty years, however, this distinction has become increasingly tenuous, and in the twenty-first century it has become virtually impossible to distinguish between the two in any meaningful way.

Frankenfiction and transmedia world-building

As I have demonstrated in the previous two sections, aspects of both the Romantic author model and the postmodern model have survived into the twenty-first century. Multimedia authorship, as we find enacted in Frankenfiction and other twenty-first-century, transmedia world-building, borrows the Romantic concept of originality (with some modifications) and combines it with postmodernism's emphasis on collaboration and transtextuality over individual authorship. Writing about the politics of twenty-first-century science fiction and fantasy, Dan Hassler-Forest defines transmedia world-building (i.e. the construction of fragmented and 'complex fantastic storyworlds') as a process that 'takes place *across* media', 'involves *audience participation*', and '*defers narrative closure*' (2016, 5, original italics). The process by which this occurs closely resembles remix.

Hassler-Forest explains how transmedia world-building has become an increasingly integral part of convergence culture since the turn of the century, citing Henry Jenkins's 2006 description of the increasing 'flow of media across multiple media platforms, the cooperation between multiple media industries, and the migratory behavior of media audiences who will go almost anywhere in search of the kinds of entertainment they want' (2006, 3). Globalization and digitization, argues Hassler-Forest, have eroded many of the 'fundamental distinctions between contemporary media', and have simultaneously 'helped transform transmedia world-building from a cultural activity that existed on the margins of mainstream culture to one of the cornerstones of popular entertainment' (2016, 6). In other words, remix is the new tool of mass culture. As Borschke suggests, remix 'may have been born analog but it has become the dominant descriptive and explanatory metaphor for the artifacts of networked new media' (Borschke 2017, 23). The link between this brand of mass culture and the emergence of popular genres like Frankenfiction, which blends stories from multiple eras, genres, and media into one coherent narrative, should not be underestimated. This does not mean distinctions between one medium and another are rendered unimportant. It simply means that in certain situations these distinctions are less important than they once were. Media 'can neither be reduced to its physical properties nor fully understood without recognizing when these material properties matter, and why' (2017, 25). This recognition of when and why media's material properties matter is something I have attempted to demonstrate throughout this book.

In his argument for the study of 'clusters of authorship' (rather than individual authors) in this twenty-first-century context, Jonathan Gray suggests that '[a]uthor*ship* is quintessentially about author*ity*', and that creators 'are *given* authority, which requires us to ask who has given this power, what parameters – if any – they have set, and how they in turn control the distribution, exhibition, and/or circulation' of texts and paratexts (J. Gray 2013, 108, 103). In the case of Frankenfiction, this authoritative figure is often not the self-declared author of the individual text, but the publishing company or distribution house that commissions, funds, and markets it. The individual author's purpose is simply to make a distinct contribution to an existing story-world or brand, overlaying it with their own particular style or perspective – though of course, the possibility of a wholly unique authorial style is itself a 'neoromantic' notion, as critics of *auteur* theory in cinema studies have noted (Cuelenaere, Joye, and Willems 2016, 1; see also Leitch 2005).

Frankenfiction is part of what Roberta Pearson has called 'non-proprietary story-worlds',[2] or professional appropriations that only make use of material in the public domain. In Frankenfiction, this includes both the stories they appropriate and the pseudo-historical Victorian universe in which they are set. Non-proprietary story-worlds do not infringe on an author's intellectual rights, but they do restrict access to public domain material in another way. The multimedia companies that produce such story-worlds protect them with copyright, but also increasingly through trademarks.[3] Unlike the copyright on individual works, trademarks on characters and concepts can be perpetually renewed, so long as the rights holder continues to use the trademarked object in works or products. In US copyright law, a 'trademark'

> [i]ncludes any word, name, symbol, or device, or any combination thereof [...] used by a person [...] to identify and distinguish his or her goods, including a unique product, from those manufactured or sold by others and to indicate the source of the goods, even if that source is unknown. ('Chapter 22: Trademarks' 2013, III §1127)

The idea of Dracula cannot be trademarked, but the specific way he appears in one adaptation or work of Frankenfiction can. In this case, what sets a commercial work of art apart as 'original' is not its uniqueness in general, but its uniqueness to a particular author or producer. Tautologically, an object's originality is whatever can be said 'to indicate the source of the goods', as well as distinguishing it 'from those manufactured or sold by others' ('Chapter 22: Trademarks' 2013, III §1127). It is the object's *legitimate* or authorized origin, rather than its own uniqueness or value, that determines originality. This allows trademarks to benefit corporations aiming to transform public domain texts and characters into sources of continual profit.

In the postmodern West, then, the godlike figure of the individual author may have been discredited, but it has been quickly and systematically replaced by the godlike figure of the global multimedia corporation. An overwhelming number of popular narratives in the twenty-first century are owned not by individuals, but by corporate franchises, which use individual stories to construct massive transmedia story-worlds. In this context the figure of the individual author returns as a creative remixer of others' intellectual property. Rather than Romantic author-geniuses, these individuals are more readily comparable to the media fans who consume and reproduce their stories. Indeed, Frankenfiction and fan fiction are similar in many ways, despite a few significant differences.

Were it not available for sale on the mass market, identifying major textual or paratextual differences between fan fiction authors and professional authors of Frankenfiction would be a challenge. Frankenfiction is also frequently miscategorized as amateurish by the mainstream press. Because the authors of Frankenfiction tend to work with material from outside their direct profession, they are often presented as self-taught, and any financial success in the genre tends to be framed as coincidence rather than skill. Seth Grahame-Smith, for instance, is the child of two book industry professionals, and has a university degree in film (Sharkey 2010, para. 15). In an interview with *The Telegraph*, however, he highlights his lack of formal training as a writer:

> I spent years trying to become a real writer [...] I wrote one terrible manuscript after another for a decade and I guess they gradually got a little less terrible. But there were many, many unpublished short stories, abandoned screenplays and novels ... a Library of Congress worth of awful literature. (Sharkey 2010, paras 7, 8)

This story reads much like that of any contemporary writer, slowly improving their craft in an oversaturated market, but this is not how it is interpreted by the interviewer, Alix Sharkey. 'Everything changed when Grahame-Smith finally found his natural genre – the literary mash-up', Sharkey writes in summary (2010, para. 9). Rather than reading Grahame-Smith's story as one of slow growth through practice, Sharkey interprets his success as luck: the simple matter of finding a genre bad enough to match his writing. Other Frankenfiction writers and artists are presented in a similar light. The dismissal of novel-as-mashup authors and their talent is compounded by the fact that many also publish in other underappreciated genres, like romance and young adult fantasy.

Many works of Frankenfiction are also distributed and marketed through online networks, in a way that would be familiar to fan communities. Their success is largely enabled by the internet, and sometimes they assume the aesthetic of these platforms as well. Camilla Nelson describes:

> [T]he first *Pride and Prejudice and Zombies* book trailer, a mashup combining the BBC production of *Pride and Prejudice* with George Romero's *Night of the Living Dead*, rendered with the kind of 'twenty dollars and four pizzas' aesthetic that is typical of amateur-made fanworks. (Nelson 2013, 340)

This trailer (and subsequent ones) appeared on YouTube, and has since garnered hundreds of thousands of views. While Nelson's generalization about the aesthetic of 'amateur-made fanworks' may sound dismissive, the fact that Quirk Books could have chosen a more traditionally professional aesthetic but instead chose to mimic fan productions is worth noting: their use of fan tactics and aesthetics lends the book an anti-establishment air.

Indeed, Frankenfiction often cites its similarities to fan fiction as proof that it challenges the conservative policies of traditional media and trademark empires. Jason Rekulak, for instance, suggests that *Pride and Prejudice and Zombies* came about because he was 'intrigued by all of the creative copyright violations that you find on the Internet – all of the people remixing songs, editing new cuts of film trailers, splicing themselves into existing TV shows, and so forth' (Wagstaff 2009, para. 3). He cites fandom as a place where artists can 'get away with' flouting copyright concerns in a way that he, as a traditional book publisher, normally cannot (2009, para. 2). In practice, however, Frankenfiction operates within the same binary author model, where a person creating derivative work must either be a professional creator (for profit), or an amateur fan (for pleasure). The resulting model of authorship and intellectual property disenfranchises minority authors in much the same way the Romantic and postmodern models did. Frankenfiction is often guilty of capitalizing on fan fiction's grassroots popularity and circulation tactics, while still operating as a product of professional mass culture.

The single greatest distinction between Frankenfiction and fan fiction is this economic and proprietary boundary between professional and amateur writing. Both appropriate intellectual property, but fan fiction authors do not generally own the resulting product, or profit from their appropriation. Frankenfiction (as I define it) thus falls outside of the typical classification of a fan product, geared as it is for the commercial market. Even free-to-view monster mashups like Kevin J. Weir's animated gifs or Pemberley Digital's YouTube series *Frankenstein, MD* have led directly to professional and financial reward. This is an important difference between Frankenfiction and fan fiction, though as fan labour is increasingly recognized and monetized, this distinction becomes steadily murkier.

In addition to profit, there is one component that separates both Frankenfiction *and* fan fiction from a potentially more innocent 'grassroots' culture – in this case standing in as the opposite of commercial culture, insofar as such a distinction is still possible (Jenkins 2014, 65). The separation lies in the distinction between myth and popular culture, and the obligations each has towards the figure of the author. As Francesca Middleton points out in her comparison between classical and contemporary textuality in fan fiction:

> [T]he contemporary text is something imagined to be much bigger and more generalized than the individual compositions and circulated material objects that are used to read it […] The purpose of literature is seen as being to express the self, and to that extent literature is seen to embody the self. (Middleton 2016, paras 1.7, 2.9)

In other words, an infringement on an author's text is seen as an attack on the author themselves (2016, para. 2.11). This too represents a socioeconomic concern, particularly in the age of global mass media, where authors (canonical or otherwise) often represent brands, estates, or corporations in their own right. As Deborah Yaffe writes in her account of Jane Austen fandom, the contemporary Austen is both a great author and an 'international profit centre […] a wrestling match between the real Austen and her fabricated everything-for-sale brand' (2013, 31). Frankenfiction has touched on this subject as well. In *Jane Bites Back* (Ford 2010), Jane Austen is living in the modern world as a vampire, and is unable to find a publisher for her latest novel. Other authors accrue wealth and fame through adaptations of her work, but despite both literal and figurative immortality, the 'real' Jane struggles to be successful in the modern age.

In contemporary consumer culture, popular mythology is severely limited as a tool to subvert dominant ideologies and power structures. Taking the example of fan fiction, Ika Willis argues that '[a]s a narrative form, fan fiction, like classical myth, is characterized by its multiple, self-contained but (at least potentially) overlapping or crisscrossing story worlds' (Willis 2016, para. 1.2). Willis cites Sarah Iles Johnson's 2015 article 'The Greek Mythic Story World', where Johnson explains how this 'crisscrossing' works in Greek mythology:

> There is no such thing as a Greek mythic character who stands completely on his or her own; he or she is always related to characters from other myths, and the narrators take some pains to tell us that (and, one assumes, to invent such relationships when they need to). The monstrous Python may have been new to some people the first time they heard the Homeric *Hymn to Apollo*, but the narrator ties her into the larger family of mythic monsters by mentioning that the Python had been the nursemaid of Typhoeus, a dreadful creature about whom Hesiod had a lot to say. And the narrator makes Apollo himself tell us a few lines later that the Python was a pal of the Chimaera, who first appeared in the *Iliad* and whom Hesiod said was the *child* of Typhoeus (as were Cerberus and the Hydra). (Johnston 2015, 293)

Likewise, while fan fictions (and Frankenfictions) are self-contained narratives, they make reference to a larger story world full of other characters, events, and texts, implying that 'everything can be made to fit together; everything can be understood as part of a single, bigger picture and thus ratified, if only you know where to look for the missing pieces – or how to fashion them yourself' (2015, 306). This echoes Kathryn Hume's description of fantastical monsters (referenced in Chapter 2), who 'have an ancestry that links them to a total network of divine and demonic powers' (1984, 67).

Both fan fiction and Frankenfiction thus serve as a kind of mythmaking, but with one important difference: the socioeconomic status of the classical myth is fundamentally different from that of a copyrighted text in modern popular culture. Referring to work by scholars like Henry Jenkins and Elizabeth Durack, who position popular culture as the myth of the modern age, and as a subversive or revolutionary domain of the masses, Willis writes:

> Such appeals to myth that frame contemporary popular culture as folk culture thus construct a historical continuity and/or a conceptual parallel between, on the one hand, texts produced and circulated by the modern culture industry and, on the other hand, premodern folk culture. (Willis 2016, para. 2.5)

In other words, the fact that fan fiction and Frankenfiction appropriate *from* popular culture is not in itself enough to subvert the normative impulse *of* popular culture, which is increasingly synonymous with mass culture. To imagine such appropriation as subversive is also in opposition, Willis argues, to the model of contemporary mythmaking posited by scholars like Barthes and Bruce Lincoln, which 'constructs myth as fundamentally and essentially hegemonic' (2016, para. 3.1). Willis cites Barthes's definition of myth as a form of 'depoliticized speech', which is conservative rather than progressive, and which 'transforms history into Nature' ([1957] 1972, 142, 148, 128). This depoliticization of myth echoes the Romantic naturalization of literature. As I have argued, such naturalization has been a central strategy in maintaining the authorial status quo, elevating certain kinds of authorship above others.

Bruce Lincoln likewise calls myth 'ideology in narrative form' (1999, 147), suggesting that we need a different approach to studying mythmaking in contemporary culture. Specifically (and perhaps counterintuitively), he advocates an author-centric approach to myth that looks more closely at the act of narration itself. We need, he argues:

> [A] more dialectic, eminently political theory of narration, one that recognizes the capacity of narrators to modify details of the stories that pass through them, introducing changes in the classificatory order as they do so, most often in ways that reflect their subject position and advance their interests. (Lincoln 1999, 149)

This approach responds to Foucault's ideal perspective on the author-figure, i.e. 'What matter who's speaking?' (1980, 138), but rather than simply dismissing the author with this rhetorical question, Lincoln suggests that we can only move beyond such paratextual questions by addressing them. What impact do the form, genre, and author/authority of an appropriating text have on the story they are relaying? This is precisely the question I have been asking in this book, and from here we can begin to consider how we might apply the concept of mythmaking, in the context of Frankenfiction, to reflect the political motivations inherent in the act of appropriation. Does Jane Austen belong to everyone, and if so, what is to be gained by associating oneself with her work? How might these gains be different from those achieved by appropriating or mythologizing the work of another artist?

Such questions have been especially central in feminist criticism. As Busse describes, 'much of literary criticism of the 1980s and 1990s grappled with the question of how to combine identity politics with the theoretical insights of postmodernism and deconstruction' (2013, 55). Battersby, for instance, finds the postmodern death of the author unconvincing in a feminist context. She writes:

> Post-modernists have proclaimed the death of the author. But for an author to die, he must first have lived [...] The emphasis on debunking the subjective

authority of an author, as well as all objective standards of 'truth' or 'greatness', means that new authors and new traditions cannot get established. (1989, 146)

In other words, by proclaiming the death of the author and the anonymity of both text and meaning, or by 'amputating all talk of genius' (1989, 15), as Battersby puts it, we inadvertently exclude all those authors who were originally denied a Romantic history (women, the poor, people of colour) an equal place in present and future art history as well. Battersby concludes:

> The concept of genius is too deeply embedded in our conceptual scheme for us to solve our aesthetic problems by simply amputating all talk of genius, or by refusing to evaluate individual authors and artists. Before we can fundamentally revalue old aesthetic values, the concept of genius has to be appropriated by feminists, and made to work for us. (Battersby 1989, 15)

This project of appropriation is ongoing, though it is unclear whether the mashup, as an inherently collaborative work, is well suited to such an endeavour. Battersby never addresses the subject of mashup directly, but does make the argument that '[t]he fact that much feminist art is, and always will be, a collaborative enterprise shouldn't obscure individual women creators' (1989, 160). She also briefly discusses Hannah Höch, an artist often associated with the Dadaist movement (cf. Battersby 1989, 142–4).

Remix and appropriation have been closely associated with feminism in the arts since the movement's institutionalization in academia. As I discussed in the introduction to this book, the feminist critic Alicia Ostriker has argued that female artists must often be 'thieves of language' (1982, 68), illicitly appropriating stories and concepts previously defined by mainstream patriarchal culture to use in new ways. Whenever an artist 'employs a figure or story previously accepted and defined by a culture, [she] is using myth, and the potential is always present that the use will be revisionist: that is, the figure or tale will be appropriated for altered ends' (1982, 72). With 'altered ends' Ostriker refers to the construction of a feminist mythopoetics, through which women can re-write the past to reclaim a place in the present. This does not seem to be what most of Frankenfiction is doing, however, and it is questionable whether such a mythopoetics is even possible in the twenty-first century's neoliberal, capitalist culture.

How and why does mass culture continue to mythologize the figure of the author, then? Austen is far from the only fictionalized author figure to appear in popular fiction, or even in Frankenfiction. In *Anno Dracula* alone, for instance, we find Bram Stoker, Oscar Wilde, Beatrice Potter, George Bernard Shaw, and many more. Edgar Allan Poe is a main character in *Anno Dracula*'s sequel, *The*

Bloody Red Baron. Frankenfiction is an active participant in the celebrity and mythologization of the canonical authors it appropriates. As I have argued, Frankenfiction is at the confluence of romantic, postmodern, and multimedia authorship, each of which privilege the figure of the 'original' author or copyright owner in different ways. Up to this point I have provided a very broad historical perspective on this argument. To illustrate in more depth how canonical authors are fictionalized and mythologized for popular consumption, and how this reflects the complex relationship between author and historical authority, I will analyse Frankenfiction's depiction of Mary Wollstonecraft Shelley, the author of *Frankenstein*, through a series of case studies. Following Battersby's argument, I suggest that Shelley's mythologization as an author is an important part of constructing a feminist mythopoetics.

Shelley is widely regarded as the 'mother of science fiction' for her authorship of *Frankenstein*, first published anonymously in 1818 (Blumberg 1993, 3). At first glance this is a formidable title. Brian Aldiss, one of those responsible for popularizing it, described Shelley as a writer of 'prophetic talent', and *Frankenstein* as 'a triumph of imagination: more than a new story, a new myth' (1973, 35, 30). Like later science fiction, he argues, *Frankenstein* combined 'social criticism with new scientific ideas, while conveying a picture of [the author's] own day' (1973, 23). In this account, *Frankenstein* becomes the origin story of the modern age, and Shelley its creator. Two hundred years after its publication, Shelley's 'hideous progeny' (Shelley [1831] 2015, xiii) looms large in the genre, and numerous retellings of *Frankenstein* have graced screens large and small worldwide. However, Shelley's role as the metaphorical 'mother' of this tradition is more complex than the above description implies. Specifically, while her feminist scholarship often portrays her symbolic motherhood as positive and powerful, popular culture offers a very different, often contradictory perspective (see De Bruin-Molé 2018).

Women's work: Mary Shelley as remixer/remixed

There are many author models through which we could examine the mythologization of Mary Shelley in popular culture, but in the context of this book I want to look specifically at Shelley as an author in (and of) Frankenfiction, as both an object of remix and a remixer herself. *Frankenstein* is an especially useful text in this context because it is so often read as a metaphor for failed or monstrous authorship. Frankenfiction is far from the first source to equate the story of *Frankenstein* with the story of its authorship. The novel is a popular allegory for Mary Shelley's authorship among feminist scholars. Anne K. Mellor, for instance, suggests that 'the book represents her authorial self' (2003, 11), and Barbara Johnson argues that *Frankenstein* is 'the story of the experience of writing *Frankenstein*' (1982, 7). In the preface to her revised 1831 edition, Shelley includes a disclaimer that creates striking parallels between her writing process and Victor Frankenstein's assemblage of the creature, but also aligns her work with the logic of remix culture:

> Invention, it must be admitted, does not consist in creating out of void, but out of chaos; the materials must, in the first place, be afforded: it can give form to dark, shapeless substances, but cannot bring into being the substance itself. In all matters of discovery and invention, even those that appertain to the imagination, we are continually reminded of the story of Columbus and his egg. Invention consists in the capacity of seizing upon the capabilities of a subject, and in the power of moulding and fashioning ideas suggested to it. (Shelley [1831] 2015, x–xi)

With the example of 'Columbus and his egg', which illustrates how a paradigm shift can make an impossible problem seem possible, Shelley is referring to the ability of the writer not to invent something from nothing, but to see the material already available in a new light. Of course, this process applies both to herself and to the titular character of her novel, who creates new life by 'seizing upon the capabilities' of existing material. Shelley goes on to describe the events that inspired her creation of *Frankenstein*, implying that without this set of stimuli her novel would never have come into being. Her preface suggests that she gave this random collection of pre-existing ideas a unique configuration, but the actual components had their own distinct forms before they came together in her waking dreams. In many ways, then, Shelley herself can be read as a remix artist, self-consciously re-combining the texts and ideas of others to reveal a new perspective, and thereby create her own story.

Several additional factors contribute to a reading of Shelley as a remixer, and an author of Frankenfiction. One is a lack of clarity among adaptors about which is the original version of *Frankenstein*. This is partly the result of *Frankenstein*'s long history of cinematic adaptations, but the 'original' version of the novel itself has long been contested. Many scholars now prefer the initial 1818 edition, but this is also the version over which Mary Shelley herself had the least editorial control (Robinson 2016, 16). In this sense, fittingly, *Frankenstein* could be framed as an early kind of Frankenfiction. Produced in multiple stages and edited by various authors, it combines modern monsters with Gothic history, drawing on identifiable stories and sources, and defies a single, unified reading or genre label. Like many of the authors of Frankenfiction who would later appropriate her work, Shelley also inserts herself into the Frankenstein narrative with her 1831 account of its conception, in which 'the hideous phantasm of a man' stirs before her much as it does before Victor Frankenstein ([1831] 2015, xi). As a creator, however, Shelley is rarely framed as a person with powerful authorial agency.

While the question of who deserves credit for Mary Shelley's creativity may initially seem like a simple one, in scholarship, as in fiction, Mary Shelley has often been identified through the men around her, from her husband and Lord Byron to the monster and the mad scientist she created in *Frankenstein*. In the introduction to a collection of her letters, editor Frederick Jones wrote that 'a collection of the present size could not be justified by the general quality of the letters or by Mary Shelley's importance as a writer. It is as the wife of [Percy] Shelley that she excites our interest' (1944, xxix). Robert Kiely, likewise, suggested that '[l]ike almost everything else about her life', Mary Shelley's authorship of *Frankenstein* 'is an instance of genius observed and admired but not shared' (1972, 161). It is only more recently that critics and adaptors have taken an interest in Shelley as an author, editor, and critic in her own right, apart from her work on *Frankenstein*.

Shelley's idea for *Frankenstein* (both text and creature) is often framed as a tale of passive conception rather than creation, even by herself (see also Baldick 1987, 35). Shelley suggests that she was the last to come up with a story for the competition, 'forced to reply with a mortifying negative' when asked whether she, too, had an idea ([1831] 2015, x). This idea is eventually conceived in the night, nourished by the input and urging of Shelley's male companions. Interestingly, this account conflicts with that of the other competitors – Polidori, for instance, claims that *Frankenstein* was the first story to emerge, not the last (Wilson 1999, 168–70). In her 1831 preface, Shelley describes the ease with which writing and imagination comes to her as a child. Much of this activity takes place in nature, and is framed as 'natural'. Shelley's childhood is spent 'beneath the trees [...] or on the bleak sides of the woodless mountains near', and this is where her 'true companions, the airy flights of my imagination, were born and fostered' (Shelley [1831] 2015, viii). Once she attains womanhood (and becomes a mother), her 'life became busier', and this natural ability to capture her imaginings in stories is lost, or becomes unnatural. Her reading and discourse with Percy becomes 'all of the literary employment that engaged [her] attention', which is again framed by Shelley as the natural course of a woman's life and intellectual state ([1831] 2015, viii). In light of this diminished capacity for authorship, Shelley then discusses how her conversation and competition with the male authors present at the Villa Diodati in 1816 inspired the novel's central events, minimizing her own role as author. Indeed, on the anonymous 1818 release of *Frankenstein* the only names directly associated with the work were that of her father, William Godwin, to whom the book was dedicated, and that of her husband, Percy Shelley, who wrote the 1818 preface (Baldick 1987, 56; Battersby 1989, 37). In her own 1831 preface, Shelley defends her authorship of *Frankenstein* by describing herself as a vessel for inspiration, framing herself as a maternal figure, reproductive rather than creative, and her novel as an unnatural, 'hideous progeny [...] an offspring of happy days' produced by her intercourse with the other writers at Villa Diodati ([1831] 2015, xiii).

As a historical figure, Shelley has received substantial attention from feminist scholars and critics since the 1970s, claiming her as a great author in her own right and as one of the 'lost foremothers who could help [women] find their distinctive female power' as writers and creators (S.M. Gilbert and Gubar 2000, 59). Jane Donawerth and Carol Kolmerten likewise argue that 'a clear and traceable tradition of women's writing often derives its permission for women's writing from the example of Mary Shelley' (1994, 9), and Debbie Shaw introduces feminist science fiction by outlining how, since 'Mary Shelley's time, many women have discovered the unique potential that sci-fi offers for social comment' (1992, 263). More recently, following the conservative 'Sad Puppies' voting campaigns at the Hugo Awards,[4] Shelley has been cited as proof that women's contributions deserve more recognition in the genre. 'Despite the fact that science fiction as a genre was literally invented by a woman – aka Mary Shelley, author of *Frankenstein* – women have often been marginalized in the world of science fiction, both as fans and as creators', writes Emma Cueto (2016, para. 2).

Given this context, one might expect Mary Shelley's increasingly frequent appearances in fictional film and television productions to reflect these empowering claims, with Shelley as a feminist role model and originary genius. After all, representation is an important tool in the negotiation of cultural equality. As Carolyn Cocca argues, in mass media 'the repetition of stereotypes exerts power' (2016, 5). In the case of sex and gender roles, if:

[T]he constantly repeated story is that women and girls are not leaders, are not working in professional settings, are not agents of their own lives but merely adjuncts to others, and are sometimes not even present at all, it can reinforce or foster societal undervaluing of women and girls. It can naturalise inequalities. (Cocca 2016, 5)

In other words, we need great women in our media if we are to value the great women we have in our society.

Shelley is an increasingly visible figure in fantastical film, television, and fiction with frequent appearances as part of the 1980s heritage industry, children's educational programming and young adult fiction in the 1990s and 2000s, and new media texts of the 2010s (see De Bruin-Molé 2018). Each of these productions dramatizes her role as the creator of *Frankenstein* and science fiction's metaphorical mother. In practice, however, Shelley's appearances in these texts are rarely flattering to the author herself, or empowering to female artists working in the genre today. This does not necessarily indicate that these texts are part of a postfeminist backlash; indeed, many claim explicitly feminist motives. However, while some feminists nominate Shelley as a 'mother' or great originary author in an attempt to create a space for female artists in the present, in popular practice her 'motherhood' (or female authorship) is still not recognized as equal to 'fatherhood' (or male authorship).

As I have suggested, in part this is how Shelley constructs herself. Much of her professional career was spent establishing the work of other, male writers, and Blumberg argues that 'what actually drove Shelley's fiction seems to have been a fundamental intellectual conflict with the men in her life, men that she loved deeply' (1993, 6). Shelley's image in popular culture is also part of a broader tradition of representing women writers in film and television. As Sonia Haiduc suggests, 'the construction of the woman writer on the screen feeds on often contradictory cultural readings of female autonomy, as her quest for self-definition is predominantly set against the background of romance and the love interest tends to overshadow all other concerns' (2013, 52). Such constructions are linked to gendered ideas about creative genius, which are also vital in interpreting popular afterlives of Shelley as the author and 'mother' of *Frankenstein*.

This does not mean such popular, overtly fictional representations are unimportant. On the contrary, liberal adaptations of an author or text are vital in ensuring their cultural longevity. In an article about the popular success of William Shakespeare and Jane Austen as author figures, for instance, Linda Troost and Sayre Greenfield argue that '[w]orks of literature prosper not through simple reproductions but through re-interpretations, quotations and transformations [...] Megastardom for a writer comes only by being adapted to interest an audience far beyond the natural one' (2010, 431, 438). More specifically, this process requires three forces: adaptation, travesty (parody or extreme transformations), and fictionalization of the author (2010, 443).

As demonstrated by their choice of authors, the actual content of the stories matters less for the immortality of a text than the cultural processes that take over once they are written. Shakespeare's wordplay and physical humour is dramatically different from Austen's understated comedy of manners, and Shelley's serious, sombre fictions again differ from Shakespeare and Austen. In Troost and Greenfield's final qualification for authorial megastardom, iconic images and 'little personal stories' are key ingredients in bringing the author to life (2010, 442). As an author Mary Shelley has not quite reached the same level of fictionalization as Shakespeare or Austen, but we have an iconic image of Mary Shelley, painted by Richard Rothwell in the mid-nineteenth century, and we have the story of *Frankenstein's* inception at Villa Diodati. Both text and author need to come alive in fiction and in history, however, and new audiences must feel free to use the author's name and work in ways they were never intended to be used. Only then does a text enter the realm of popular myth. It is precisely this mythologization (of text and author) that allows Frankenfictions to be formed in response.

Fictionalized retellings of Shelley's experiences at the Villa in 1816 often link her inspiration for the novel *Frankenstein* with the events of the novel. They mythologize Shelley as an author figure, but also frame her as an initiator of remix culture, appropriative storytelling, and Frankenfiction. Such retellings are an important part of Shelley's establishment as a literary genius and celebrity author, but the manner in which Frankenfictions narrate and alter the 'stories that pass through' them also promotes familiar author models and exclusions, even when the narrative itself can be said to contain transgressive or revolutionary elements (Lincoln 1999, 149). As Gaston Franssen and Rick Honings note in their recent edited collection *Celebrity Authorship and Afterlives in English and American Literature*, the textual 'afterlife' is a concept 'rooted in the mid-twentieth-century art theory of, among others, cultural scientist Aby Warburg; in the past decade, however, it has received a reappraisal in the discipline of cultural memory studies' (2016, 11). The afterlives of authors in fiction and popular culture are effectively a means of ensuring 'a prolonged afterlife for their idol, but at the same time they *re-author*, in a sense, the author's image and oeuvre' (2016, 3). As Astrid Erll suggests, literary afterlives have much to teach us about 'transcultural memory' and 'the incessant wandering of carriers, media, contents, forms and practices of memory, their continual "travels" and ongoing transformations through time and space' (2011, 11). Not only does Mary Shelley's cultural afterlife inform how we view her as an author, it also hints at the ways the construction and transmission of authorship has changed or remained the same since Shelley's own time.

Although Shelley's establishment as a 'great author' may be part of a feminist process, her primary use in film and television has overwhelmingly been to promote the products that fictionalize her, not initiate fundamental change in the industry more broadly. She is more often used as a vehicle for a male character or author's vision than to advocate for women in the arts. Often, Shelley's motherhood of *Frankenstein* is only possible through her metaphorical (or literal) impregnation by some greater seed of genius, inevitably from a male source. For example, in the late 1980s a trio of films imagined the inception of *Frankenstein* in dramatically different but similarly sexualized terms. Where Branagh's film is best linked to Francis Ford Coppola's *Bram Stoker's Dracula* (1992), and the revival of the sympathetic monster in 1990s cinema (Weinstock 2013, 278), these three films respond more clearly to the wave of heritage films coming out of the UK, adapting the literature and literary idols of the nineteenth century to comment on the relationship between past and present. They even cast familiar faces from the heritage industry, including Hugh Grant, Alice Krige and Julian Sands. In Ken Russell's camp horror film *Gothic* (1986), Shelley and the others at Villa Diodati combine ghost stories with experimental drugs, causing their worst fears to come to life as gory hallucinations. The film plays on the glamorous depiction of Romantic poets as the equivalent of twentieth-century rock stars, immersed in an almost metaphysical world of sex, drugs and art. *Haunted Summer* (1988), based on Anne Edwards's 1972 novel of the same name, indulges in a similarly glorified sex-and-drugs lifestyle, but characterizes the Shelleys and their companions as gentle hippies rather than boisterous rock stars. *Rowing with the Wind* (1988) begins as a costume drama but slowly morphs into an erotic, psychological horror. Shelley is literally haunted by her past, and imagines her fictional creature has somehow come to life to murder her friends and family.

In all three films Shelley's character follows a similar arc, and Byron is the central figure. His relationship with Percy Shelley, an equally passionate but more naïve character, is the initial focus. Mary begins as a silent and reserved figure – particularly in contrast with Claire Claremont – clothed in bonnet, gloves and several layers of dress and coat. This accords with a larger biographical mythology that depicts Shelley as 'cold' and reserved (Mellor 1988, 153). In each film, her cool exterior is gradually worn down by her proximity to

Lord Byron and (to a lesser degree) Percy. Her relationship to Byron, whether directly sexual or a sexualized power struggle for Percy's affections, plays a key role in each film's climax. As the films proceed, Mary's sensuality and sexual receptiveness is revealed, visually symbolized by her undressing from braids and gowns into a thin, white cotton nightgown and a loose halo of blonde hair. This sexual awakening also coincides with her establishment as a more vital and outspoken part of the narrative. It is her physical relationship with Byron and Percy and immersion in their world of drugs and poetry that enables her vision of *Frankenstein*. Her creativity is thus directly linked to her sexuality, and her ability to be receptive to the sexual and creative prowess of these Romantic poets.

In these three films, Shelley's inspiration for *Frankenstein* and the Frankenstein narrative itself become symbolic of sexual and spiritual revelation. This psychoanalytical reading is one many *Frankenstein* scholars have explored in a feminist context, and it is certainly no coincidence that Shelley's rising popularity as a fictionalized author closely follows her reclamation by feminist theory. This period also sees the more general advent of biopics about historical women artists (Codell 2014, 163). As Adams suggests, although:

[S]ome critics still contend that Shelley's impressionistic and dream-laden account of the summer of 1816 does much to diminish her own role in the genesis of Frankenstein, most scholars endorse feminist readings of the introduction that see it and the tale that follows as a peculiarly 'feminine' creation. (2009, 408)

These feminist critics are also responsible for many of the resulting psychoanalytic readings popularized by later adaptations. As Brian Stableford notes, however, when determining whether there are biographical origins for the diverse themes found in *Frankenstein*, popular fiction tends to oversimplify psychoanalytical theory, and popular 'champions of these various meanings are usually content to interpret them as the result of a coincidence of inspirational forces in which the author's role was that of semi-conscious instrument' (1995, 47). This effectively allows authors to frame the text as a blank slate on which to inscribe their own, authoritative reading.

While the heritage industry primarily produced fictions in the realist mode, with occasional forays into Gothic romance, 1980s science fiction also began to delve regularly into the past for its narratives. In addition to psychoanalytical or superficial adaptations of Shelley and the *Frankenstein* inspiration story, several retellings are themselves science fiction or fantasy, bringing in characters from entirely different, often futuristic, storyworlds. In some, the *Frankenstein* origin story offers an attractive opportunity for the main character – often a time traveller – to insert himself into Shelley's legend. This has the added effect of transforming the inserted character into a kind of viewer surrogate – someone who already knows the larger story and can predict its progression. Again, such Frankenfictions tend to depict Shelley as an object of idolization and sexual attraction for a more modern, male character, who is inevitably a fan of *Frankenstein*. This constructs Shelley as a celebrity author within the text as well as paratextually.

Frankenstein Unbound (1990), based on Brian Aldiss's 1974 science fiction novel of the same name, marks Shelley's last appearance on the big screen for nearly three decades. Scientist Joe Buchanan travels from 2030 to 1817 through a tear in time and space created by his own failed experiments. Emerging in Geneva, he meets Victor Frankenstein and his creature, who has helped his creator to continue his monstrous experiments. Joe, suffering the consequences of his own brush with hubris, determines to stop them. He attends the trial of Justine Moritz, another character from Shelley's novel, and there meets Mary Godwin. The villagers identify her as 'Byron's mistress', but Joe is a great admirer of *Frankenstein* and realizes that she is the future Mary Shelley. In this adaptation, then, Shelley's inspiration comes not from a series of ghost stories, but from real-life events unfolding in Geneva. This 'based on a true story' revelation is a common trope in time-travel adaptations, allowing original characters (often men) from other storyworlds to assume ownership or authority over past texts and events.

Despite Mary Godwin's early appearance in the film, she plays a relatively minor role in the narrative. She serves two key purposes, enabling the film to make *Frankenstein*'s themes and context explicit to uninitiated viewers, and becoming Joe's love interest. Taking her on a drive in his futuristic car, he reveals that he is a scientist from the future and an avid fan of the book she will someday write. Fearful of learning too much about her own work and future, Mary chooses not to accompany him on his mission to stop Frankenstein – but she does sleep with him, citing her belief in 'free love'. Again, Mary serves as an inspiration or muse in a way that directly objectifies her, rather than elevating her as a great author in her own right. She is science fiction's 'mother' only in that she brings the seed of a male character's genius to fruition.

Given that the film speaks very little about the actual work of authorship, or the details of Shelley's novel, Joe's infatuation with Mary is more clearly attributable to her physical attractiveness. Aldiss's source novel also paints Shelley in this light, focusing not on her artistic genius but her solemn beauty:

> Seen in the soft green light of the window, speaking with her serious calm air, Mary Shelley was beautiful to behold. There might be a melancholy here, but

there was none of Shelley's madness, none of Byron's moodiness. She seemed like a being apart, a very sane but extraordinary young woman, and a slumbering thing in my breast woke and opened to her. (Aldiss 1974, 93)

This description mirrors Aldiss's own response to Edward John Trelawney's description of Shelley, in which he associates the validity of her authorship with her physical beauty.[5] In *Frankenstein Unbound*, then, Shelley's value as science fiction's 'mother' is once again sexual and reproductive. Her function is to inspire great men, and be inspired by them. Even as Aldiss linked Shelley to science fiction in *Billion Year Spree*, this was more to the science fiction's benefit than to hers. He notes that just as 'the standing of Mary's reputation is still in the balance, so is science fiction's' (Aldiss 1973, 36), but reinforces many of the value judgements that originally stopped work by Shelley and other women from being recognized as artists in their own right. Aldiss even suggests that Shelley's success with Frankenstein was accidental. Describing her 1826 novel *The Last Man* as failed science fiction, Aldiss laments: 'If only Mary had been a great writer instead of merely a good one! What a sombre masterpiece she could have given us!' (1973, 34).

Interestingly, more recent productions often frame Shelley as the story's 'mad scientist', attempting to offer her the role of 'genius' she is denied by Aldiss and earlier adaptors. While a number films and television productions have explored the possibilities of a female Frankenstein, however, only rarely have they placed Shelley in this role. Often such adaptations serve as allegories for women in traditionally male-dominated fields. In Shelley Jackson's hypertext novel *Patchwork Girl* (1994), for instance, 'it is Mary Shelley (not Frankenstein) who assembles the monster, and this patching is specifically identified with the characteristically feminine work of sewing or quilting' (Hayles 2000, para. 33). *Patchwork Girl* represents an effort to highlight the embodied difference between male and female creators. As N. Katherine Hayles argues, in *Patchwork Girl* 'Mary's acts of creation are hedged with qualifications that signal her awareness that she is not so much conquering the secrets of life and death as participating in forces greater than she' (2000, para. 34). Here, then, Shelley is again a model for remix authorship, though specifically in a feminist context.

Combining original text with derivative, *Patchwork Girl* borrows entire sections of Shelley's *Frankenstein*, re-stitching and re-contextualizing them so that the homosocial bonds in the tale are converted from male relationships to female ones. As Hayles suggests, Jackson's text is full of 'subtle suggestions that the monster and Mary [Shelley] share something Mary and her husband do not, an intimacy based on equality and female bonding rather than subservience and female inferiority' (2000, para. 34). Accordingly, in *Patchwork Girl* the lost 'companion' described in Shelley's preface, 'who, in this world, I shall never see more', is not Percy Shelley. Instead the female creature becomes the '"lover, friend, collaborator" without whom *Patchwork Girl* could not have been written' (2000, para. 37). This alteration draws the reader's attention to the many ambiguities and possibilities present in Shelley's relationship to her 'hideous progeny', the text that transformed her into an author, and for which she still has 'an affection [...] as it was the offspring of happy days' (Shelley [1831] 2015, xiii; Hayles 2000, para. 36).

Many other adaptations of Shelley-as-scientist also offer explicitly feminist – or STEMinist, as the recent buzzword among feminist scientists would have it (see Kantor 2014) – readings of *Frankenstein* that vilify the value contemporary culture places, to the detriment of women, on certain kinds of originality, individuality and success. The genderswapped YouTube series *Frankenstein, MD* (2014) features Victoria Frankenstein (Anna Lore), a final-year medical student determined to become a world-renowned doctor and scientist, and to succeed in a male-dominated industry where her mother did not, rewrites the female 'author' or genius into the Frankenstein story. It is framed as her informational video blog, where she catalogues her research for the public. On it, she recruits her friends – including other genderswapped characters from the novel, such as Eli Lavenza (Brendan Bradley) and Rory Clerval (Sara Fletcher) – to help demonstrate certain practical aspects of her work. Some characters retain their traditional genders, including Frankenstein's teacher Dr Abraham Waldman (Kevin Rock), Iggy DeLacey (Steve Zaragoza) – based on the Igor character from various film adaptations – and the creature (Evan Strand), a reanimated version of Robert the cameraman, who serves as an analogue to Robert Walton, the frame narrator in Shelley's novel.

Frankenstein, MD clearly drew from numerous texts and authors during the process of its creation, including Whale's *Frankenstein* (1931) and Mel Brooks' *Young Frankenstein* (1974), with which it arguably has more in common. However, the show's creators persist in acknowledging Shelley as their inspiration, and Victoria is explicitly linked to her through efforts to succeed in a male-dominated field. Head writer Lon Harris explains that what drew him to the idea of 'Frankenstein as a gender-bending character is that Mary Shelley wrote it on a dare to a bunch of dudes that she could write a better horror novel than they could' (McNutt 2014). Harris not only reframes the character of Frankenstein to better align it with its author (and with what he perceived to be Shelley's own cultural situation), but he also reframes the novel's origin story as an overtly feminist endeavour.

Harris frequently engages with critical fans in the comments section of *Frankenstein, MD* videos, occasionally referencing Shelley's novel and defending his own creative decisions with claims of fidelity to it. In the final episode, 'Alone Together' (2014), Victoria decides to abandon her career in the natural sciences and run away with Eli, but before they can make their escape, the creature appears at Victoria's hideout, demanding that she make him a friend. As she has done in previous episodes, Victoria rejects his request. Furious at her refusal, he strangles Eli, ensuring that Victoria will be as alone as her creation. The episode ends with a shot of a weeping Victoria holding Eli's broken body. In the comments below the video, one viewer asks: 'What the hell kind of way to end is this'? Harris replies: 'The Mary Shelley way! It's not really a happy ending kind of story' (Pemberley Digital and PBS Digital Studios 2014). Of course, this dramatic final scene is very different from the novel's drawn-out ending, in which Victor eventually dies of exhaustion, and the creature vanishes into the Arctic wasteland, presumably to end his life. This takes place months, possibly even years, after the creature murdered Elizabeth. It also results in the (somewhat) happy ending of Robert Walton returning home to his country and his family. Although there is no reason to assume that Harris or Pemberley Digital are disingenuous in their desire to promote female authors and creators, positioning Shelley as the 'author' of their narrative is nevertheless misleading.

At the same time as *Frankenstein, MD* works to mythologize Shelley as both the 'original' author of their adaptation and an inspiration to women, many elements of the show's production undercut its promotion of female authorship. First, while Victoria is capable and intelligent, she is also depicted as a lone female hero in male-dominated STEM work, indirectly reinforcing the Romantic stereotype of the 'great woman' as being the exception rather than the rule (Battersby 1989, 24). Second, perhaps because *Frankenstein, MD* represented Pemberley Digital's first foray into horror, or perhaps because of its broadcast on PBS Digital (a science-heavy network), the scripts and sets for the show are noticeably masculinized in comparison to Pemberley Digital's earlier productions. In *The Lizzie Bennet Diaries* (2012–13), *Emma Approved* (2013–14) and *The March Family Letters* (2014–15), most scenes take place in a domestic space (bedroom, living room or home office). The backgrounds are painted in bright or pastel colours, and filled with images and trinkets that reflect the personal nature of the space. Likewise, most episodes centre around inner conflict or relationship dynamics, and the dialogue is accordingly colloquial. *Frankenstein, MD*, in contrast, is set at Engle State University (a play on *Frankenstein*'s Ingolstadt), against relatively stark, sparse backgrounds decorated in blues, whites and greys. Because it is framed as a research and teaching vlog, the dialogue includes many technical explanations of scientific concepts, and numerous jokes about blood and other bodily fluids, as well as gruesome or macabre medical experiments. Finally, although Pemberley Digital is a network that employs a high number of female creators and directors, *Frankenstein, MD*'s head writer, director, executive producers, cinematographer and editor are all men. While the narrative advertised a feminist message, the steps the network took to adapt the story to this new platform ironically suggest that they fell prey to familiar stereotypes about women's interests and genre preferences. While this adaptation claims Shelley as a great, original author, it does not imply a role for other female creators in the genre.

Discussing women's writing and the tradition of pseudonymity, Busse suggests that women's work often fits the wrong mould to be counted as art: amateur, private, and sentimental. Writing about female authors in the eighteenth century, she concludes that '[t]heir work effectively had to be ignored because the ideological context in which it was created spoke directly against the aesthetic models men needed to create, in order to justify owning and selling their works' (2013, 61). Because of the context and culture in which it occurs, women's work often goes unrecognized in the pages of art history, and in definitions of authorship. That Mary Shelley is now being selected as an object of adaptation, remix, and mythologization ultimately has less to do with her actual status as a great female writer, and more with the advantage that mainstream authors can derive from framing her as such.

As an author whose literary portrayals of other women in *Frankenstein* are admittedly complex, Shelley does not always facilitate feminist readings of herself or this work. Theodora Goss addresses this issue at the very end of *The Strange Case of the Alchemist's Daughter*. Here the narrator Catherine Moreau adds an author's note dedicated to Mary Shelley, questioning why she wrote *Frankenstein* (in light of the novel's appropriation of this book as a historical account) and why she hides 'the truth' about the novel's villainous Société des Alchimistes and its colonizing mission (Goss 2017, 398). Moreau also speculates on why Shelley would 'lie' about the survival of Frankenstein's female creature, who is a major character in the book (2017, 398). She comes to the following conclusion:

> Why did Mary Shelley never join the Société des Alchimistes? Because she was the daughter of Mary Wollstonecraft and the stepsister of Claire Clairmont, whom Lord Byron was treating as a mistress he had already tired of. He would later abandon her daughter Allegra, who died in a convent in Italy. She knew the truth: that Frankenstein had created a female monster,

and that the female monster had escaped. And she hid that truth. Knowing of Justine, she did the best she could, for another woman. She erased her from the story. (Goss 2017, 398–9)

Here the lack or silence of women in Shelley's novel is read as an invitation, not just to resurrect Shelley or other marginalized authors, but to comb historical works and writings for absent voices, 'de-monstrating' them to contemporary audiences (Foucault 1967, 68–70), and offering a 're-vision' of the texts in which they appear (Rich 1972). Goss walks a fine line between appropriation, re-vision, and Romantic valorization throughout the *Athena Club* novels. Unfortunately, as we have seen throughout this book not all Frankenfictions are equally successful in this balancing act – especially where issues of gender and authorship are concerned.

Feminist Frankenfiction?

I have argued that the impetus of much feminist re-vision, like that performed by Adreinne Rich, has been fundamentally different from the appropriative remixing of mainstream Frankenfiction. This does not imply that the one is not indebted to the other, or that Frankenfiction could never serve feminist ends. As the work of Theodora Goss and other creators in this book has demonstrated, sometimes Frankenfiction attempts to do exactly that. There are certainly links between Frankenfiction's 'appropriations' and feminism's 're-visions'. After all, monstrosity is a theme with a lengthy (perhaps even defining) history in feminist criticism. Gilbert and Gubar describe how, '[i]n their attempts at the escape that the female pen offers from the prison of the male text, women [...] begin [...] by alternately defining themselves as angel-women or as monster-women' (2000, 44). Historically, however, popular culture has been dismissed as impossible to reconcile with feminism, with popular feminism representing an 'alliance with the commercial marketplace' that is 'tantamount to political betrayal' (Munford and Waters 2013, 2). Frankenfiction's basis in popular culture, as well as its tendencies towards camp and commercialism, may render it unattractive or inaccessible to many feminist artists.

The issue might also be in our own systems of classification. What conditions must be met before an artwork is no longer dismissed as a Frankensteinian appropriation, but classified as a re-vision? I have already mentioned Charlotte Cory as a precursor to Colin Batty, but the work of British-Canadian photographer Janieta Eyre also bears many similarities to that of the visual artists

I discussed in Chapter 3. Like Travis Louie, for example, Eyre communicates a 'narrative of photographic desire to make the imaginary real' in her art, constructed of historical and popular imagery that suggests 'an accumulation of impossible memories' (Hickey 2006, para. 3). Like Louie much of her work deals with migration and immigration, and with how it feels 'not to have a land or a people' (Mierins 2013, para. 7). In 'Twin Manicurists' (Eyre 1996; Figure 5.1), two women (both Eyre) pose in an approximation of historical costume – matching fox furs, a lace mantilla, and floral dresses. Their antiquated clothing, twin poses, and the beckoning hand of the left figure frame them as mystical,

Figure 5.1 'Twin Manicurists' (1996) © Janieta Eyre.

and their feet, bare and clawed, mark them as 'somewhere between animal and human' (Jonjak 2013, para. 1).

Eyre's work is not nearly as commercial as any of the 'mainstream' Frankenfictions I have chosen as case studies in this thesis, however, nor does she directly appropriate familiar, branded monsters in a way that might make her work more accessible to a general or popular audience. This does not make Eyre's work less accessible, though – in her art she constantly attempts to reconcile the 'artistic' with the popular. In one interview she suggests: 'I've been thinking of different ways to get out of the gallery and to be in a more public space because sometimes it seems a little sad to me that it's a bit academic' (Mierins 2013, para. 46). In terms of whether monstrous adaptations can still be Frankenfictions when they are not mainstream, but are part of the realm of 'serious' or overtly revisionist art, as Eyre points out 'seriousness' is determined as much by audiences as it is by artists. She writes:

> I do have humour when I'm making the work. Sometimes I think people miss the humour and they think it's provocation instead, but some of it is silliness and humour. Not many artists work with that in the art world, or you start being silly or using humour and it's not considered art anymore. (Mierins 2013, para. 40)

Because many marginal artists are already working at the edge of what is recognized as 'art', their work is less likely to be called Frankensteinian in the same way works by a 'popular' (i.e. hegemonic) company or author might. As more past texts are appropriated by feminist artists, and as more of women's work is becomes recognized for the humour and playful parody it already contains, more feminist Frankenfictions will come to light.

The mashup's own history is a notable example of how gendered categorizations and exclusions continue to function. In the world of collecting, European records of women's collections are largely domestic (Pearce 1995, 207). Although they might easily be catalogued as collections in the more grand and 'masculine' sense, and though 'women seem to have actually collected things as much as men', it was 'frequently in ways which emerge much less often into specific and recorded social practice' (Pearce 1995, 222). This elision continues today. 'If Picasso and Braque's invention of collage is recognized as a fundamental moment in the emergence of mashup methodology', writes curator Bruce Grenville in his introduction to the book accompanying the Vancouver Art Gallery's 2016 exhibition, *MashUp: The Birth of Modern Culture*, 'then the other great benchmark in the early twentieth century must certainly be attributed to Marcel Duchamp's proposition of the readymade' (2016, 23). But these men were certainly not the first people to engage in mashup techniques, and as journalist Robin Laurence pointed out on viewing the exhibition, '[d]espite the large number of women among the show's 28 collaborating curators, female artists are dramatically underrepresented in *MashUp*' – 36 out of 156 (2016, para. 7).

The exhibition alludes to some of these absent women. One plaque describes how '[d]ecades before the collage experiments of [...] the 20th century European avant-garde, the manipulation of photographs had already become a popular technique', citing a work of photomontage by Kate Edith Gough in the late 1870s (2016, paras 8–9). And an essay by Hannah Höch in the *MashUp* artbook points out that the earliest forms of collage 'may sometimes be found in the boxes of our grandmothers', in the form of scrapbooks and albums (2016, 62). No mention is made of the renowned eighteenth-century gentlewoman Mary Delany, however, whose paper 'mosaicks' were a precursor to collage (Peacock 2010, 4). Although the author continues to be a central figure, some authors remain marginalized. This is partly because our definitions of 'good' or 'valuable' art – like our definition of good and valuable authors – continues to be defined through Romantic ideals. In her 1998 presentation 'Stitch Bitch', Jackson writes that hypertext (like *Patchwork Girl*) 'is amorphous, indirect, impure, diffuse, multiple, evasive. So is what we learned to call bad writing. Good writing is direct, effective, clean as a bleached bone. Bad writing is all flesh, and dirty flesh at that [...] Hypertext then, is what literature has edited out: the feminine' (1998, para. 39). This is because, even as Frankenfiction adopts precisely those styles of creation and authorship that the Romantic model deemed bad or marginal, and confuses the meaning of the term 'author', it holds fast to key Romantic definitions of authorship and genius.

Fortunately, there are still ways future Frankenfictions can resist this exclusionary perspective. As Katrin Horn points out, 'the acknowledgment that popular culture cannot be radical in the sense of being anti-capitalist should not exclude the notion that it is still capable of transporting other forms of resistance within the limitations of a capitalistic framework and market logic' (Horn 2017, 6). Firstly, the creators and consumers of mainstream culture must continue to challenge our popular definitions of 'greatness', seeking out monstrous and marginal texts to revise through adaptation, travesty, and author fictionalization (Troost and Greenfield 2010, 443). In the short term, however, we also need *better* fictionalizations of marginalized artists, who serve as heroes and 'original' authors in their own right. Such depictions may be historically inaccurate or over-simplistic, but they serve an important inspirational and representational function in popular culture, which has a long and deeply entrenched engagement with the Romantic genius, and a resulting lack of women in mainstream creative roles. In this case, 'bad' or ahistorical adaptations – perhaps more accurately called remixes in this instance – can have a vital function. They serve to inspire contemporary creators, even if this is sometimes at the expense of highlighting the real, historical marginalization such creators have faced in the past. Whether or not Frankenfiction will play a progressive role in this process of 'mainstreaming' marginalized artists and perspectives remains to be seen, though I certainly believe it has the potential to do so.

Notes

1 Other creators to whom the saying 'bad artists copy. Good artists steal' has been attributed include the critic Lionel Trilling and the poet T.S. Eliot. More recently (and in a slightly different wording), it was also associated with former Apple CEO, Steve Jobs (Farber 2014).

2 This term is was presented as part of a paper on 'The Cohesion and Expansion of Fictional Worlds' at the International Conference on Narrative, University of Amsterdam, 16–18 June 2016.

3 The legal concept of the trademark emerged in the mid-nineteenth century – in France with the Manufacture and Goods Mark Act in 1857, in the UK with the Merchandise Marks Act of 1862 and the Trade Marks Registration Act of 1875, and in the United States with a trademark act in 1881. The latter would be finalized in the Lanham Act of 1946, which serves as the basis for much US and international trademark law today.

4 The Sad Puppies first aimed to influence Hugo nominations in 2013, campaigning 'for slates of nominees made up mostly of white men', and claiming 'that the Hugos had become dominated by what Internet conservatives call Social Justice Warriors … who value politics over plot' (A. Wallace 2015, paras 4, 16). In 2015 this campaign was largely successful, and they have returned in the years since to promote their agenda.

5 In *Billion Year Spree*, Brian Aldiss (quoting Trelawney) writes: "'The most striking feature in her face was her calm grey eyes; she was rather under the English standard of woman's height, very fair and light-haired, witty, social, and animated in the society of friends, though mournful in solitude." It is hard to resist the idea that this is a portrait of the first writer of science fiction' (Aldiss 1973, 21).

Conclusion: The Monster Always Escapes

Before, I looked upon the accounts of vice and injustice that I read in books or heard from others as tales of ancient days or imaginary evils; at least they were remote and more familiar to reason than to the imagination; but now misery has come home, and men appear to me as monsters thirsting for each other's blood.
(Shelley [1831] 2015, 86)

Dan Hassler-Forest describes how 'the figure of the undead' has become '[i]nstantly recognizable to general audiences, yet flexible enough to serve both as a legitimate monster and as the punchline to a bad joke' (2016, 156). Living monsters are numbered among these ranks as well, with adaptations of beasts like *Godzilla* (2014) and King Kong (*Kong: Skull Island,* 2017) dominating global box offices, and a multi-movie series of Universal Monster reboots underway. With the 200th anniversary of *Frankenstein*'s publication now behind us, Mary Shelley's creature also seems set to retake the cultural spotlight. So does James Whale's—at the time of this writing, Universal's *The Bride of Frankenstein* is in pre-production (Kroll 2017). With the recent triumph of lobbyists against American copyright extensions, a wealth of new material is also poised to enter the public domain (Lee 2019). The future of Frankenfiction looks bright, at least for the monster studies scholar.

With so many monstrous adaptations on the horizon, it becomes clear that as soon as we define Frankenfiction – distancing it from other genres and theories – it develops its own margins, gaps, and boundaries, distinct from those to which it is grafted (adaptation, remix, and historical fiction). Even messy definitions are necessarily exclusionary, and as we reveal, dissect, and catalogue one part of Frankenfiction, other parts shift further into the margins. As Cohen asserts, 'the monster always escapes', continuously returning in new guises for new contexts (1996, 4). Alongside its continued presence in Western mass, mainstream culture, over the last several years Frankenfiction has appeared in unexpected places.

Throughout this book I have focused my definitions of Frankenfiction around the particularly Anglo-American ways contemporary stories are recycled and appropriated, but since the emergence of Frankenfiction in this context, non-English-language instances have materialized in response. In 2011, Panini Books (the German publisher responsible for several translations of Quirk Books titles) released both *Die Leichen des jungen Werther* – a *Pride and Prejudice and Zombies*-style parody of Johann Wolfgang von Goethe's *Die Leiden des jungen Werther* (1774) by Susanne Picard – and *Sissi: Die Vampirjägerin* by Claudia Kern – a novel similar in concept to A.E. Moorat's *Queen Victoria: Demon Hunter* (2009) or Grahame-Smith's *Abraham Lincoln, Vampire Hunter* (2010), but featuring Empress Elisabeth of Austria. Fantasy author Martijn Adelmund has given the Dutch colonial classic *Max Havelaar* (1860) a postcolonial novel-as-mashup makeover in *Max Havelaar met zombies* (2016). In 2013, the Japanese manga series 文豪ストレイドッグス (trans. *Bungo Stray Dogs*, lit. *Great Writer Stray Dogs*) presented a supernatural crime-fighting and detective agency that draws its inspiration from *The League of Extraordinary Gentlemen*. Although it is set in the present day, the main characters are great historical authors, including Agatha Christie, Osamu Dazai, Fyodor Dostoyevsky, Rampo Edogawa, Edgar Allan Poe, and Mark Twain. In 2016, the series was also adapted as an anime, and English editions of the manga were released. Project Itoh's 2012 novel 屍者の帝国 (trans. *The Empire of Corpses*) performs a similar move, mashing up the Frankenstein legend with Sherlock Holmes and historical figures like Charles Babbage. This text also has manga and film versions, with translations into English and several other languages. These kinds of transnational appropriations offer an entirely new, but equally interesting set of questions, given the ways these texts inevitably migrate across national borders, and the differing models of authorship and heritage culture that operate in each country.

There is also much work to be done in exploring the expressions of Frankenfiction in fan and craft cultures. By its very nature, such fictions connect disparate texts and fanbases. In fact, Frankenfictions have much in common with 'crossover' fan fiction, where two separate storyworlds or universes are brought together. Part of the genre's success involves its juxtaposition of seemingly opposed media fandoms – horror and costume drama, opposed because they are mistakenly assumed to represent extreme poles in audience gender and taste. As I discussed in Chapter 5, acts of Frankenfiction also creatively perform the texts they collect in recognizably fannish ways. The steampunk movement, likewise, which encompasses a wide range of aesthetic and political standpoints on nineteenth-century industrialism, is arguably engaged in a kind of historical mashup. Steampunk is a highly diverse subculture, commonly defined by its aesthetics and 'practices of vernacular craft', and driven by the utopian idea of the self-made man or woman (Onion 2008, 138, 151–2). Steampunk often takes monstrous stories of British colonialism, racism, and patriarchy and diffuses them, sometimes using literal monsters. In many cases, it seeks to undo the white, masculine, imperialist versions of the past that historical accuracy and historical traces have constructed. In some cases, it does so by constructing alternate histories and aesthetics. In other cases, it simply works through existing ones. As Margaret Rose writes, steampunk's 'deliberate breaks with the realism of historical representation draw attention to the fictional (and fantastic) [...] narrative-making processes at work in any representation of history' (2009, 324). Steampunk is also a useful example of a subculture in which fan ethics and aesthetics have merged with professional ones.

These and other monstrous historical fictions on the margins of this book await further scholarly analysis. In any case, mainstream Frankenfiction is already a worthy heir to the legacy of Mary Shelley's *Frankenstein*. Like the creature to Victor Frankenstein, Frankenfictions force us to reckon with our past judgements, actions, and creations, making us responsible for what happens next, and calling us to choose how we will respond. Like the creature, Frankenfictions carelessly destroy the things we hold dear, daring us to reply. Like the creature, they illuminate new opportunities and ways of looking at the world, echoing through history and fiction long after it has ceased to speak. Increasingly, Frankenfictions are even used as metaphors in non-fictional contexts. As Elizabeth Lavenza laments in the above excerpt from *Frankenstein*, horror is no longer an abstract concept 'read in books or heard from others as tales of ancient days or imaginary evils'. Instead, 'misery has come home, and men appear [...] as monsters thirsting for each other's blood' (Shelley [1831] 2015, 86). 'We live in an age of monsters', writes McNally, before beginning his litany of the many ways in which, in the twenty-first century, fantastical monstrosity has slowly but aggressively emerged from the margins of genre fiction into the public and popular spheres, becoming part of 'real' history as well as fictional (2012, 1). During this period, '*Pride and Prejudice and Zombies* rocketed up bestseller-lists, and seemingly endless numbers of vampire- and zombie-films and novels flooded the market' (2012, 1). But the fantastical monster has seeped into political discourse as well. In 2009, *Time* magazine declared the zombie 'the official monster of the recession' (Grossman 2009b, para. 8); in 2016, Donald Trump was described as the 'Frankenstein monster' of the Republican party

(Kagan 2016; D. Smith 2016); and in June 2017, the New Statesman featured an undead Theresa May on its front cover, beneath the headline 'The Zombie PM' (see Heffer 2017).

At the beginning of the twenty-first century, Fred Botting suggested that in 'Gothic times margins may become the norm and occupy a more central cultural place. Consequently, that center is now characterized by a dispersal, emptied of both core and apex. [...] To live in Gothic times at present means that Gothic loses its older intensity, shedding some of the allure of darkness, danger, and mystery' (2002, 286–7). Botting describes a dystopian future in which Gothic fiction

> [H]as become too familiar after two centuries of repetitive mutation and seems incapable of shocking anew. Inured to Gothic shocks and terrors, contemporary culture recycles its images in the hope of finding a charge intense enough to stave off the black hole within and without, the one opened up by postmodernist fragmentation and plurality. (Botting 2002, 298)

Nearly two decades on from this assertion, I would argue that the opposite has happened. It is indeed the 'postmodernist fragmentation and plurality' of mainstream culture that historical monster mashups and Frankenfictions are attempting to fend off with the recycling of Gothic images. But while this recycling is certainly hopeful, it is not as futile as Botting's black hole analogy would suggest. Instead, we have seen a whole new range of meanings, shocks, and terrors open up in its wake, as Frankenfiction denaturalizes figures and fictions that seemed to have lost their transgressive impulse, and resurrects them once more.

Bibliography

Adams, A.M. 2009. 'What's in a Frame?: The Authorizing Presence in James Whale's *Bride of Frankenstein*'. *Journal of Popular Culture* 42 (3): 403–18.

Adelmund, Martijn, and Multatuli. 2016. *Max Havelaar met zombies*. Amsterdam: Luitingh Sijthoff Fantasy.

Aldana Reyes, Xavier. 2017. *Spanish Gothic: National Identity, Collaboration and Cultural Adaptation*. London: Palgrave.

Aldiss, Brian. 1973. *Billion Year Spree: The True History of Science Fiction*. Garden City, NY: Doubleday.

Aldiss, Brian. 1974. *Frankenstein Unbound*. London: Random House.

Alexander, Isabella. 2010. *Copyright Law and the Public Interest in the Nineteenth Century*. Oxford: Hart Publishing.

Anders, Charlie Jane. 2009. 'Literary Mashups Meet Tentacles. Has All of Western Literature Been Leading up to This'. *io9*. 15 July 2009. http://io9.com/5315301/literary-mashups-meet-tentacles-has-all-of-western-literature-been-leading-up-to-this.

andycimex. 2010. 'Man Falling from One of the WTC-Towers'. *Documenting Reality*. 28 March 2010. https://www.documentingreality.com/forum/f10/man-falling-one-wtc-towers-44325/.

Appelbaum, Stanley. 1976. 'Publisher's Note'. In *Une semaine de bonté: A Surrealistic Novel in Collage by Max Ernst*, edited by Stanley Appelbaum, v–xi. New York: Dover.

Arewa, Olufunmilayo B. 2013. 'Making Music: Copyright Law and the Creative Processes'. In *A Companion to Media Authorship*, edited by Jonathan Gray and Derek Johnson, 69–87. Malden, MA: John Wiley & Sons.

Armitt, Lucie. 2011. *History of the Gothic: Twentieth-Century Gothic*. Cardiff: University of Wales.

Arthurs, Jane. 2004. *Television and Sexuality: Regulation and the Politics of Taste*. New York: Open University Press.

Asagiri, Kafka, and Sango Harukawa. 2017. *Bungo Stray Dogs*. Translated by Kevin Gifford. Vol. 1. New York: Yen Press.

Augaitis, Daina, Bruce Grenville, and Stephanie Rebick, eds. 2016. *MashUp: The Birth of Modern Culture*. London: Black Dog Publishing.

Austen, Jane. (1813) 2008. *Pride and Prejudice*. Rockville, MD: Arc Manor LLC.

Baker, Daniel. 2011. 'History as Fantasy: Estranging the Past in *Jonathan Strange and Mr Norrell*'. *Otherness: Essays & Studies* 2 (1): 1–16.

Baker, Jo. 2013. *Longbourn*. New York: Knopf.

Baldick, Chris. 1987. *In Frankenstein's Shadow: Myth, Monstrosity, and Nineteenth-Century Writing*. Oxford: Clarendon.

Baldick, Chris. 1992. 'Introduction'. In *The Oxford Book of Gothic Tales*, edited by Chris Baldick, xi–xxiii. Oxford: Oxford University Press.

Barr, Stuart. 2015. 'Interview: Kim Newman on Vampires and Horror'. *Maxrennblog*. 25 March 2015. https://maxrennblog.wordpress.com/2015/03/25/interview-kim-newman-on-vampires-and-horror/.

Barthes, Roland. (1957) 1972. 'Myth Today'. In *Mythologies*, translated by Annette Lavers, 107–64. London: Jonathan Cape.

Barthes, Roland. 1978. *Image, Music, Text*. Translated by Stephen Heath. New York: Hill and Wang.

Barton, Charles, dir. 1948. *Abbott and Costello Meet Frankenstein*. Universal Pictures.

Bassett, Jordan. 2015. '10 Weird Literary Mash-Ups Inspired by "Pride and Prejudice and Zombies"'. *NME*. 28 October 2015. http://www.nme.com/blogs/nme-blogs/10-weird-literary-mash-ups-inspired-by-pride-and-prejudice-and-zombies-14498.

Battersby, Christine. 1989. *Gender and Genius: Towards a Feminist Aesthetic*. London: The Women's Press.

Batty, Colin. 2014a. 'Alien in Crowd'. Acrylic paint on cabinet card. *Peculiarium*. http://www.peculiarium.com/colin-batty/cabinet-card-alien-in-crowd.

Batty, Colin. 2014b. 'Alien Tree Man'. Acrylic paint on cabinet card. *Peculiarium*. http://www.peculiarium.com/colin-batty/cabinet-card-alien-tree-man.

Batty, Colin. 2014c. 'Brainiac and Son'. Acrylic paint on cabinet card. *Peculiarium*. http://www.peculiarium.com/colin-batty/cabinet-card-brainiac-and-son.

Batty, Colin. 2014d. 'Captain Clevage'. Acrylic paint on cabinet card. *Peculiarium*. http://www.peculiarium.com/colin-batty/cabinet-card-captain-clevage.

Batty, Colin. 2014e. 'Chimp Siblings'. Acrylic paint on cabinet card. *Peculiarium*. http://www.peculiarium.com/colin-batty/cabinet-card-chimp-siblings.

Batty, Colin. 2014f. 'Elephant Dude'. Acrylic paint on cabinet card. *Peculiarium*. http://www.peculiarium.com/colin-batty/cabinet-card-elephant-dude.

Batty, Colin. 2014g. 'Fembot'. Acrylic paint on cabinet card. *Peculiarium*. http://www.peculiarium.com/colin-batty/cabinet-card-fembot.

Batty, Colin. 2014h. 'Frankenvintage Seated'. Acrylic paint on cabinet card. *Peculiarium*. http://www.peculiarium.com/colin-batty/cabinet-card-frankenvintage-seated.

Batty, Colin. 2014i. 'Girl and Frank'. Acrylic paint on cabinet card. *Peculiarium*. http://www.peculiarium.com/colin-batty/cabinet-card-girl-and-frank.

Batty, Colin. 2014j. 'Half Dowager Half Squid?' Acrylic paint on cabinet card. *Peculiarium*. http://www.peculiarium.com/colin-batty/cabinet-card-half-dowager-half-squid.

Batty, Colin. 2014k. 'I'm Your Puppet'. Acrylic paint on cabinet card. *Peculiarium*. http://www.peculiarium.com/colin-batty/cabinet-card-im-your-puppet.

Batty, Colin. 2014l. 'Melissa Muscles'. Acrylic paint on cabinet card. *Peculiarium*. http://www.peculiarium.com/colin-batty/cabinet-card-melissa-muscles.

Batty, Colin. 2014m. 'Mild Mannered Man of Superness'. Acrylic paint on cabinet card. *Peculiarium*. http://www.peculiarium.com/colin-batty/cabinet-card-mild-mannered-man-of-superness.

Batty, Colin. 2014n. 'Mr. Brundle'. Acrylic paint on cabinet card. *Peculiarium*. http://www.peculiarium.com/colin-batty/cabinet-card-mr-brundle.

Batty, Colin. 2014o. 'Smoking Smiling Demon'. Acrylic paint on cabinet card. *Peculiarium*. http://www.peculiarium.com/colin-batty/cabinet-card-smoking-smiling-demon.

Batty, Colin. 2014p. 'Snake Boy'. Acrylic paint on cabinet card. *Peculiarium*. http://www.peculiarium.com/colin-batty/cabinet-card-snake-boy.

Batty, Colin. 2014q. 'Wolfman Jacket'. Acrylic paint on cabinet card. *Peculiarium*. http://www.peculiarium.com/colin-batty/cabinet-card-wolfman-jacket.

Bayor, Ronald H. 2014. *Encountering Ellis Island: How European Immigrants Entered America*. Baltimore, MD: Johns Hopkins University Press.

Beattie, Stuart, dir. 2014. *I, Frankenstein*. Lionsgate.

Bekmambetov, Timur, dir. 2012. *Abraham Lincoln: Vampire Hunter*. 20th Century Fox.

Benjamin, Walter. 2004. 'The Work of Art in the Age of Mechanical Reproduction'. In *Literary Theory: An Anthology*, edited by Julie Rivkin and Michael Ryan, 2nd ed., 1235–41. Malden, MA: Blackwell.

Ben-Porat, Ziva. 1979. 'Method in Madness: Notes on the Structure of Parody, Based on MAD TV Satires'. *Poetics Today* 1 (1/2): 245–72.

Binder, Heiko. 2009. 'Word of Mouth and Zombies'. MA diss. Burnaby, BC: Simon Fraser University. http://summit.sfu.ca/system/files/iritems1/9916/ETD4916.pdf.

Bird, Kathryn. 2014. '"Civilised Society Doesn't Just Happen": The Animal, the Law, and "Victorian Values" in Kim Newman's *Anno Dracula*'. *Neo-Victorian Studies* 7 (1): 1–24.

Bloom, Edward A., and Lillian D. Bloom. 1979. *Satire's Persuasive Voice*. Ithaca, NY: Cornell University Press.

Blumberg, Jane. 1993. *Mary Shelley's Early Novels: 'This Child of Imagination and Misery'*. London: Macmillan.

Boehm-Schnitker, Nadine, and Susanne Gruss. 2014. 'Introduction: Fashioning the Neo-Victorian – Neo-Victorian Fashions'. In *Neo-Victorian Literature and Culture: Immersions and Revisitations*, edited by Nadine Boehm-Schnitker and Susanne Gruss, 1–17. London: Routledge.

Borschke, Margie. 2017. *This Is Not a Remix: Piracy, Authenticity and Popular Music*. New York: Bloomsbury Academic.

Botelho, Derek. 2012. 'Exclusive Interview: Author Kim Newman Talks *Anno Dracula*'. *Daily Dead*. 20 April 2012. http://dailydead.com/exclusive-interview-author-kim-newman-talks-anno-dracula/.

Botting, Fred. 1992. 'Frankenstein and the Language of Monstrosity'. In *Reviewing Romanticism*, edited by Robin Jarvis and Philip W. Martin, 51–9. Houndmills: Palgrave.

Botting, Fred. 1995. 'Introduction'. In *Frankenstein/Mary Shelley*, edited by Fred Botting, 1–20. New York: St. Martin's.

Botting, Fred. 2002. 'Aftergothic: Consumption, Machines, and Black Holes'. In *The Cambridge Companion to Gothic Fiction*, edited by Jerrold E. Hogle, 277–300. Cambridge: Cambridge University Press.

Botting, Fred. 2008. *Limits of Horror: Technology, Bodies, Gothic*. Manchester: Manchester University Press.

Botting, Fred, and Dale Townshend. 2004. *Twentieth Century Gothic: Our Monsters, Our Pets*. Vol. IV. Gothic: Critical Concepts in Literary and Cultural Studies.

Bradley, Laura. 2017. 'Universal Invented Movie Universes; Why Are They Having Such a Hard Time with Them Now?' Vanity Fair. 13 June 2017. https://www.vanityfair. com/hollywood/2017/06/the-mummy-dark-universe.

Braidotti, Rosi. 1997. 'Mothers, Monsters, and Machines'. In *Writing on the Body: Female Embodiment and Feminist Theory*, edited by Katie Conboy, Nadia Medina, and Sarah Stanbury, 59–79. New York: Columbia University Press.

Branagh, Kenneth, dir. 1994. *Mary Shelley's Frankenstein*. TriStar Pictures.

Brantlinger, Patrick. 1988. *Rule of Darkness: British Literature and Imperialism, 1830–1914*. Ithaca, NY: Cornell University Press.

Brecht, Bertolt. 1964. 'Alienation Effects in Chinese Acting'. In *Brecht on Theatre: 1933–1947*, edited and translated by John Willett, 91–99. London: Shenval Press.

Brennan, Matt. 2016. '"Pride and Prejudice and Zombies": World War Zzzzzs'. *IndieWire*. 3 February 2016. http://www.indiewire.com/2016/02/pride-and-prejudice-and-zombies-world-war-zzzzzs-review-roundup-175087/.

Bridgeman, Sharon, dir. 2004. *Van Helsing: The London Assignment*. Animation. Universal Pictures.

Briggs, Nicholas, and Lisa Bowerman, dirs. 2009. 'The Company of Friends: Mary's Story'. Radio. *Doctor Who*. Big Finish.

Britt, Ryan. 2011. 'Genre in the Mainstream: Mary Wollstonecraft Shelley's Frankenstein'. *Tor.Com*. 25 October 2011. http://www.tor.com/2011/10/25/genre-in-the-mainstream-mary-wollstonecraft-shelleys-frankenstein/.

Bromwich, Kathryn. 2015. 'Colin Batty's Sci-Fi Portraiture – in Pictures'. *The Guardian*. 31 January 2015. http://www.theguardian.com/artanddesign/gallery/2015/jan/31/colin-battys-sci-fi-portraiture-in-pictures.

Brooks, Mel, dir. 1975. *Young Frankenstein*. 20th Century Fox.

Brophy, Brigid. 1968. *Black and White: A Portrait of Aubrey Beardsley*. London: Jonathan Cape.

Brownstein, Rachel. 2011. *Why Jane Austen?* New York: Columbia University Press.

Bruin-Molé, Megen de. 2016. '"I'm Just a Guy on the Internet": An Interview with Kevin J. Weir'. *Frankenfiction*. 2 November 2016. http://frankenfiction.com/im-just-guy-internet-interview-kevin-j-weir/.

Bruin-Molé, Megen de. 2017. '"Now with Ultraviolent Zombie Mayhem!": The Neo-Victorian novel-as-mashup and the limits of postmodern irony'. In *Neo-Victorian Humour: The Rhetorics and Politics of Comedy, Irony and Parody*, edited by Marie-Luise Kohlke and Christian Gutleben, 249–276. Amsterdam: Brill.

Bruin-Molé, Megen de. 2018. '"Hail, Mary, the Mother of Science Fiction": Popular Fictionalisations of Mary Wollstonecraft Shelley in Film and Television, 1935–2018'. *Science Fiction Film and Television* 11 (2): 233–55.

Bruin-Molé, Megen de, and Martin Stiff. 2015. 'Anatomy of a Cover'. Frankenfiction. 29 April 2015. http://frankenfiction.com/anatomy-of-a-cover/.

Burke, K. (1969a) A Grammar of Motives [1945], Berkeley: University of California Press.

Burne-Jones, Edward. 1856. 'Essay on *The Newcomes*'. *The Oxford and Cambridge Magazine*, January 1856.

Burstein, Miriam. 2006. 'Rules for Writing Neo-Victorian Novels'. *The Little Professor*. 15 March 2006. http://littleprofessor.typepad.com/the_little_professor/2006/03/rules_for_writi.html.

Burton, Tim, dir. 1996. *Mars Attacks!* Warner Bros.

Burton, Tim, dir. 2016. *Miss Peregrine's Home for Peculiar Children*. Film. 20th Century Fox.

Burton, Tim, and Mike Johnson, dirs. 2005. *Corpse Bride*. Warner Bros.

Busse, Kristina. 2013. 'The Return of the Author: Ethos and Identity Politics'. In *A Companion to Media Authorship*, edited by Jonathan Gray and Derek Johnson, 48–67. Malden, MA: John Wiley & Sons.

Butler, Judith. 2004. *Undoing Gender*. London: Routledge.

Cabezas, Paco, dir. 2016a. 'This World Is Our Hell'. *Penny Dreadful*. Showtime/Sky.

Cabezas, Paco, dir. 2016b. 'No Beast So Fierce'. *Penny Dreadful*. Showtime/Sky.

Cabezas, Paco, dir. 2016c. 'Ebb Tide'. *Penny Dreadful*. Showtime/Sky.

Cabezas, Paco, dir. 2016d. 'The Blessed Dark'. *Penny Dreadful*. Showtime/Sky.

Cahir, Linda Costanzo. 2006. *Literature into Film: Theory and Practical Applications*. Jefferson, NC: McFarland.

Campbell, Joseph. (1949) 2008. *The Hero with a Thousand Faces*. Novaro, CA: New World Library.

Carroll, Samantha J. 2010. 'Putting the "Neo" Back into Neo-Victorian: The Neo-Victorian Novel as Postmodern Revisionist Fiction'. *Neo-Victorian Studies* 3 (2): 172–205.

Carter, Angela. 1995. 'Appendix: Afterword to *Fireworks*'. In *Burning Your Boats: Collected Short Stories*, 459–60. New York: Henry Holt.

Cartmell, Deborah, and Imelda Whelehan, eds. 1999. *Adaptations: From Text to Screen, Screen to Text*. New York: Routledge.

Cavallaro, Dani, and Alexandra Warwick. 1998. *Fashioning the Frame: Boundaries, Dress and the Body*. London: Bloomsbury Academic.

'Chapter 1: Subject Matter and Scope of Copyright'. 2013. In *United States Code*. Vol. 17. Washington, DC: U.S. Government Publishing.

'Chapter 22: Trademarks'. 2013. In *United States Code*. Vol. 15. Washington, DC: U.S. Government Publishing.

Clarke, Susanna. 2004. *Jonathan Strange and Mr Norrell*. London: Bloomsbury.

Clery, E.J. 2002. 'The Genesis of "Gothic" Fiction'. In *The Cambridge Companion to Gothic Fiction*, edited by Jerrold E. Hogle, 21–39. Cambridge: Cambridge University Press.

Cleto, Fabio. 1999. 'Introduction: Queering the Camp'. In *Camp: Queer Aesthetics and the Performing Subject: A Reader*, 1–42. Edinburgh: Edinburgh University Press.

Cocca, Carolyn. 2016. *Superwomen: Gender, Power, and Representation*. New York: Bloomsbury Academic.

Cocozza, Paula. 2014. 'Ghostly Gifs Made from Archive Photos – the Haunting Work of Kevin Weir'. *The Guardian*. 28 September 2014. http://www.theguardian.com/artanddesign/shortcuts/2014/sep/28/gif-archive-photos-kevin-weir-flux-machine.

Codell, Julie. 2014. 'Gender, Genius, and Abjection in Artist Biopics'. In *The Biopic in Contemporary Film Culture*, edited by Tom Brown and Bélel Vidal, 159–75. New York: Routledge.

Codell, Julie. 2016. 'Art Periodicals'. In *The Routledge Handbook to Nineteenth-Century British Periodicals and Newspapers*, edited by Andrew King, Alexis Easley, and John Morton, 377–89. London: Routledge.

Cohen, Jeffrey Jerome. 1996. 'Monster Culture (Seven Theses)'. In *Monster Theory: Reading Culture*, edited by Jeffrey Jerome Cohen, 3–25. Minneapolis: University of Minnesota Press.

Cohen, Jeffrey Jerome. 1999. *Of Giants: Sex, Monsters, and the Middle Ages*. Minneapolis: University of Minnesota Press.

Colebrook, Claire. 2004. *Irony*. London: Routledge.

'Conceptual Realism – Travis Louie'. 2013. *The Artillerist*. 26 September 2013. http://theartillerist.com/wjbean/conceptual-realism-travis-louie/.

Cook, Nickolas, and Lewis Carroll. 2011. *Alice in Zombieland*. Chicago, IL: Sourcebooks.

Coppola, Francis Ford, dir. 1992. *Bram Stoker's Dracula*. Columbia Pictures.

Corman, Roger, dir. 1990. *Roger Corman's Frankenstein Unbound*. 20th Century Fox.

Cornwell, Neil. 2012. 'European Gothic'. In *A New Companion to the Gothic*, edited by David Punter, 64–76. Oxford: Blackwell Publishing.

Cory, Charlotte. 2007. *The Visitors*. Stockport: Dewi Lewis.

Cory, Charlotte. 2018. 'About Charlotte Cory, Artist'. *CharlotteCory.Com*. February 2018. http://www.charlottecory.com/Home/View/ABOUT.

Côté, Marc-Alexis, dir. 2015. *Assassin's Creed Syndicate*. PlayStation 4. Quebec: Ubisoft.

Craft, Christopher. 1997. '"Kiss Me with Those Red Lips": Gender and Inversion in Bram Stoker's *Dracula*'. In *Dracula*, edited by Nina Auerbach and David J. Skal, 444–59. New York: Norton Critical Editions.

Creed, Barbara. 1993. *The Monstrous-Feminine: Film, Feminism, Psychoanalysis*. London: Routledge.

Crenshaw, Kimberle. 1991. 'Mapping the Margins: Intersectionality, Identity Politics, and Violence against Women of Color'. *Stanford Law Review* 43 (6): 1241–99.

Critchley, Simon. 2002. *On Humour*. London: Routledge.

Cuelenaere, Eduard, Stijn Joye, and Gertjan Willems. 2016. 'Reframing the Remake: Dutch-Flemish Monolingual Remakes and Their Theoretical and Conceptual Implications'. *Frames Cinema Journal* 10: 1–19.

Cueto, Emma. 2016. 'Women Clean Up at Nebula Awards, but Sci-Fi Still Has Work to Do with Gender Equality'. *Bustle*. 16 May 2016. https://www.bustle.com/articles/161143-women-clean-up-at-nebula-awards-but-sci-fi-still-has-work-to-do-with-gender-equality.

Currie, Mark. (1995) 2013. *Metafiction*. London: Routledge.

D'Alessandro, Anthony. 2017. '"The Mummy" Will Lose $95M: Here's Why'. *Deadline*. 19 June 2017. http://deadline.com/2017/06/the-mummy-tom-cruise-box-office-bomb-loss-1202114482/.

'Dan Hillier: Artist Interview'. 2015. *Artrepublic*. 23 March 2015. http://www.artrepublic.com/posts/httpwww-artrepublic-comarticles506-dan-hillier-artist-interview-html/.

'Dan Hillier: Isn't Life Surreal?' 2012. *Ladies and Gents*. 12 December 2012. http://www.ladiesngents.com/en/curator/DAN-HILLIER-Interview.asp?thisPage=4.

'Dan Hillier's IIllustrations [*sic*]'. 2014. *Creative Mapping*. 16 April 2014. http://www.creative-mapping.com/dan-hillier-london-artist-illustrator-ink/.

Daniels, Nia. 2015. 'Showrunner John Logan: "To Me, *Penny Dreadful* Is a Dance with Eva Green"'. *The Knowledge*. 27 August 2015. http://www.theknowledgeonline.com/the-knowledge-bulletin/post/2015/08/27/showrunner-john-logan-to-me-penny-dreadful-is-a-dance-with-eva-green.

da Silva, Patrícia Dias, and José Luís Garcia, 'YouTubers as Satirists: Humour and Remix in Online Video', JeDEM-EJournal of EDemocracy and Open Government, 4 (2012), 89–144.

Davies, Helen. 2015. *Neo-Victorian Freakery: The Cultural Afterlife of the Victorian Freak Show*. Houndmills: Palgrave Macmillan.

Deahl, Rachel. 2009. 'Quirk Has Unlikely Hit with Jane Austen-Zombie Mash-Up'. *Publishers Weekly*. 7 April 2009. http://web.archive.org/web/20100302075649/http://www.publishersweekly.com/article/409276-Quirk_Has_Unlikely_Hit_with_Jane_Austen_Zombie_Mash_up.php.

Defoe, Daniel. 1840. *The Political History of the Devil*. Oxford: Thomas Tegg.

Desforges, Luke, and Joanne Maddern. 2004. 'Front Doors to Freedom, Portal to the Past: History at the Ellis Island Immigration Museum, New York'. *Social & Cultural Geography* 5 (3): 437–57.

Dias da Silva, Patrícia and José Luís Garcia. 2012. 'YouTubers as Satirists: Humour and Remix in Online Video'. *JeDEM – EJournal of EDemocracy and Open Government* 4: 89–114.

Domsch, Sebastian. 2012. 'Monsters against Empire: The Politics and Poetics of Neo-Victorian Metafiction in *The League of Extraordinary Gentlemen*'. In *Neo-Victorian*

Gothic: Horror, Violence and Degeneration in the Re-Imagined Nineteenth Century, edited by Marie-Luise Kohlke and Christian Gutleben, 97–121. Amsterdam: Rodopi.

Donawerth, Jane L., and Carol A. Kolmerten. 1994. 'Introduction'. In *Utopian and Science Fiction by Women: Worlds of Difference*, edited by Jane L. Donawerth and Carol A. Kolmerten, 1–14. Syracuse, NY: Syracuse University Press.

Donoghue, Steve. 2012. 'An Interview with Kim Newman'. *Open Letters Monthly*. 25 May 2012. http://www.openlettersmonthly.com/an-interview-with-kim-newman/.

Doyle, Sir Arthur Conan. 1922. *The Coming of the Fairies*. New York: George H. Doran. https://archive.org/details/comingoffairies00doylrich.

Duchamp, Marcel. 1964. 'L.H.O.O.Q., or La Joconde'. Acrylic on paper. Norton Simon Museum. https://www.nortonsimon.org/art/detail/P.1969.094.

Dysart, Joshua, and Jason Shawn Alexander. 2004. *Van Helsing: From Beneath the Rue Morgue*. Milwaukie, OR: Dark Horse.

Elliott, Kamilla. 2003. *Rethinking the Novel/Film Debate*. Cambridge: Cambridge University Press.

Elliott, Kamilla. 2008. 'Gothic – Film – Parody'. *Adaptation* 1 (1): 24–43.

Ellis, Markman. 2000. *The History of Gothic Fiction*. Edinburgh: Edinburgh University Press.

Erlanson, Amanda. 2009. 'Travis Louie's "Portrait of the Artist as a Young Monster"'. *Erratic Phenomena*. 21 August 2009. http://www.erraticphenomena.com/2009/08/travis-louies-portrait-of-artist-as.html.

Erll, Astrid. 2011. 'Travelling Memory'. *Parallax* 17 (4): 4–18.

Erwin, Sherri Browning, and Charlotte Brontë. 2010. *Jane Slayre*. New York: Gallery Books.

Erwin, Sherri Browning, and Charles Dickens. 2011. *Grave Expectations*. New York: Gallery Books.

Eyre, Janieta. 1996. 'Twin Manicurists'. Black and white photograph. Diane Farris Gallery. http://www.dianefarrisgallery.com/artist/eyre/available.htm.

Faraci, Devin. 2013. 'Showtime Is Ripping Off LEAGUE OF EXTRAORDINARY GENTLEMEN'. *Birth.Movies.Death*. 14 January 2013. https://birthmoviesdeath.com/2013/01/14/showtime-is-ripping-off-league-of-extraordinary-gentlemen.

Farber, Dan. 2014. 'What Steve Jobs Really Meant When He Said "Good Artists Copy; Great Artists Steal"'. *CNET*. 28 January 2014. https://www.cnet.com/news/what-steve-jobs-really-meant-when-he-said-good-artists-copy-great-artists-steal/.

Ferguson, Christine. 2011. 'Surface Tensions: Steampunk, Subculture, and the Ideology of Style'. *Neo-Victorian Studies* 4 (2): 66–90.

Fleegler, Robert L. 2013. *Ellis Island Nation: Immigration Policy and American Identity in the Twentieth Century*. Philadelphia: University of Pennsylvania Press.

Flint, Kate. 1992. *The Woman Reader: 1837–1914*. Oxford: Clarendon.

Ford, Michael Thomas. 2010. *Jane Bites Back: A Novel*. New York: Ballantine Books.

Foucault, Michel. 1967. *Madness and Civilization: A History of Insanity in the Age of Reason*. Translated by Richard Howard. London: Routledge.

Foucault, Michel. 1980. 'What Is an Author?' In *Language, Counter-Memory, Practice: Selected Essays and Interviews*, edited by Donald F. Bouchard, 113–38. Ithaca, NY: Cornell University Press.

Fowles, John. 1969. *The French Lieutenant's Women*. London: Jonathan Cape.

'Frankenstein, MD'. 2014. *Pemberley Digital*. http://www.pemberleydigital.com/frankenstein-md/.

Franssen, Gaston, and Rick Honings. 2016. 'Introduction: Starring the Author'. In *Celebrity Authorship and Afterlives in English and American Literature*, edited by Gaston Franssen and Rick Honings, 1–21. Houndmills: Palgrave Macmillan.

Freud, Sigmund. (1819) 2001. 'The Uncanny'. In *'An Infantile Neurosis' and Other Works*, edited by Anna Freud, Alix Strachey, and Alan Tyson, translated by James Strachey, 217–56. London: Vintage Classics.

Frye, Northrop. (1957) 2002. *Anatomy of Criticism*. London: Penguin Books.

Gaiman, Neil. 2007. *Fragile Things*. London: Headline Review.

Gaskell, Elizabeth. 1849. *Mary Barton, a Tale of Manchester Life*. Leipzig: Bernhard Tauchnitz.

Genette, Gérard. 1997. *Palimpsests: Literature in the Second Degree*. Translated by Channa Newman and Claude Doubinsky. Lincoln: University of Nebraska Press.

Gibson, William. 2005. 'God's Little Toys: Confessions of a Cut & Paste Artist'. *WIRED Magazine*. July 2005. http://archive.wired.com/wired/archive/13.07/gibson.html.

Gilbert, Sandra M., and Susan Gubar. 2000. *The Madwoman in the Attic: The Woman Writer and the Nineteenth-Century Literary Imagination*. 2nd ed. New Haven, CT: Yale University Press.

Gilbert, Sophie. 2016. 'Pride and Prejudice and Zombies: Classic Romance with a Nasty Bite'. *The Atlantic*. 5 February 2016. https://www.theatlantic.com/entertainment/archive/2016/02/pride-and-prejudice-and-zombies-review/460194/.

Goldman, Paul. 2004. *Victorian Illustration: The Pre-Raphaelites, the Idyllic School, and the High Victorians*. 2nd ed. Aldershot: Lund Humphries.

Golomb, Jacob. 1995. *In Search of Authenticity: From Kierkegaard to Camus*. London: Routledge.

Goodwin, Christopher. 2009. 'Lizzie Bennet as a Zombie Slayer: Who'd Have Believed It?' *Sunday Times*, 4 May 2009.

Goss, Theodora. 2012. 'The Monster in the Mirror: Late Victorian Gothic and Anthropology'. Doctoral thesis. Boston, MA: Boston University.

Goss, Theodora. 2017. *The Strange Case of the Alchemist's Daughter*. New York: Saga Press.

Goss, Theodora. 2018. *European Travel for the Monstrous Gentlewoman*. New York: Saga Press.

Grahame-Smith, Seth. 2010. *Abraham Lincoln, Vampire Hunter*. New York: Grand Central Publishing.

Grahame-Smith, Seth, and Jane Austen. 2009. *Pride and Prejudice and Zombies*. Quirk Classics. Philadelphia, PA: Quirk Books.

Gray, Jonathan. 2013. 'When Is the Author?' In *A Companion to Media Authorship*, edited by Jonathan Gray and Derek Johnson, 88–111. Malden, MA: John Wiley & Sons.

Gray, Sarah, and Emily Brontë. 2010. *Wuthering Bites*. New York: Kensington.

Green, Hank. 2012. 'The Lizzie Bennet Diaries'. *Tumblr*. 9 April 2012. http://edwardspoonhands.com/post/20791746020/the-lizzie-bennet-diaries.

Grenville, Bruce. 2016. 'MashUp: The Birth of Modern Culture'. In *MashUp: The Birth of Modern Culture*, edited by Daina Augaitis, Bruce Grenville, and Stephanie Rebick, 18–41. London: Black Dog Publishing.

Groot, Jerome de. 2016. *Remaking History: The Past in Contemporary Historical Fictions*. London: Routledge.

Grossman, Lev. 2009a. 'Pride and Prejudice, Now with Zombies!' *Time*. 2 April 2009. http://content.time.com/time/arts/article/0,8599,1889075,00.html.

Grossman, Lev. 2009b. 'Zombies Are the New Vampires'. *Time*. 9 April 2009. http://www.time.com/time/magazine/article/0,9171,1890384,00.html?imw=Y.

Gunkel, David J. 2012. 'What Does It Matter Who Is Speaking? Authorship, Authority, and the Mashup'. *Popular Music and Society* 35 (1): 71–91.

Gunkel, David J. 2016. *Of Remixology: Ethics and Aesthetics after Remix*. Cambridge, MA: MIT Press.

Gutleben, Christian. 2001. *Nostalgic Postmodernism: The Victorian Tradition and the Contemporary British Novel*. Amsterdam: Rodopi.

Haiduc, Sonia. 2013. '"Here Is the Story of My Career …": The Woman Writer on Film'. In *The Writer on Film: Screening Literary Authorship*, edited by Judith Buchanan, 50–63. Houndmills: Palgrave Macmillan.

Halberstam, J. 1993. 'Technologies of Monstrosity: Bram Stoker's *Dracula*'. *Victorian Studies* 36 (3): 333–52.

Halberstam, J. 1995. *Skin Shows: Gothic Horror and the Technology of Monsters*. Durham, NC: Duke University Press.

Halsband, Robert. 1976. 'Women and Literature in Eighteenth-Century England'. In *Woman in the Eighteenth Century and Other Essays*, edited by Paul Fritz and Richard Morton, 55–71. Toronto: Hakkert.

Haraway, Donna J. 1990. 'A Manifesto for Cyborgs: Science, Technology, and Social Feminism in the 1980s'. In *Feminism/Postmodernism*, edited by Linda J. Nicholson, 190–233. New York: Routledge.

Hardaway, Elizabeth. 1999. '"Ourselves Expanded": The Vampire's Evolution from Bram Stoker to Kim Newman'. In *Blood Is the Life: Vampires in Literature*, edited by Leonard G. Heldreth and Mary Pharr, 177–86. Madison, WI: Popular Press.

Hardison, Jim. 2014. 'Foreword'. In *Meet the Family: Altered Photographs by Colin Batty*, edited by Mike Wellins and Lisa Freeman, 1–2. Portland, OR: Freakybuttrue.

Hartcher, Peter. 2017. 'Is the Right-Wing Populist Monster Dying?' *The Sydney Morning Herald*. 27 May 2017. http://www.smh.com.au/comment/is-the-rightwing-populist-monster-dying-20170526-gwdo7m.html.

Harvey, Benjamin. 2016. 'Dan Hillier's New Art Histories'. *Le BonBon*. 15 February 2016. https://www.lebonbon.co.uk/culture/dan-hilliers-new-art-histories/.

Harvey, John. 2007. *Photography and Spirit*. London: Reaktion Books.

Harvison, Anthony. 2009. '*Pride and Prejudice and Zombies* Review and Seth Grahame-Smith Interview'. *Den of Geek*. 11 June 2009. http://www.denofgeek.com/books-comics/5872/pride-and-prejudice-and-zombies-review-and-seth-grahame-smith-interview.

Hassler-Forest, Dan. 2014. '*Game of Thrones*: Quality Television and the Cultural Logic of Gentrification'. *TV/Series* 6 (December): 160–77.

Hassler-Forest, Dan. 2016. *Science Fiction, Fantasy, and Politics: Transmedia World-Building beyond Capitalism*. London: Rowman & Littlefield.

Hawcroft, Emily. 2011. 'Fair or Foul Dealing?: Parody, Satire and Derogatory Treatment'. *Intellectual Property Forum: Journal of the Intellectual and Industrial Property Society of Australia and New Zealand* 87 (December): 29–38.

Hawthorne, Nathaniel. (1846) 1863. 'Rappaccini's Daughter'. In *Mosses from an Old Manse*, 1: 106–49. Boston, MA: Ticknor and Fields.

Hayles, N. Katherine. 1999. *How We Became Posthuman: Virtual Bodies in Cybernetics, Literature, and Informatics*. Chicago: University of Chicago Press.

Hayles, N. Katherine. 2000. 'Flickering Connectivities in Shelley Jackson's *Patchwork Girl*: The Importance of Media-Specific Analysis'. *Postmodern Culture* 10 (2).

Heffer, Simon. 2017. 'The Humbling of Theresa May'. *The New Statesman*. 26 June 2017. http://www.newstatesman.com/politics/uk/2017/06/humbling-theresa-may.

Heilmann, Ann, and Mark Llewellyn. 2010. *Neo-Victorianism: The Victorians in the Twenty-First Century, 1999–2009*. Houndmills: Palgrave Macmillan.

Hesse, Monica. 2009. 'Zombie? Let Austen Flesh It Out'. *The Washington Post*. 17 April 2009. http://www.washingtonpost.com/wp-dyn/content/article/2009/04/16/AR2009041604348.html.

Hickey, Andria. 2006. 'Art Fiction'. *Art Mur*. 1 October 2006. http://artmur.com/en/exhibitions/past-exhibitions/art-fiction/.

Hillier, Dan. 2006a. 'Snake'. Ink and digital collage. https://www.danhillier.com/artwork/Snake.

Hillier, Dan. 2006b. 'Mother'. Ink and digital collage. https://www.danhillier.com/artwork/Mother.

Hillier, Dan. 2006c. 'Father'. Ink and digital collage. https://www.danhillier.com/artwork/Father.

Hillier, Dan. 2011. 'The Way'. Ink and digital collage. https://www.danhillier.com/artwork/theway.

Hillier, Dan. 2013. 'Lunar Seas'. Ink and digital collage. https://www.danhillier.com/artwork/LunarSeas.

Hillier, Dan. 2014a. 'Throne'. Ink and digital collage. https://www.danhillier.com/artwork/Throne.

Hillier, Dan. 2014b. 'Untitled'. Ink and digital collage. *Instagram*. https://www.instagram.com/p/l17pT0ONEn/.

Hillier, Dan. 2015a. 'Aperture'. Ink and digital collage. https://www.danhillier.com/artwork/aperture.

Hillier, Dan. 2015b. 'Cellar Door'. Ink and digital collage. https://www.danhillier.com/artwork/cellar-door.

Hine, Lewis W. 1908. 'Glassworks. Midnight. Location: Indiana'. Photograph. LC-DIG-nclc-01151. Library of Congress.

Hine, Lewis W. 1911. 'Little Lottie, a Regular Oyster Shucker in Alabama Canning Co. She Speaks No English. Note the Condition of Her Shoes Caused by Standing on the Rough Shells So Much. A Common Sight. Bayou La Batre, Ala'. Photograph. Still Picture Records Section, NWCS-S. National Archives and Records Administration.

Ho, Elizabeth. 2012. *Neo-Victorianism and the Memory of Empire*. London: Continuum.

Höch, Hannah. 2016. 'A Few Words on Photomontage'. In *MashUp: The Birth of Modern Culture*, edited by Daina Augaitis, Bruce Grenville, and Stephanie Rebick, 62–65. London: Black Dog Publishing.

Hogle, Jerrold E. 2002. 'Introduction: The Gothic in Western Culture'. In *The Cambridge Companion to Gothic Fiction*, edited by Jerrold E. Hogle, 1–20. Cambridge: Cambridge University Press.

Hogle, Jerrold E. 2012. 'The Gothic Ghost of the Counterfeit and the Progress of Abjection'. In *A New Companion to the Gothic*, edited by David Punter, 496–509. Oxford: Blackwell Publishing.

Holland, Patricia. 2004. '"Sweet It Is to Scan … ": Personal Photographs and Popular Photography'. In *Photography: A Critical Introduction*, edited by Liz Wells, 105–32. London: Routledge.

Holmes, Adam. 2018. 'It's Been One Year since the Dark Universe Was Announced, So What Happened?' *CINEMABLEND*. 22 May 2018. https://www.cinemablend.com/news/2423971/its-been-one-year-since-the-dark-universe-was-announced-so-what-happened.

Horn, Katrin. 2017. *Women, Camp, and Popular Culture: Serious Excess*. Houndmills: Palgrave Macmillan.

Horner, Avril, ed. 2002. *European Gothic: A Spirited Exchange 1760–1960*. Manchester: Manchester University Press.

Horner, Avril, and Sue Zlosnik. 2005. *Gothic and the Comic Turn*. Houndmills: Palgrave Macmillan.

Hume, Kathryn. 1984. *Fantasy and Mimesis: Responses to Reality in Western Literature*. New York: Methuen.

Hurst, Rochelle. 2008. 'Adaptation as an Undecidable: Fidelity and Binarity from Bluestone to Derrida'. In *In/Fidelity: Essays on Film Adaptation*, edited by David L. Kranz and Nancy C. Mellerski, 172–96. Cambridge: Cambridge Scholars Publishing.

Hutcheon, Linda. 1985. *A Theory of Parody*. London: Methuen.

Hutcheon, Linda. 1988. *A Poetics of Postmodernism*. New York: Routledge.

Hutcheon, Linda. 1994. *Irony's Edge: The Theory and Politics of Irony*. London: Routledge.

Hutcheon, Linda. 2013. *A Theory of Adaptation*. 2nd ed. New York: Routledge.

Hutcheon, Linda, and Mario J. Valdés. 2000. 'Irony, Nostalgia, and the Postmodern: A Dialogue'. *Poligrafías* 3: 29–54.

Huyda, Richard J. 1977. 'Photographs and Archives in Canada'. *Archivaria: The Journal of the Association of Canadian Archivists* 5: 5–16.

Iversen, Margaret. 1994. 'What Is a Photograph?' *Art History* 17 (3): 450–63.

Jackson, Shelley. 1995. *Patchwork Girl; or, a Modern Monster*. CD-ROM. Watertown, MA: Eastgate Systems.

Jackson, Shelley. 1998. 'Stitch Bitch: The Patchwork Girl'. Presented at the Transformations of the Book Conference, Massachusetts Institute of Technology, Cambridge, MA. http://web.mit.edu/m-i-t/articles/jackson.html.

Jameson, Fredric. 1984. 'Foreword'. In *The Postmodern Condition: A Report on Knowledge*, translated by Geoff Bennington and Brian Massumi, vii–xxi. Manchester: Manchester University Press.

Jameson, Fredric. 1988. 'Postmodernism and Consumer Society'. In *Postmodernism and Its Discontents*, edited by E. Ann Kaplan, 192–205. New York: Verso.

Jameson, Fredric. 1991. *Postmodernism, or, the Cultural Logic of Late Capitalism*. Durham, NC: Duke University Press.

Jan, Dana, and Ru Weerasuriya, dir. 2015. *The Order: 1886*. PlayStation 4. Ready at Dawn.

Jenkins, Henry. 2006. *Convergence Culture: Where Old and New Media Collide*. New York: New York University Press.

Jenkins, Henry. 2010. 'Multiculturalism, Appropriation, and the New Media Literacies: Remixing Moby Dick'. In *Mashup Cultures*, edited by Stefan Sonvilla-Weiss, 98–119. Wien: Springer.

Jenkins, Henry. 2014. 'Fan Activism and Participatory Politics: The Case of the Harry Potter Alliance'. In *DIY Citizenship: Critical Making and Social Media*, edited by Matt Ratto and Megan Boler, 65–73. Cambridge, MA: MIT Press.

Jeralds, Scott, dir. 1998. 'Super Writers'. *Histeria!* The WB.

Johnson, Barbara. 1982. 'My Monster/My Self'. *Diacritics* 12 (2): 2–10.

Johnston, Sarah Iles. 2015. 'The Greek Mythic Story World'. *Arethusa* 48 (3): 283–311.

Jones, David J. 2011. *Gothic Machine: Textualities, Pre-Cinematic Media and Film in Popular Visual Culture, 1670–1910*. Cardiff: University of Wales Press.

Jones, David J. 2014. *Sexuality and the Gothic Magic Lantern: Desire, Eroticism and Literary Visibilities from Byron to Bram Stoker*. Houndmills: Palgrave Macmillan.

Jones, Frederick L. 1944. 'Introduction'. In *The Letters of Mary W. Shelley*, 1: i–xxxii. Norman, OK: University of Oklahoma Press.

Jonjak, Marti. 2013. 'Worn Out – Janieta Eyre: Leech Gowns and Manicures'. *The Stranger*. 13 March 2013. https://www.thestranger.com/seattle/worn-out/Content?oid=16235839.

Joseph, Anthony. 2017. 'Facebook Users Share Sick "Grenfell Tower Candle" Meme'. *Mail Online*. 29 June 2017. http://www.dailymail.co.uk/~/article-4651134/index.html.

Kagan, Robert. 2016. 'Trump Is the GOP's Frankenstein Monster. Now He's Strong Enough to Destroy the Party'. *Washington Post*. 25 February 2016.

https://www.washingtonpost.com/opinions/trump-is-the-gops-frankenstein-monster-now-hes-strong-enough-to-destroy-the-party/2016/02/25/3e443f28-dbc1-11e5-925f-1d10062cc82d_story.html.

Kantor, Julie. 2014. 'STEMinism'. *Huffington Post*. 20 August 2014. https://www.huffingtonpost.com/julie-kantor/steminism_b_5691586.html.

Kechiche, Abdellatif, dir. 2010. *Black Venus*. Film. MK2.

Kellogg, Carolyn. 2009. '"Pride and Prejudice and Zombies" by Seth Grahame-Smith'. *BBC News*. 4 April 2009. http://www.latimes.com/entertainment/la-et-zombies4-2009apr04-story.html.

Kern, Claudia. 2011. *Sissi: Die Vampirjägerin*. Stuttgart: Panini.

Khoury, George. 2003. *The Extraordinary Works of Alan Moore*. Raleigh, NC: TwoMorrows Publishing.

Kiely, Robert. 1972. *The Romantic Novel in England*. Cambridge, MA: Harvard University Press.

Kilgore, Maggie. 1995. *The Rise of the Gothic Novel*. New York: Routledge.

Kit, Borys. 2014. 'Forget Franchises: Why 2014 Will Be Hollywood's Year of the "Shared Universe"'. *The Hollywood Reporter*. 6 January 2014. http://www.hollywoodreporter.com/heat-vision/x-men-amazing-spider-man-668376.

Klipspringer, S. A., and F. Scott Fitzgerald. 2012. *The Late Gatsby*. Shay K. Azoulay.

Knickerbocker, Conrad, and William S. Burroughs. 1965. 'William S. Burroughs, The Art of Fiction No. 36'. *The Paris Review*. http://www.theparisreview.org/interviews/4424/the-art-of-fiction-no-36-william-s-burroughs.

Kohlke, Marie-Luise. 2014. 'Mining the Neo-Victorian Vein: Prospecting for Gold, Buried Treasure and Uncertain Metal'. In *Neo-Victorian Literature and Culture: Immersions and Revisitations*, edited by Nadine Boehm-Schnitker and Susanne Gruss, 21–37. London: Routledge.

Kohlke, Marie-Luise, and Christian Gutleben. 2012. 'The (Mis)Shapes of Neo-Victorian Gothic: Continuations, Adaptations, Transformations'. In *Neo-Victorian Gothic: Horror, Violence and Degeneration in the Re-Imagined Nineteenth Century*, edited by Marie-Luise Kohlke and Christian Gutleben, 1–48. Amsterdam: Rodopi.

Kristeva, Julia. 1982. *Powers of Horror: An Essay on Abjection*. Translated by Leon S. Roudiez. New York: Columbia University Press.

Kroll, Justin. 2017. 'Universal's "Bride of Frankenstein" to Open February 2019 as Part of Studio's "Dark Universe"'. *Variety*. 22 May 2017. http://variety.com/2017/film/news/bride-of-frankenstein-opens-february-2019-1202439874/.

Kukkonen, Karin. 2010. 'Navigating Infinite Earths: Readers, Mental Models, and the Multiverse of Superhero Comics'. *Storyworlds: A Journal of Narrative Studies* 2 (1): 39–58.

Laderman, David, and Laurel Westrup. 2014. *Sampling Media*. Oxford: Oxford University Press.

Laurence, Robin. 2016. 'MashUp Reveals Pivotal Role of Women in Pioneering of Modern Art Methods'. *The Georgia Straight: Arts*. 23 February 2016. http://www.straight.com/arts/643691/mashup-reveals-pivotal-role-women-pioneering-modern-art-methods.

Le Fanu, Joseph Sheridan. 1872. 'Carmilla'. In *In a Glass Darkly*, 3: 47–270. London: Richard Bentley & Son.

Leavitt, Glen. 2013. 'Travis Louie'. *Georgie Magazine*. 1 August 2013. http://georgiemagazine.com/art/travis-louie/.

Lee, Timothy B. 'Mickey Mouse Will Be Public Domain Soon—Here's What That Means', *Ars Technica*, 1 January 2019. Accessed 6 January 2019. https://arstechnica.com/tech-policy/2019/01/a-whole-years-worth-of-works-just-fell-into-the-public-domain/.

Leitch, Thomas. 2005. 'The Adapter as Auteur: Hitchcock, Kubrick, Disney'. In *Books in Motion: Adaptation, Intertextuality, Authorship*, edited by Mireia Aragay, 107–24. Amsterdam: Rodopi.

Leitch, Thomas. 2012. 'Adaptation and Intertextuality, or, What Isn't an Adaptation and What Does It Matter?' In *A Companion to Literature, Film, and Adaptation*, edited by Deborah Cartmell, 87–104. Hoboken, NJ: Wiley-Blackwell.

Leitch, Thomas. 2015. 'History as Adaptation'. In *The Politics of Adaptation: Media Convergence and Ideology*, edited by D. Hassler-Forest and P. Nicklas, 7–20. Houndmills: Palgrave Macmillan.

Lessig, Lawrence. 2001. *The Future of Ideas: The Fate of the Commons in a Connected World*. New York: Random House.

Lessig, Lawrence. 2008. *Remix: Making Art and Commerce Thrive in the Hybrid Economy*. London: Penguin.

Levina, Marina, and Diem-My T. Bui. 2013. 'Introduction: Toward a Comprehensive Monster Theory in the 21st Century'. In *Monster Culture in the 21st Century: A Reader*, edited by Marina Levina and Diem-My T. Bui, 1–13. New York: Bloomsbury.

Lincoln, Bruce. 1999. *Theorizing Myth: Narrative, Ideology, and Scholarship*. Chicago, IL: University of Chicago Press.

Lloyd-Smith, Allan. 2004. *American Gothic Fiction: An Introduction*. London: Continuum.

Logan, John. 2014. 'Penny Dreadful: The Literary Origins'. *YouTube*. 27 April 2014. https://www.youtube.com/watch?v=UlfPyW1A__Q.

Louie, Travis. 2006a. 'Emily'. Acrylic on board. *Flickr*. https://www.flickr.com/photos/travis37a/315734310/.

Louie, Travis. 2006b. 'Pals'. Acrylic on board. *William Baczek Fine Arts*. http://www.wbfinearts.com/index.php?id=2855.

Louie, Travis. 2008. 'Sea Monkey Princess'. Acrylic on board. *Flickr*. https://www.flickr.com/photos/travis37a/2263215464/in/photostream/.

Louie, Travis. 2009. 'The Ghost of Abigail'. Acrylic on board. *Flickr*. https://www.flickr. com/photos/travis37a/4017043248/in/photostream/.

Louie, Travis. 2011a. 'Dorothy and Her Damsel Fly'. Acrylic on board. http:// travislouieartworks.com/artworks/damsel-fly/.

Louie, Travis. 2011b. 'Oscar and the Truth Toad'. Acrylic on board. http:// travislouieartworks.com/artworks/oscar-and-the-truth-toad/.

Louie, Travis. 2011c. 'The Family Yeti'. Acrylic on board. http://travislouieartworks.com/ artworks/the-family-yeti/.

Louie, Travis. 2013a. 'Miss Lucy and Her Hat Monkey'. Acrylic on board. http:// travislouieartworks.com/artworks/gallery-2/miss-lucyand-her-hat-monkey/.

Louie, Travis. 2013b. 'The Thompson'. Acrylic on board. KP Projects/MKG. https:// www.artsy.net/artwork/travis-louie-the-thompson.

Louie, Travis. 2014a. 'Miss Emily Fowler & Her Spider'. Acrylic on board. *Instagram*. https://www.instagram.com/p/2gjc66EKPT/?taken-by=travislouie.

Louie, Travis. 2014b. 'Mr. Sam'. Acrylic on board. *Instagram*. https://www.instagram. com/p/p1TU1wkKE-/?taken-by=travislouie.

Louie, Travis. 2014c. 'Oscar and the Giant Tarsier'. Acrylic on board. *Roq La Rue gallery*. http://www.roqlarue.com/files/Oscar-and-the-Giant-Tarsier-150dpi-8X10. ADJ_.jpg.

Louie, Travis. 2015a. 'The Bat of Exmoor'. Acrylic on board. *William Baczek Fine Arts*. https://www.artsy.net/artwork/travis-louie-the-bat-of-exmoor.

Louie, Travis. 2015b. 'Roq La Rue Gallery Show'. *TravisLouieArtwork.Com*. 8 September 2015. http://travislouieartworks.com/roq-la-rue-gallery-show/.

Lovecraft, H.P. 2017. *The Call of Cthulhu & Other Weird Stories*. Edited by S.T. Joshi. London: The Folio Society.

Lyall, Sarah. 2013. 'Pride, Prejudice, Promotion? Mr. Darcy Rising'. *The New York Times*. 9 July 2013. http://www.nytimes.com/2013/07/10/arts/design/pride-prejudice-promotion-mr-darcy-rising.html.

Lyotard, Jean-François. 1984. *The Postmodern Condition: A Report on Knowledge*. Translated by Geoff Bennington and Brian Massumi. Manchester: Manchester University Press.

MacDonald, Tara, and Joyce Goggin. 2013. 'Introduction: Neo-Victorianism and Feminism'. *Neo-Victorian Studies* 6 (2): 1–14.

Mandal, Anthony. 2007. *Jane Austen and the Popular Novel: The Determined Author*. Houndmills: Palgrave Macmillan.

Marx, Karl. 1976. *Capital: Volume I*. Translated by Ben Fowkes. Harmondsworth: Penguin Books.

Mattin, David. 2012. 'Trendspotter: Mash-up Literature'. *The National (Arts & Lifestyle)*. 3 September 2012. http://www.thenational.ae/arts-culture/books/trendspotter-mash-up-literature.

Maxwell, Mike. 2015. *Episode 165: Travis Louie*. Podcast. Live Free. http://mikemaxwellart. com/livefreepodcast/LiveFreeCast165.mp3.

Maybee, Spencer, dir. 2014. *Carmilla*. YouTube.

McNally, David. 2012. *Monsters of the Market: Zombies, Vampires and Global Capitalism*. Chicago, IL: Haymarket Books.

McNutt, Myles. 2014. 'Cultural Interview: PBS Digital Studios' Frankenstein M.D. [Part One]'. *Cultural Learnings*. 18 August 2014. https://cultural-learnings.com/2014/08/18/interview-frankenstein-md-bernie-su-anna-lore-pbs-digital-studios/.

Mellor, Anne K. 1988. *Mary Shelley: Her Life, Her Fiction, Her Monsters*. New York: Routledge.

Mellor, Anne K. 1993. *Romanticism and Gender*. London: Routledge.

Mellor, Anne K. 2003. 'Making a "Monster": An Introduction to *Frankenstein*'. In *The Cambridge Companion to Mary Shelley*, edited by Esther Schor, 9–25. Cambridge: Cambridge University Press.

Messina, Lynn, and Louisa May Alcott. 2010. *Little Vampire Women*. New York: HarperTeen.

Meyer, Moe. 1994. 'Introduction: Reclaiming the Discourse of Camp'. In *The Politics and Poetics of Camp*, edited by Moe Meyer, 1–22. London: Routledge.

Meyers, Lee Roy, and Seth Beard. 2013. *WoodRocket Ep. 30: Travis Louie*. Podcast. WoodRocket. http://woodrocket.com/episodes/woodrocket-ep-30-travis-louie.

Meylikhov, Matthew. 2014. 'Multiversity Turns 5 with: Nemo and All Things "League of Extraordinary Gentlemen," with Kevin O'Neill [Interview]'. *Multiversity Comics*. 9 May 2014. http://www.multiversitycomics.com/interviews/multiversity-turns-5-with-nemo-and-all-things-league-of-extraordinary-gentlemen-with-kevin-oneill-interview/.

Middleton, Francesca. 2016. 'Abusing Text in the Roman and Contemporary Worlds'. *Transformative Works and Cultures* 21: n.p.

Mierins, Krystina. 2013. 'Messy Comedies: Janieta Eyre Creates Strange Worlds of Beauty and Humour'. Magenta. 18 July 2013. https://www.thestranger.com/seattle/worn-out/Content?oid=16235839.

Miller, I.J., and Emily Brontë. 2013. *Wuthering Nights: An Erotic Retelling of Wuthering Heights*. New York: Grand Central Publishing.

Miller, Zara. n.d. 'The Psychedelic Butcher: Dan Hillier on Art and Acid'. Kids of Dada. http://www.kidsofdada.com/blogs/magazine/14456249-the-psychedlic-butcher.

Milton, John. (1819) 2003. *Paradise Lost*. Edited by Merritt Yerkes Hughes. Indianapolis, IN: Hackett.

Mitchell, Kate. 2008. 'Ghostly Histories and Embodied Memories: Photography, Spectrality and Historical Fiction in *Afterimage* and *Sixty Lights*'. *Neo-Victorian Studies* 1 (1): 81–109.

Mitchell, Kate. 2010. *History and Cultural Memory in Neo-Victorian Fiction: Victorian Afterimages*. Houndmills: Palgrave Macmillan.

Mitchell, Kaye. 2012. 'Gender and Sexuality in Popular Fiction'. In *The Cambridge Companion to Popular Fiction*, edited by David Glover and Scott McCracken, 122–40. Cambridge: Cambridge University Press.

Mittman, Asa Simon. 2013. 'Introduction: The Impact of Monsters and Monster Studies'. In *The Ashgate Research Companion to Monsters and the Monstrous*, edited by Asa Simon Mittman and Peter J. Dendle, 1–16. Farnham: Ashgate.

Moore, Alan, and Kevin O'Neill. 2000. *The League of Extraordinary Gentlemen: Volume I*. New York: America's Best Comics.

Moore, Alan, and Kevin O'Neill. 2003. *The League of Extraordinary Gentlemen: Volume II*. New York: America's Best Comics.

Moore, Alan, and Kevin O'Neill. 2007. *The League of Extraordinary Gentlemen: Black Dossier*. New York: America's Best Comics.

Mulvey, Laura. 2006. *Death 24x a Second: Stillness and the Moving Image*. London: Reaktion Books.

Munford, Rebecca, and Melanie Waters. 2013. *Feminism and Popular Culture: Investigating the Postfeminist Mystique*. London: I.B. Tauris.

Murphy, Bernice M., and Stephen Matterson. 2018. 'Introduction: "Changing the Story" – Popular Fiction Today'. In *Twenty-First-Century Popular Fiction*, edited by Bernice M. Murphy and Stephen Matterson, 1–8. Edinburgh: Edinburgh University Press.

Nathan, Terrence R. 2011. 'Review: Photography and Science by Kelley Wilder'. *Visual Resources* 27 (4): 379–85.

Navas, Eduardo. 2009. 'Remix: The Bond of Repetition and Representation'. *Remix Theory*. 16 January 2009. http://remixtheory.net/?p=361.

Nazarian, Vera, and Jane Austen. 2009. *Mansfield Park and Mummies: Monster Mayhem, Matrimony, Ancient Curses, True Love, and Other Dire Delights*. The Supernatural Jane Austen Series 1. Los Angeles: Curiosities.

Ndalianis, Angela. 2009. 'Enter the Aleph: Superhero Worlds and Hypertime Realities'. In *The Contemporary Comic Book Superhero*, edited by Angela Ndalianis, 270–90. New York: Routledge.

Nelson, Camilla. 2013. 'Jane Austen … Now with Ultraviolent Zombie Mayhem'. *Adaptation* 6 (3): 338–54.

Nevins, Jess. 2003. *Heroes and Monsters: The Unofficial Companion to The League of Extraordinary Gentlemen*. Austin, TX: MonkeyBrain.

Nevins, Jess. 2004. *A Blazing World: The Unofficial Companion to The League of Extraordinary Gentlemen, Volume Two*. Austin, TX: MonkeyBrain.

Nevins, Jess. 2008. *Impossible Territories: An Unofficial Companion to The League of Extraordinary Gentlemen*. Austin, TX: MonkeyBrain.

Nevins, Jess. 2018. 'Comic Book Annotations'. *JessNevins.Com*. 30 July 2018. http://jessnevins.com/annotations.html.

Newman, Kim. 2011. *Anno Dracula*. London: Titan Books.

Newman, Kim. 2012. *The Bloody Red Baron*. New York: Titan Books.

Newman, Kim. 2013. 'Anno Dracula: Appropriation of Characters'. *Lit Reactor*. 13 September 2013. https://litreactor.com/columns/anno-dracula-appropriation-of-characters.

Noriega, Chon. 1987. 'Godzilla and the Japanese Nightmare: When "Them!" Is U.S.' *Cinema Journal* 27 (1): 63–77.

Novák, Caterina. 2013. 'Those Very "Other" Victorians: Interrogating Neo-Victorian Feminism in *The Journal of Dora Damage*'. *Neo-Victorian Studies* 6 (2): 114–36.

Ó Méalóid, Pádraig. 2011. 'It's 1969, OK? Pádraig Talks with Kevin O'Neill'. *Forbidden Planet*. 30 September 2011. http://www.forbiddenplanet.co.uk/blog/2011/its-1969-ok-padraig-talks-with-kevin-oneill/.

O'Keeffe, Alice. 2014. 'Sarah Waters: Interview'. *The Bookseller*. 13 June 2014. http://www.thebookseller.com/profile/sarah-waters-interview.

Onion, Rebecca. 2008. 'Reclaiming the Machine: An Introductory Look at Steampunk in Everyday Practice'. *Neo-Victorian Studies* 1 (1): 138–63.

O'Reilly, Lara, and Will Heilpern. 2016. 'The 30 Most Creative People in Advertising under 30'. *Business Insider UK*. 27 January 2016. http://uk.businessinsider.com/30-most-creative-people-in-advertising-under-30-2016?r=US&IR=T.

Ostriker, Alicia. 1982. 'The Thieves of Language: Women Poets and Revisionist Mythmaking'. *Signs* 8 (1): 68–90.

'Oxford Living Dictionaries'. 2016. Oxford Living Dictionaries. 27 October 2016. https://en.oxforddictionaries.com.

Passer, Ivan, dir. 1988. *Haunted Summer*. Cannon Films.

Paul, Adrian, dir. 1997. 'The Modern Prometheus'. *Highlander: The Series*. Gaumont Television.

Peacock, Molly. 2010. *The Paper Garden: An Artist Begins Her Life's Work at 72*. New York: Bloomsbury.

Pearce, Susan M. 1995. *On Collecting: An Investigation into Collecting in the European Tradition*. London: Routledge.

Peeren, Esther. 2008. *Intersubjectivities and Popular Culture: Bakhtin and Beyond*. Stanford, CA: Stanford University Press.

Pemberley Digital, and PBS Digital Studios. 2014. 'Alone Together: Frankenstein, MD – Ep. 24'. *YouTube*. 31 October 2014. https://youtu.be/bm4vURGaQ30.

Penny Dreadful. 2014. 'Penny Dreadful | Behind Episode 6: Professor Van Helsing | Season 1'. *YouTube*. 16 June 2014. https://www.youtube.com/watch?v=KHPOXIBkmZE.

Phillips, Jordan. 2017. '"There Is Some Thing within Us All": Queer Desire and Monstrous Bodies in Penny Dreadful'. *Refractory* 28. https://refractory-journal.com/phillips/.

Picard, Susanne. 2011. *Die Leichen des jungen Werther*. Stuttgart: Panini.

Pip, Scroobius. 2014. *Episode 3: Alan Moore*. Podcast. Distraction Pieces Podcast (Episode 3). https://www.acast.com/distractionpieces/db34aae9-7596-4a55-a9d1-81d031b6d9a7.

van Poecke, Niels. 2014. 'Beyond Postmodern Narcolepsy: On Metamodernism in Popular Music Culture'. *Notes on Metamodernism*. 4 June 2014. http://www.metamodernism.com/2014/06/04/beyond-postmodern-narcolepsy/.

Poore, Benjamin. 2016. 'The Transformed Beast: *Penny Dreadful*, Adaptation, and the Gothic'. *Victoriographies* 6 (1): 62–81.

'Pride and Prejudice and Zombies'. 2016. *Box Office Mojo*. 28 February 2016. http://www.boxofficemojo.com/movies/?page=main&id=prideprejudicezombies.htm.

Primorac, Antonija. 2013. 'The Naked Truth: The Postfeminist Afterlives of Irene Adler'. *Neo-Victorian Studies* 6 (2): 89–113.

Primorac, Antonija. 2015. 'Cultural Nostalgia, Orientalist Ideology, and Heritage Film'. In *The Politics of Adaptation: Media Convergence and Ideology*, edited by D. Hassler-Forest and P. Nicklas, 35–49. Houndmills: Palgrave Macmillan.

Prince, Gerald. 1997. 'Preface'. In *Palimpsests: Literature in the Second Degree*, edited by Gérard Genette, translated by Channa Newman and Claude Doubinsky, ix–xii. Lincoln: University of Nebraska Press.

Punter, David. 1996. *The Literature of Terror: A History of Gothic Fictions from 1765 to the Present Day*. 2nd ed. Vol. 2. London: Longman.

Punter, David. 2012. 'Introduction: The Ghost of a History'. In *A New Companion to the Gothic*, edited by David Punter, 1–10. Oxford: Blackwell Publishing.

Quéma, Anne. 2007. 'The Gothic and the Fantastic in the Age of Digital Reproduction'. *English Studies in Canada* 30 (4): 81–119.

Quentel, Debra L. 1996. '"Bad Artists Copy. Good Artists Steal": The Ugly Conflict between Copyright Law and Appropriationism'. *Entertainment Law Review* 4 (1): 39–80.

Ramsey, Liz. 2014. 'Interview – Dan Hillier'. *Blank Space BLOG*. 8 August 2014. https://blankspaceblog.com/2014/08/08/interview-dan-hillier/.

Randall, Marilyn. 2001. *Pragmatic Plagiarism: Authorship, Profit, and Power*. Toronto: University of Toronto Press.

Rekulak, Jason. 2009. 'How to Mash Up Jane Austen and the Zombies'. *The Washington Post*. 27 October 2009. http://voices.washingtonpost.com/shortstack/2009/10/how_to_mash_up_jane_austen_and.html.

Rich, Adrienne. 1972. 'When We Dead Awaken: Writing as Re-Vision'. *College English* 34 (1): 18–30.

Riter, Amanda V. 2017. 'The Evolution of Mashup Literature: Identifying the Genre through Jane Austen's Novels'. MA diss. Leicester: De Montfort University.

Robinson, Charles E. 2016. '*Frankenstein*: Its Composition and Publication'. In *The Cambridge Companion to Frankenstein*, edited by Andrew Smith, 13–25. Cambridge: Cambridge University Press.

Rodgers, Troy, and Kim Newman. 2013. 'Interview – Kim Newman'. *SciFiFx.Com*. 8 April 2013. http://www.scififx.com/2013/04/interview-kim-newman/.

Roediger, David R. 2005. *Working toward Whiteness: How America's Immigrants Became White: The Strange Journey from Ellis Island to the Suburbs*. New York: Basic Books.

Rogers, Richard A. 2006. 'From Cultural Exchange to Transculturation: A Review and Reconceptualization of Cultural Appropriation'. *Communication Theory* 16: 474–503.

Rose, Gillian. 2005. 'Visual Methodologies'. In *Research Methods for English Students*, edited by Gabrielle Griffin, 67–89. Edinburgh: Edinburgh University Press.

Rose, Margaret. 2009. 'Extraordinary Pasts: Steampunk as a Mode of Historical Representation'. *Journal of the Fantastic in the Arts* 20 (3): 319–33.

Rose, Mark. 2003. 'Nine-Tenths of the Law: The English Copyright Debates and the Rhetoric of the Public Domain'. *Law and Contemporary Problems* 66 (1/2): 75–87.

Roth, Jenny, and Monica Flegel. 2014. 'It's Like Rape: Metaphorical Family Transgressions, Copyright Ownership and Fandom'. *Continuum* 28 (6): 901–13.

Runciman, David. 2016. 'How the Education Gap Is Tearing Politics Apart'. *The Guardian*. 5 October 2016. https://www.theguardian.com/politics/2016/oct/05/trump-brexit-education-gap-tearing-politics-apart.

Russell, Ken, dir. 1986. *Gothic*. Vestron Pictures.

Ryan, Maureen. 2014. '"Penny Dreadful" Creator on What's Next for the Engaging and Underrated Horror Show'. *Huffington Post*. 16 October 2014. http://www.huffingtonpost.com/2014/10/16/penny-dreadful-showtime_n_5998428.html.

Said, Edward. 1993. *Culture and Imperialism*. New York: Alfred A. Knopf.

SanAngelo, David, dir. 2006. 'Nightmare on Joe's Street'. *Time Warp Trio*. Discovery Kids.

Sanders, Julie. 2006. *Adaptation and Appropriation*. London: Routledge.

Sardar, Ziauddin. 1998. *Postmodernism and the Other: The New Imperialism of Western Culture*. London: Pluto Press.

Scott, Suzanne. 2013. 'Fangirls in Refrigerators: The Politics of (In)Visibility in Comic Book Culture'. *Transformative Works and Cultures* 13.

Scott, Walter. (1820) 1877. *Waverley Novels: Ivanhoe*. London: Routledge.

Sedgwick, Eve Kosofsky. 2003. *Touching Feeling: Affect, Pedagogy, Performativity*. Durham, NC: Duke University Press.

Seville, Catherine. 2006. *The Internationalisation of Copyright Law: Books, Buccaneers and the Black Flag in the Nineteenth Century*. Cambridge: Cambridge University Press.

Sharkey, Alix. 2010. 'Seth Grahame-Smith Interview'. *The Telegraph*. 30 April 2010. http://www.telegraph.co.uk/culture/books/7656909/Seth-Grahame-Smith-interview.html.

Shaw, Debbie. 1992. 'In Her Own Image: The Constructed Female in Women's Science Fiction'. *Science as Culture* 3 (2): 263–81.

Shelley, Mary. (1831) 2015. *Frankenstein; or, the Modern Prometheus*. London: The Folio Society.

Sherman, Augustus F., and Peter Mesenhöller. 2005. *Augustus F. Sherman: Ellis Island Portraits 1905–1920*. New York: Aperture.

Shildrick, Margrit. 2002. *Embodying the Monster: Encounters with the Vulnerable Self*. London: Sage.

Shugart, Helene A., and Catherine Egley Waggoner. 2008. *Making Camp: Rhetorics of Transgression in U.S. Popular Culture*. Tuscaloosa: University of Alabama Press.

Silver, Sean. 2014. 'The Politics of Gothic Historiography, 1660–1800'. In *The Gothic World*, edited by Glennis Byron and Dale Townshend, 3–14. London: Routledge.

Simone, Gail. 1999. 'Character List'. *Women in Refrigerators*. 15 March 1999. http://lby3.com/wir/.

Sinclair, Eve, and Charlotte Brontë. 2012. *Jane Eyre Laid Bare: The Classic Novel with an Erotic Twist*. New York: St. Martin's Griffin.

Sinfield, Alan. 1997. *Literature, Politics and Culture in Postwar Britain*. London: Athlone Press.

Singer, Marc. 2002. '"Black Skins" and White Masks: Comic Books and the Secret of Race'. *African American Review* 36 (1): 107–19.

Slayton, Nicholas. 2014. 'How Penny Dreadful Reanimated the Gothic-Horror Genre'. *The Atlantic*. 27 June 2014. http://www.theatlantic.com/entertainment/archive/2014/06/a-good-fright-is-hard-to-find/373597/.

Smith, Andrew, ed. 2016. *The Cambridge Companion to Frankenstein*. Cambridge: Cambridge University Press.

Smith, David. 2016. 'Donald Trump's Ghostwriter on Being the "Dr Frankenstein" Who Made a Monster'. *The Guardian*. 30 October 2016. https://www.theguardian.com/us-news/2016/oct/30/donald-trump-tony-schwartz-art-of-the-deal-out-of-control.

Solicari, Sonia. 2013a. 'Is This Neo-Victorian? Planning an Exhibition on Nineteenth-Century Revivalism'. *Neo-Victorian Studies* 6 (1): 180–88.

Solicari, Sonia, ed. 2013b. *Victoriana: A Miscellany*. London: Guildhall Art Gallery.

Sommers, Stephen, dir. 2004. *Van Helsing*. Universal Pictures.

Sontag, Susan. 1967. *Against Interpretation and Other Essays*. New York: Dell.

Sontag, Susan. 1999. 'Notes on Camp'. In *Camp: Queer Aesthetics and the Performing Subject – A Reader*, edited by Fabio Cleto, 53–65. Edinburgh: Edinburgh University Press.

Sonvilla-Weiss, Stefan. 2010. 'Introduction: Mashups, Remix Practices and the Recombination of Existing Digital Content'. In *Mashup Cultures*, edited by Stefan Sonvilla-Weiss, 8–23. Wien: Springer.

Spector, Nicole Audrey, and Oscar Wilde. 2013. *Fifty Shades of Dorian Gray*. New York: Skyhorse Publishing.

Spooner, Catherine. 2004. *Fashioning Gothic Bodies*. Manchester: Manchester University Press.

Spooner, Catherine. 2006. *Contemporary Gothic*. London: Reaktion Books.

Spooner, Catherine. 2014. 'Twenty-First-Century Gothic'. In *Terror & Wonder: The Gothic Imagination*, edited by Dale Townshend, 180–205. London: British Library Publishing.

Spooner, Catherine. 2017. *Post-Millennial Gothic: Comedy, Romance and the Rise of Happy Gothic*. London: Bloomsbury Publishing.

Stableford, Brian. 1995. 'Frankenstein and the Origins of Science Fiction'. In *Anticipations: Essays on Early Science Fiction and Its Precursors*, edited by David Seed, 46–57. Syracuse, NY: Syracuse University Press.

Stamets, Bill. 2012. 'Black Venus: A Study in Exploitation'. *RogerEbert.Com*. 2 March 2012. http://www.rogerebert.com/festivals-and-awards/black-venus-a-study-in-exploitation.

Starling, Belinda. 2007. *The Journal of Dora Damage*. London: Bloomsbury.

Starrs, D. Bruno. 2004. 'Keeping the Faith: Catholicism in *Dracula* and Its Adaptations'. *Journal of Dracula Studies* 6: 1–6.

Steiner, George. 1992. *After Babel: Aspects of Language and Translation*. 2nd ed. Oxford: Oxford University Press.

Stevenson, Robert Louis. 1886. *Strange Case of Dr Jekyll and Mr Hyde*. London: Longmans, Green, and Co.

Stoker, Bram. (1897) 1997. *Dracula*. Edited by Nina Auerbach and David J. Skal. New York: Norton Critical Editions.

Storey, John. 2001. *Cultural Theory and Popular Culture: An Introduction*. 5th ed. London: Pearson Longman.

Stribling, William J., dir. 2016. 'The Purloined Letter'. *Edgar Allan Poe's Murder Mystery Dinner Party*. YouTube.

Suárez, Gonzalo, dir. 1988. *Rowing with the Wind*. Buena Vista Home Video.

Tartakovsky, Genndy, dir. 2012. *Hotel Transylvania*. Film. Sony.

'The Slender Man'. 2015. *Creepypasta Wiki*. 10 October 2015. http://creepypasta.wikia.com/wiki/The_Slender_Man.

Thielman, Sam. 2014. '*Penny Dreadful* Creator John Logan Explains Why He Loves Monsters'. *AdWeek*. 27 June 2014. http://www.adweek.com/news/television/penny-dreadful-creator-john-logan-explains-why-he-loves-monsters-158656.

Thomas, Damon, dir. 2016a. 'The Day Tennyson Died'. *Penny Dreadful*. Showtime/Sky.

Thomas, Damon, dir. 2016b. 'Predators Far and Near'. *Penny Dreadful*. Showtime/Sky.

Thomas, Damon, dir. 2016c. 'Good and Evil Braided Be'. *Penny Dreadful*. Showtime/Sky.

Thomas, Julia. 2016. 'Illustrations and the Victorian Novel'. In *The Oxford Handbook of Victorian Literary Culture*, edited by Juliet John, 617–36. Oxford: Oxford University Press.

Thomas, June. 2014. '"The Thing that Made Me Monstrous to Some People Is Also the Thing that Empowered Me"'. *Slate*. 9 May 2014. http://www.slate.com/blogs/outward/2014/05/09/penny_dreadful_s_john_logan_why_a_gay_writer_feels_a_kinship_with_frankenstein.html.

Thompson, Emily G. 2016. 'One of the Most Haunting Scenes from the September 11 Attacks'. *Tumblr*. 11 September 2016. http://congenitaldisease.tumblr.com/post/128850497710/one-of-the-most-haunting-scenes-from-the-september.

Tomaiuolo, Saverio. 2018. *Deviance in Neo-Victorian Culture: Canon, Transgression, Innovation*. Houndmills, Basingstoke: Palgrave Macmillan.

Tondro, Jason. 2011. *Superheroes of the Round Table: Comics Connections to Medieval and Renaissance Literature*. Jefferson, NC: McFarland.

Tough, David. 2010. 'The Mashup Mindset: Will Pop Eat Itself?' In *Play It Again: The Cover Songs in Popular Music*, edited by George Plasketes, 205–12. London: Ashgate.

Townshend, Dale. 2014. 'Introduction'. In *The Gothic World*, edited by Glennis Byron and Dale Townshend, xxiv–xlvi. London: Routledge.

Travers, Andrew. 1993. 'An Essay on Self and Camp'. *Theory, Culture and Society* 10 (1): 127–43.

'Travis Louie Profile'. 2010. Joshua Liner Gallery. http://joshualinergallery.com/artists/travis_louie/.

Trilling, Lionel. 1972. *Sincerity and Authenticity*. Oxford: Oxford University Press.

Troost, Linda, and Sayre Greenfield. 2010. '"Strange Mutations": Shakespeare, Austen and Cultural Success'. *Shakespeare* 6 (4): 431–45.

Tushnet, Rebecca. 2011. 'Scary Monsters: Hybrids, Mashups, and Other Illegitimate Children'. *Notre Dame Law Review* 86: 2133–56.

Twain, Mark. 1997. *Mark Twain Speaks for Himself*. Edited by Paul Fatout. West Lafayette, IN: Purdue University Press.

Uhlin, Graig. 2014. 'Playing in the Gif(t) Economy'. *Games and Culture* 9 (6): 517–27.

Vallee, Mickey. 2013. 'The Media Contingencies of Generation Mashup: A Žižekian Critique'. *Popular Music and Society* 36 (1): 76–97.

Vidler, Mark. 2006. 'Mashup Genius: Mark Vidler Interview'. *Disc Jockey 101*. http://www.discjockey101.com/tipofthemonth.html.

Voynovskaya, Nastia. 2015. 'Travis Louie Imagines New Mythical Beasts in "Archive of Lost Species"'. *Hi-Fructose: The New Contemporary Art Magazine*. 5 May 2015. http://hifructose.com/2015/05/05/travis-louie-imagines-new-mythical-beasts-in-archive-of-lost-species/.

Wagstaff, Dan. 2009. 'Q & A with Jason Rekulak'. *(Un)Death-Match Presents: Free for All*. 2 September 2009. undeathmatch.wordpress.com/2009/09/02/q-a-with-jason-rekulak/.

Wakeman, Geoffrey. 1973. *Victorian Book Illustration: The Technical Revolution*. Detroit, MI: Gale Research.

Wallace, Amy. 2015. 'Sci-Fi's Hugo Awards and the Battle for Pop Culture's Soul'. *WIRED Magazine*. 30 October 2015. https://www.wired.com/2015/10/hugo-awards-controversy/.

Wallace, Diana. 2012. 'The Gothic Reader: History, Fear and Trembling'. In *Reading Historical Fiction: The Revenant and Remembered Past*, edited by K. Mitchell and N. Parsons, 136–52. Wien: Springer.

Wallace, Diana. 2013. *Female Gothic Histories: Gender, History and the Gothic*. Cardiff: University of Wales Press.

Wallop, Henry. 2010. 'Wuthering Heights Sales Quadruple Thanks to Twilight Effect'. *The Telegraph*. 10 April 2010. http://www.telegraph.co.uk/culture/books/booknews/7570922/Wuthering-Heights-quadruple-double-thanks-to-Twilight-effect.html.

Walpole, Horace. (1765) 2004. *The Castle of Otranto*. 2nd ed. Mineola, NY: Dover Thrift.

Walsh, Dearbhla, dir. 2014. 'Resurrection'. *Penny Dreadful*. Showtime/Sky.

Walz, Robin. 2000. *Pulp Surrealism: Insolent Popular Culture in Early Twentieth-Century Paris*. Berkeley: University of California Press.

Weinstock, Jeffrey Andrew. 2013. 'Invisible Monsters: Vision, Horror, and Contemporary Culture'. In *The Ashgate Research Companion to Monsters and the Monstrous*, edited by Asa Simon Mittman and Peter J. Dendle, 275–89. Farnham: Ashgate.

Weir, Kevin J. 2011. 'Czar Michael'. GIF digitised photographs. http://fluxmachine.tumblr.com/post/12477880410/czar-michael.

Weir, Kevin J. 2012a. 'Krupp Von Bohlen'. GIF, digitised photographs. http://fluxmachine.tumblr.com/post/19249023207/krupp-von-bohlen.

Weir, Kevin J. 2012b. 'Bangor Fire'. GIF, digitised photographs. http://fluxmachine.
tumblr.com/post/20119289081/bangor-fire.

Weir, Kevin J. 2012c. 'Peekskill'. GIF, digitised photographs. http://fluxmachine.tumblr.
com/post/20789836142/peekskill.

Weir, Kevin J. 2012d. 'Prince of Solms-Baruth'. GIF, digitised photographs. http://
fluxmachine.tumblr.com/post/24968598269/prince-of-solms-baruth.

Weir, Kevin J. 2012e. 'Doberitz'. GIF, digitised photographs. http://fluxmachine.tumblr.
com/post/29070606556/doberitz.

Weir, Kevin J. 2012f. 'Decoy Howitzer'. GIF, digitised photographs. http://fluxmachine.
tumblr.com/post/34180724587/movingthestill-title-decoy-howitzer.

Weir, Kevin J. 2012g. 'Bruges'. GIF digitised photographs. http://fluxmachine.tumblr.
com/post/34842573672/movingthestill-title-bruges-artist-flux.

Weir, Kevin J. 2016. 'Miss Peregrine's Home for Peculiar Children'. *Flux Machine*.
3 October 2016. http://fluxmachine.tumblr.com/post/151307693404/animated-
artwork-photography-animations-gifs-kevin-weir.

Wellins, Mike. n.d. 'Colin Batty Cabinet Cards'. *Peculiarium*. Accessed 23 March 2017.
http://www.peculiarium.com/colin-batty/.

Wellins, Mike, and Lisa Freeman, eds. 2014. *Meet the Family: Altered Photographs by
Colin Batty*. Portland, OR: Freakybuttrue.

Wells, H.G. 1896. *The Island of Doctor Moreau*. London: Heinemann, Stone and
Kimball.

Werf, Maarten van der, and Megen de Bruin-Molé. 2015. 'Translating *Pride and
Prejudice and Zombies*'. Translated by Megen de Bruin-Molé. *Frankenfiction*.
18 February 2015. http://frankenfiction.com/translating-pride-and-prejudice-and-
zombies/.

Weston, Paula. 2009. 'Pride and Prejudice and Zombies'. *Other Worlds*. 20 December
2009. https://paulawestonotherworlds.wordpress.com/2009/12/20/pride-and-
prejudice-and-zombies/.

Whale, James, dir. 1931. *Frankenstein*. Universal Pictures.

Whale, James, dir. 1935. *Bride of Frankenstein*. Universal Pictures.

Wharton, Lawrence. 1974. 'Godzilla to Latitude Zero: The Cycle of the Technological
Monster'. *Journal of Popular Film* 3 (1): 31–38.

Whelehan, Imelda. 2000. *Overloaded: Popular Culture and the Future of Feminism*.
London: Women's Press.

White, Hayden. 1978. *Tropics of Discourse: Essays in Cultural Criticism*. Baltimore, MD:
Johns Hopkins University Press.

Wilde, Oscar. 1890. 'The Picture of Dorian Gray'. *Lippincott's Monthly Magazine*, 1890.

Williams, Gilda. 2014. 'Defining a Gothic Aesthetic in Modern and Contemporary
Visual Art'. In *The Gothic World*, edited by Glennis Byron and Dale Townshend,
412–24. London: Routledge.

Williams, Linda. 1991. 'Film Bodies: Gender, Genre, and Excess'. *Film Quarterly* 44 (4):
2–13.

Willis, Ika. 2016. 'Amateur Mythographies: Fan Fiction and the Myth of Myth'. *Transformative Works and Cultures* 21.

Wilson, Frances. 1999. '"A Playful Desire of Imitation": The Ghost Stories at Diodati and *a Single Summer with L.B.*'. In *Biofictions: The Rewriting of Romantic Lives in Contemporary Fiction and Drama*, edited by Martin Middeke and Werner Huber, 162–74. Rochester, NY: Camden House.

Wimsatt, William Kurtz, and Monroe C. Beardsley. 1954. 'The Intentional Fallacy'. In *The Verbal Icon: Studies in the Meaning of Poetry*, edited by William Kurtz Wimsatt, 3–19. Lexington, KY: University of Kentucky Press.

Winters, Ben H., and Jane Austen. 2009. *Sense and Sensibility and Sea Monsters*. Quirk Classics. Philadelphia, PA: Quirk Books.

Winters, Ben H., and Leo Tolstoy. 2010. *Android Karenina*. Quirk Classics. Philadelphia, PA: Quirk Books.

Winters, Julie Antolick. 2015. 'Interview: Travis Louie'. *BienArt Gallery*. 23 July 2015. http://beinart.org/interview-travis-louie/.

Wolf-Meyer, Matthew. 2003. 'The World Ozymandias Made: Utopias in the Superhero Comic, Subculture, and the Conservation of Difference'. *Journal of Popular Culture* 36 (3): 497–517.

Wolfson, Julie. 2011. 'Travis Louie'. *Cool Hunting*. 2 November 2011. http://www.coolhunting.com/culture/travis-louie.

Woodmansee, Martha, and Peter Jaszi. 1994. 'Introduction'. In *The Construction of Authorship: Textual Appropriation in Law and Literature*, edited by Martha Woodmansee and Peter Jaszi, 1–13. Durham, NC: Duke University Press.

Wordsworth, William. (1815) 1911. 'Essay, Supplement to the Preface'. In *The Complete Poetical Works of William Wordsworth in Ten Volumes*, 10: 104–6. Boston, MA: Houghton Mifflin.

Wordsworth, William. (1815) 1974. 'To the Editor of Kendal Mercury'. In *The Prose Works of William Wordsworth*, edited by W.J.B. Owen and Jane Worthington Smyser, 3: 308–11. Oxford: Oxford University Press.

Wu, Harmony H. 2003. 'Trading in Horror, Cult and Matricide: Peter Jackson's Phenomenal Bad Taste and New Zealand Fantasies of Inter/National Cinematic Success'. In *Defining Cult Movies: The Cultural Politics of Oppositional Tastes*, edited by Mark Jancovich, Antonio Lázaro Reboll, Julian Stringer, and Andy Willis, 84–108. Manchester: Manchester University Press.

Wyett, Jodi, Laura Gray, Lisa Ottum, Crystal B. Lake, and Cynthia Richards. 2013. 'Teaching *Pride and Prejudice*: A Pedagogy'. Presented at the *Pride and Prejudice*: The Bicentennial conference, Wright State University, October 12. https://corescholar.libraries.wright.edu/cgi/viewcontent.cgi?article=1023&context=celia_pride.

Yaffe, Deborah. 2013. *Among the Janeites: A Journey through the World of Jane Austen Fandom*. New York: Houghton Mifflin Harcourt.

Index

CPSIA information can be obtained
at www.ICGtesting.com
Printed in the USA
LVHW080401150721
692658LV00005B/11

9 781350 234468